PRAISE FOR

Prime Time

"Reassuring . . . upbeat . . . *Prime Time* is part autobiographical con-
fessional, part life advice, the two intertwined, so that reading the
book is often like talking to a friend." —*Los Angeles Times*

"Warm, informative and incredibly life-affirming." —*Woman's Day*

"A how-to book about being happy and self-aware at 73 [that] cites
research and interviews with upbeat, lively, sexually active older
people to extract some all-purpose lessons about endurance."
—*The New York Times*

"Inspirational and highly informative . . . a comprehensive guide to
living life to the fullest, particularly beyond middle age. [Fonda]
thoroughly addresses all the essential components that contribute
to one's physical, mental, emotional and spiritual health, such as
fitness, nutrition, meditation, romantic love and sex, friendship
and financial planning. . . . Although geared toward those sixty
years of age and over, the author's wealth of wisdom can benefit
readers of any age." —*Kirkus Reviews*

"Read this, age gracefully."   —*InStyle*

"Fonda has clearly done her research. . . . Readers will empathize with [her] laudable mission to change the cultural perception of aging, and enjoy her appealing, straightforward tone. Her older female readers will likely feel that she speaks directly to them."
                                                    —*Publishers Weekly*

My Life So Far

"[*My Life So Far*] belongs alongside the memoirs of Gloria Steinem, Bella Abzug, Marilyn French and Katharine Graham. . . . To hold this book in your hands is to be astonished by how much living can be packed into sixty-plus years."   —*Los Angeles Times*

"Fonda's fiercely intelligent, detailed, probing, rigorously revealing memoir should be required reading for any woman eager to excavate and understand her own past and present, and uncover her own outspoken, singular voice."   —*O: The Oprah Magazine*

"[A] sisterly, enveloping memoir . . . an intimate, haunting book that might as well be catnip."   —*The New York Times*

"Terrific . . . rich . . . unexpectedly quite moving."

—*San Francisco Chronicle*

"Jane Fonda's autobiography is as beguiling . . . as Jane Fonda herself. Smart, gifted, accomplished, principled, and entirely fetching."

—*The Washington Post Book World*

"*My Life So Far* is perhaps the most frank memoir by a seminal cultural figure in modern memory. Fonda possesses a raw and affecting candor. . . . Her honesty [is] a force. . . . The leitmotiv of her life is to do good, and be good, [and] it is sincere."

—*The Philadelphia Inquirer*

PRIME TIME

Jane Fonda

PRIME TIME

Random House Trade Paperbacks / New York

2012 Random House Trade Paperback Edition

Copyright © 2011 by Jane Fonda

Illustrations copyright © 2011 by Angela Martini

Published in the United States by Random House Trade Paperbacks, an imprint of The Random House Publishing Group, a division of Random House, Inc., New York.

RANDOM HOUSE TRADE PAPERBACKS and colophon are trademarks of Random House, Inc.

Originally published in hardcover in the United States by Random House, an imprint of The Random House Publishing Group, a division of Random House, Inc., in 2011.

Permissions credits for previously published material are located on page 393.

LIBRARY OF CONGRESS CATALOGING-IN-PUBLICATION DATA
Fonda, Jane
Prime time / by Jane Fonda.
p. cm.
Includes bibliographical references.
ISBN 978-0-8129-7858-2
eBook ISBN 978-0-679-64387-6
1. Aging—Prevention. 2. Aging—Psychological aspects. 3. Rejuvenation.
4. Fonda, Jane, 1937— —Health. 5. Motion picture actors and actresses—
United States—Biography. I. Title.
RA776.75.F655 2011   612.3—dc22   2011007454

Part-title page credits: © 2011 Brigitte Lacombe (1), Justin Marcel Lubin (81), Lee Celano/AFP/Getty Images (155), Scott Gries/Getty Images (253), © 2011 Brigitte Lacombe (315)

Printed in the United States of America

www.atrandom.com

9 8 7 6 5 4 3 2 1

Book design by Barbara M. Bachman

Contents

PART FIVE

THE SPIRAL OF BECOMING

The Arch and the Staircase

The past empowers the present, and the groping footsteps leading to this present mark the pathways to the future.[1]

—MARY CATHERINE BATESON

SEVERAL YEARS AGO, I WAS COMING TO THE END OF MY SIXTIES and facing my seventies, the second decade of what I thought of as the Third Act of my life—Act III, which, as I see it, begins at age sixty. I was worried. Being in my sixties was one thing. Given good health, we can fudge our sixties. But seventy—now, that's serious. In our grandparents' time, people in their seventies were considered part of the "old old" . . . on their way out.

However, a revolution has occurred within the last century—a longevity revolution. Studies show that, on average, thirty-four years have been added to human life expectancy, moving it from an average of forty-six years to eighty! This addition represents an entire second adult lifetime, and whether we choose to confront it or not, it changes everything, including what it means to be human.

Adding a Room

The social anthropologist (and a friend of mine) Mary Catherine Bateson has a metaphor for living with this longer life span in view. She writes in her recent book *Composing a Further Life: The Age of Active Wisdom*, "We have not added decades to life expectancy by simply extending old age; instead, we have opened up a new space partway through the life course, a second and different kind of adulthood that precedes old age, and as a result every stage of life is undergoing change."[2] Bateson uses the identifiable metaphor of what happens when a new room is added to your home. It isn't just the new room that is different; every other part of the house and how it is used is altered a bit by the addition of this room.

In the house that is our life, things such as planning, marriage, love, finances, parenting, travel, education, physical fitness, work, retirement—our very identities, even!—all take on new meaning now that we can expect to be vital into our eighties and nineties . . . or longer.

But our culture has not come to grips with the ways the longevity revolution has altered our lives. Institutionally, so much of how we do things is the same as it was early in the twentieth century, with our lives segregated into age-specific silos: During the first third we learn, during the second third we produce, and the last third we presumably spend on leisure. Consider, instead, how it would look if we tore down the silos and integrated the activities. For example, let's begin to think of learning and working as a lifelong challenge instead of something that ends when you retire. What if the wonderfully empowering feeling of being productive can be experienced by children early in life, and if they know from first grade that education will be an expected part of their entire lives? What if the second, traditionally productive silo is braided with leisure and education? And seniors, with twenty or more productive years left, can enjoy leisure time while remaining in the workforce in some form and attending to education if for no other reason than to challenge their minds? Envisioned this way, longevity becomes like a symphony with echoes of different times recurring with slight modifications, as in music, across the life arc.

Except that we don't have the sheet music to this new symphony. We—today's boomers and seniors—are the pioneer generations, the ones who need to compose together a template for how to maximize the potential of this amazing gift of time, so as to become whole, fully realized people over the longer life arc.

In attempting to chart a course for myself into my sixties and beyond, I've found it helpful to view the symphony of my own life in three acts, or three major developmental stages: Act I, the first three decades; Act II, the middle three decades; and Act III, the final three decades (or however many more years one is granted).

As I searched for ways to understand the new realities of aging, I discovered the arch and the staircase.

The Arch and the Staircase

Here you see two diagrams that I have had drawn, because they make visualizable two conceptions of human life that have come to mean a lot to me.

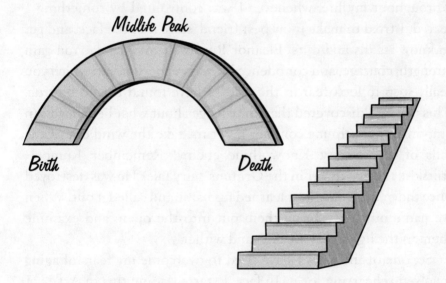

One diagram, the arch, represents a biological concept, taking us from childhood to a middle peak of maturity, followed by a decline into infirmity.

The other, a staircase, shows our potential for upward progression toward wisdom, spiritual growth, learning—toward, in other words, consciousness and soul.

The vision behind these diagrams was developed by Rudolf Arnheim, the late professor emeritus of the psychology of art at Harvard

University, and for me they are clear metaphors for ways we can choose to view aging. Our youth-obsessed culture encourages us to focus on the arch—age as physical decline—more than on the stairway—age as potential for continued development and ascent. But it is the stairway that points to late life's promise, even in the face of physical decline. Perhaps it should be a spiral staircase! Because the wisdom, balance, reflection, and compassion that this upward movement represents don't just come to us in one linear ascension; they circle around us, beckoning us to keep climbing, to keep looking both back and ahead.

Rehearsing the Future

Throughout my life, whenever I was confronted by something I feared, I tried to make it my best friend, stare it in the face, and get to know its ins and outs. Eleanor Roosevelt once said, "You gain strength, courage, and confidence by every experience in which you really stop to look fear in the face." I have found this to be true. This is how I discovered that knowledge about what lies ahead can empower me, help me conquer my fears, take the wind out of the sails of my anxiety. Know thine enemy! Remember Rumpelstiltskin, the evil dwarf in the Grimms' fairy tale? He was destroyed once the miller's daughter learned his name and called it out. When we name our fears, bring them out into the open, and examine them in the light, they weaken and wither.

So, one of the ways I have tried to overcome my fears of aging involved rehearsing for it. In fact, I started doing this in Act II. I believe that this rehearsal for the future (along with doing a life review of the past) is part of why I have been able—so far—to live Act III with relative equanimity.

Being with my father when he was in his late seventies and in decline due to heart problems was what began to shatter any childhood illusions I'd had of immortality. I was in my mid-forties, and it hit me that with him gone, I would be the oldest one left in the family and, before too long, next at the turnstile. I realized then that it was

*Kissing my father as
I brought his Oscar
for* On Golden
Pond *home to him,
because he was too
sick to attend
the ceremony*
JOHN BRYSON
© 2011 BRYSON PHOTO

not so much the idea of death itself that frightened me as it was being faced with regrets, the "what if"s and the "if only"s when there is no time left to do anything about them. I didn't want to arrive at the end of the Third Act and discover too late all that I had not done.

I began to feel the need to project myself into the future, to visualize who I wanted to be and what regrets I might have that I would need to address before I got too old. I wanted to understand as much as possible what cards age would deal me; what I could realistically expect of myself physically; how much of aging was negotiable; and what I needed to do to intervene on my own behalf with what appeared to be a downward slope.

The birth of my two children had taught me the importance of knowledge and preparation. The first birth had been a terrifying, lonely experience; I went through it unprepared and unrehearsed, swept along passively in a sea of pain. The second birth was quite the opposite. My husband and I worked with a birth educator in the months leading up to my due date, so that I was able to visualize what would happen and know what to do. The physical ordeal was no less grueling, the process no faster, but the experience itself was transformed. With knowledge and rehearsal, I found it easier to ride atop the sequence of events rather than be totally submerged by the pain.

I brought what I'd learned from childbirth to my experience facing late midlife. As I said, I was scared back then—it is hard to let go of children, of the success that came with youth, of old identities when new ones aren't yet clearly defined. I felt I could choose whether to be blindly propelled into later life, in denial with my eyes wide shut, or I could take charge and seek out what I needed to know in order to make informed decisions in the many changing areas of my life. That's why, in 1984, at age forty-six, before I'd even had my first hot flash, I wrote *Women Coming of Age,* with Mignon McCarthy, about what women can expect, physically, as they age, and what parts of aging are negotiable. It was a way to force myself to confront and rehearse the future. I was shocked to discover how little research had been devoted to women's health. Most medical studies I found had been done on men. I'm happy to say this has started to change.

At forty-six, I began to envision the old woman I wished to be, and I described her in that book:

> I see an old woman walking briskly, out-of-doors, in every season. She's feisty. She's not afraid of being alone. Her face is lined and full of life. There's a ruddy flush to her cheeks and a bright curious look in her eye because she's still learning. Her husband often walks with her. They laugh a lot. She likes to be with young people and she's a good listener. Her grandchildren love to tell her stories and to hear hers because she's got some really good ones that contain sweet, hidden lessons about life. She has a conscious set of values and the knack to make them compelling to her young friends.

This is an example of rehearsing the future . . . good to do at any age! I'm glad I wrote it down, because it's fun for me to read my forty-six-year-old vision of my senior self, almost thirty years later, as a reality check to see how well I'm doing. Some days, I actually think I'm doing pretty well. I'm still feisty, and my solitude (which I cherish) doesn't feel like loneliness. Humor has definitely come to the fore. I'm no longer married, but I do walk together with my—what to call the man I am with when I'm seventy-two and unmarried? "Boyfriend" sounds too juvenile, don't you think? So then, what? "Lover?" That seems too in-your-face. I think I'll go with "honey." Anyway, my honey and I walk together, we laugh a lot, and we try to swing-dance for fifteen or twenty minutes every night—when we can. I feel I may have finally conquered my difficulties with intimacy. (Or maybe I just found a man who isn't scared of it!)

Richard and me in 2009
MARY VINETTE
MARYVINETTE.COM

Gerontologists such as Bernice Neugarten have learned from their studies of the aged that traumatic events—widowhood, menopause, loss of a job, even imminent death—are not experienced as traumas "if they were anticipated and, in effect, *rehearsed* as part of the life cycle."[3]

Betty Friedan, in her book *The Fountain of Age,* wrote, "The finding emerges that the difference between knowing and planning, and not knowing what to expect (or denial of change because of false expectations) can be the crucial factor between moving on to new growth in the last third of life, or succumbing to stagnation, pathology, and despair."

With the help of many friends of all ages, as well as gerontologists, sexologists, urologists, biologists, psychologists, experts in cognitive research and health care, and a physicist or two, I have written this book. Even though I was already in my own Act III, doing this has been a form of rehearsal—for myself and for you, the reader. I wanted to be prepared and learn all I could. I wanted to be able to say to myself and to you, "Let's make the most of the years that take us from midlife to the end, and here's how!"

I do not want to romanticize the process of aging. Obviously, there is no guarantee that this will be a time of growth and fruition. There are negatives to any stage of life, including potentially serious issues of mental and physical health. I cannot address all these things within the scope of this book. As we know, some of how life unfolds is a matter of luck. Some of it—about one-third, actually— is genetic and beyond our control. The good news is that this means that for a lot of it, maybe two-thirds of the life arc, we *can* do something about how well we do.

This book is for those of us who, like me, believe that luck is opportunity meeting preparation; that with preparation and knowledge, with information and reflection, we can try to raise the odds of being lucky, and of making our last three decades—our Third Acts—the most peaceful, generous, loving, sensual, transcendent time of all; and that planning for it, especially during one's middle years, can help make this so.

Wholeness

Arnheim's staircase made me realize how important it can be to see life as an interplay between one's beginning, middle, and end. I found out that if we understand more deeply what Act I and Act II are (or were) about, who we are (or were becoming) during those foundational years, what dreams are still to be realized and which regrets addressed, then we can see Act III as a coming to fruition, rather than simply a period of marking time, or the absence of youth. We can understand it not as the far side of the arch—as the decline after the peak—but as *a stage of development* in its own terms. We can experience it as part of the staircase—with its own challenges and joys, pitfalls and rewards, a stage as evolving and as satisfying and different from midlife or youth as adolescence is from childhood.

In 1996, Erik and Joan Erikson wrote, in *The Life Cycle Completed,* "Lacking a culturally viable ideal of old age, our civilization does not really harbor a concept of the whole of life."[4] The old ways of thinking about age, the fears of losing our youth and facing our own mortality, have kept us from seeing Act III as a vital, inte-

*With my dog
Tulea in 2004*
MAX COLIN/ELIOT PRESS

grated part of our overall story, the potential-filled culmination of the first two acts. This old thinking is even more tragic now, in light of the extension of the life span. It can rob us of wholeness, and it can rob society of what we each, in our ripeness, have to offer.

Those of us now entering our Third Acts are, on the whole, physically stronger and healthier than ever before. There is every likelihood that, if we work at it individually and collectively, we can develop a new "culturally viable ideal of old age" and see our lives as a series of stages that build one upon the other. Our doing so will not be just for us; it will represent a major cultural shift for the world around us and will help younger generations reconceive of their own life spans.

I have been inspired and encouraged by what I have learned while writing this book. I hope reading it will do the same for you.

In Part One, I set the stage by discussing the three acts of life, the challenges and gifts that each of them presents, and ways for you to begin to step back—now, at whatever act you are in—and become a witness to your own life, in all its stages, and thus see better how to live the rest of it with greater intention, freedom, and clarity. I also write about how doing a life review transformed how I am living my Third Act.

In Part Two, I write about the body, the brain, and our attitudes. There's some pretty good news there, as well as a new word: Positivity! I also, in Chapter 10, go into detail about how to write a life review.

Part Three goes into every dimension of love, friendship, and sex, including how to meet new people. You'll find a few good laughs in there, along with a lot of handy tips.

Part Four isn't what you'd expect in a book like this. But some of the most respected experts on aging believe—as do I—that to mount that staircase of late-life development as a fully realized person, we need to become advocates for the future. This can mean mentoring young children or protecting abused women; it can mean caring for the planet, feeling some responsibility for the big picture beyond ourselves. The psychiatrist Erik Erikson referred to this as "Generativity," and here's more good news: The thirty-year-long Harvard Study of Adult Development shows that among the women in the sample, "mastering Generativity . . . was the best predictor of whether they reported attaining regular orgasm"!⁵

Part Four is also about the importance of facing our mortality and planning for late life—emotionally, financially, legally, and in terms of what we can do, individually and together, to make our society more supportive of seniors and help create a happier environment for them.

Part Five shows us how learning to go inward—spiritually and metaphysically—allows us to look outward with new eyes.

And so let's begin.

PART ONE

SETTING *the* STAGE *for* *the* REST *of* YOUR LIFE

CHAPTER 1

Act III: Becoming Whole

The greatest potential for growth and self-realization exists in the second half of life.

—Carl Jung

HOW OLD DO YOU FEEL?" SOMEONE ASKED ME RECENTLY. I THOUGHT for a moment before answering. I wanted to really consider the question and not give a glib "I feel forty" sort of answer. "I feel seventy," I said, remembering a retort of Pablo Picasso's: "It takes a long time to become young."

Ageism

A while back, I spoke to a group of adolescent girls, and when I mentioned my age, some of them winced. They whispered to me that I should not let on how old I was, because I didn't look seventy. They meant this to be a compliment, but I found it sad and a little scary. Like a lot of us when we were their age, and like our culture in general, these young women viewed age as something to hide, as if youth were the pinnacle of life. Well, maybe it is the pinnacle in terms of body tautness or sperm and egg count or thickness of cartilage and bilateral activation of the parahippocampal gyrus! But I'm not the only one who wouldn't want to go back to adolescence—not for anything! It's too hard! There's too much anxiety about trying to fit in! I also wouldn't care to repeat my twenties and thirties, for that matter. For me, those years were too fraught with trying to make my mark. And heaven forbid,

*Richard and me
on the red
carpet at the*
Vanity Fair
Oscar Party,
2011
CRAIG BARRITT/
GETTY IMAGES

let's not repeat the "in between" time of the late forties and early fifties.

For me, the "good old days" were really the "so-so old days." I spent far too much time worrying that I wasn't good enough, smart enough, thin enough, talented enough. I can honestly say that in terms of feelings of well-being, right now is the best time of my life. All those enoughnesses I worried about just don't matter as much anymore. I have come to believe that when you're actually *inside* oldness, as opposed to anticipating it from the outside, the fear subsides. You discover that you are still yourself, probably even more so.

For me, right now, this time in my life feels like I am beginning to become who I was meant to be all along. Act III isn't at all what

I expected. I never envisioned myself as a happy, learning-to-be-wise older woman.

It didn't just happen. I have worked at it. I have been fortunate in myriad ways, and I have (sometimes despite myself) done what I needed to do to make the most of what I was given.

In society's terms I may be seen as "over the hill," but I've discovered a new, different, challenging landscape on the other side—a landscape filled with new depths of love, new ways of interacting with friends and strangers, new ways of expressing myself and facing setbacks, and, by the way, more hills . . . literally.

Hiking Machu Picchu in 2000

Carl Jung pondered whether "the afternoon of human life [was] merely a pitiful appendage to life's morning" or if it had a significance of its own.[1]

I believe that Rudolf Arnheim's diagrams of the arch and the staircase (which I wrote about in the Preface) answer Jung's question perfectly. Yes, Act III has its own significance! This is when we are meant to go deeper, to become whole. It is the time to move from ego to soul, as the spiritual teacher Ram Dass says.

Professor Arnheim further illustrated his point by showing his students slides of the early and late life works of some of the world's greatest artists. He felt that the paintings of the Impressionists, for example, were the "products of detached contemplation" that age can bring. The character and practical value of the material things they painted were no longer considered relevant; the specificity became blurred, so that, he says, what the Impressionists give us is "a world view that transcends outer appearance to search out the underlying essentials."[2]

Slowing Down, Going Deeper

Over breakfast at a restaurant in Ann Arbor, Michigan, I interviewed Dr. Marion Perlmutter, who is with the Center for Human Growth and Development and the Department of Psychology at the University of Michigan. Expanding on Professor Arnheim's point, she told me, "It may be that it is only by suppression of certain things that we can actually get to higher levels. Was it that Monet had cataracts and couldn't see well or was it that because of the suppression of that detail of vision he was able to get to the deeper level of the Impressionist essence? Cézanne had macular degeneration when he did his later pastels. Beethoven was deaf when he composed his Ninth Symphony. In late life we talk about slowing down as this horrible thing, but we also know that cognition is time-bound; the longer you take, the deeper you get to conceptualization. I think physiology helps us get there. It may be that only by slowing down can we really get more of a global perspective."[3]

The poem "Monet Refuses the Operation," by Lisel Mueller, explains so artfully how age and infirmities can bring deeper insights. Here is an excerpt:

> *Doctor, you say there are no haloes*
> *around the streetlights in Paris*
> *and what I see is an aberration*
> *caused by old age, an affliction.*
> *I tell you it has taken me all my life*
> *to arrive at the vision of gas lamps as angels,*

to soften and blur and finally banish
the edges you regret I don't see,
to learn that the line I called the horizon
does not exist and sky and water,
so long apart are the same state of being. . . .
and now you want to restore
my youthful errors: fixed
notions of top and bottom,
the illusion of three dimensional space.

33 *VARIATIONS*

Right after my seventy-first birthday, I was working on this book when I was asked to star on Broadway in *33 Variations,* a new play by Moisés Kaufman. My character was a contemporary music scholar trying to understand why Beethoven spent three of his later years, when he was deaf and very ill, writing thirty-three variations on what was generally considered to be a mediocre waltz composed by Anton Diabelli, a well-known music publisher of the time. Imagine my surprise and pleasure when I discovered that my character's

A scene in 33 Variations, *with my character leaning against Beethoven* CRAIG SCHWARTZ

final monologue touches upon this very theme: how the exigencies of late life that cause us to slow down also permit a different, deeper kind of seeing.

The character I play explains how at first she had assumed that Beethoven had written the thirty-three variations in order to show mid-eighteenth-century Vienna what a grand masterpiece he could make out of a mediocre waltz. What she learned, however, was very different: She realized that Beethoven knew that the waltz was a simple, popular waltz that people danced to in beer halls. In delving to its depths, Beethoven pierced and dissected it in his thirty-three variations, turning a fifty-second waltz into a brilliant fifty-minute composition. He was sick and deaf, but he was showing us how, when we allow ourselves (or are forced) to slow down and see, what may appear banal on the surface can flower into magnificence.

Ripening Consciousness

We're not all Monet, Cézanne, or Beethoven, but we all have the potential to achieve the flowering of consciousness—to learn to really *see*—and this can occur later in life, even in the presence of terrible physical infirmities.

The day of my final performance in *33 Variations,* I read an article in *The New York Times*[4] about Neil Selinger, a fifty-seven-year-old lawyer who, following retirement, had begun tutoring at the local high school. He volunteered for Habitat for Humanity, and signed up for The Writing Institute at Sarah Lawrence College, where he discovered his "writer's voice." Two years later, he was diagnosed with fatal amyotrophic lateral sclerosis, commonly known as Lou Gehrig's disease. The disease wastes your body, but your brain remains untouched by it. I know quite a bit about the disease because my character in *33 Variations* died of it every night. So, for me, the appearance of this article on that day felt like a little miracle.

In an unpublished essay, Mr. Selinger described what he felt happening to him. "As my muscles weakened, my writing became stronger. As I slowly lost my speech, I gained my voice. As I diminished, I grew. As I lost so much, I finally started to find myself."

Selinger's writing teacher, Steve Lewis, says that his student has had to lose his lawyer's voice and that "he's got sort of a Zen countenance now. And it's reflected in what he writes. He doesn't duck anger and despair, he doesn't duck anything, but it's all there without self-pity. His writing is richer because his experience of the moment is richer." Neil Selinger is the embodiment of mounting the Third Act staircase!

Slowing Down

Unlike during childhood, Act III is a quiet ripening. It takes time and experience and, yes, perhaps the inevitable slowing down.

You have to learn to sort out what's fundamentally important to you from what's irrelevant. A life review, which we'll take up in the next chapter, can help you do this.

Letting Go of What's No Longer Needed: Flexibility and the Shift from Ego to Soul

My brother, Peter, once pointed out to me that on the Fonda family crest is the word *perseverate,* Latin for "persevere." We have been proud, my brother and I, over the years, of our perseverance through some challenging times.

While I still appreciate the value of persistence, it occurs to me that in the Third Act, part of the shift from ego to soul requires flexibility more than perseverance—the flexibility, for instance, to take stock of who and what surround us and to see if maybe we should let some of it go.

Think about gardening. My daughter taught me that if I want to maximize the spring and summer blooms on the English lavender that fills my garden, I have to cut back the dead blooms of fall. Deadheading, it's called (not the Jerry Garcia variety!). The Third Act is the time for deadheading. Like plants in the winter, we have less energy to spare trying to resurrect old, dead growth, trying to blow life into the escapades and behaviors of youth in order to prove we're still young. I don't want to become a hollow old fool, squandering my precious remaining life force on stuff that doesn't serve this stage of life. It takes flexibility and a dose of courage to slough off the clutter, the gadgets, the obsessions, the pursuits, the whatever or whoever doesn't resonate with who we are now or want to become. I understand now what it is that I really need to know and so am freer to discard the rest.

Sure, I forget things, but I also remember a whole lot of things with more vividness because I know *why* I want to remember them and what significance they have for my life. With age, as Stephen Levine says, we "lose memory but gain insight."[5] My time now is dependent on no one but myself, so I, myself, must be sure that the various tasks I choose to occupy my time are the right ones. I have no time to waste as I once did, going down wrong paths. If I want to make ripples, I better be sure I am throwing my pebbles into the right pond.

Getting to Essences

Like the Impressionists, by rendering life down to its concentrated essences, we can begin to live more lightly and to put our energies into activities and people who enrich what may be the only thing that still retains the capacity for growth—our spirit.

SPIRIT

It has been explained to me that soul is the substance of who a person is, while spirit—or consciousness—is a way for a person to communicate with God . . . which, as I see it, means becoming whole. Spirit is the uncapturable essence that makes us unique among animals.

Every other single thing in the world operates on the principle of entropy; in fact, the second law of thermodynamics says that everything is in a continual state of decline and decay (think of

Arnheim's arch). The one thing that defies this universal law is the human spirit (Arnheim's stairway). This alone continues to evolve upward. And, like energy—which it is—spirit can be changed from one form to another, but it cannot be created or destroyed (the first law of thermodynamics!).

The philosopher, poet, and novelist George Santayana wrote, "Never have I enjoyed youth so thoroughly as I have in my old age. . . . Nothing is inherently and invincibly young except spirit. And spirit can enter a human being perhaps better in the quiet of old age and dwell there more undisturbed than in the turmoil of adventure."

We're all born with spirit, but for some of us it is buried deep beneath the detritus of life—violence, abuse, neglect, disease, chronic depression. That's when addictions can happen. We become "empty chalices," in the words of the psychologist Marion Woodman, and so we try to fill ourselves with clutter, including addictions. Psychiatrists call this "self-medicating." For example, alcoholics try to replace spirit with spirits . . . alcohol. There are many other ways in which people in whom spirit is damped down seek to fill themselves: compulsive shopping, gambling, violence, workaholism, sex, drugs, food, drama. One of the great ideas of Alcoholics Anonymous's twelve-step program is that we can't be fully healed until we've opened ourselves to our spirit or "Higher Power."

It took me a long time to get this. The whole "Higher Power" business used to feel so touchy-feely to me. Now that I have experienced it myself—overcoming a long-standing food addiction— I understand that it has more to do with love than it does with God (unless you understand these two as one). The humility needed to take the step of acceptance and love softens the hard, empty place at our center, permitting spirit to flood in and fill the emptiness.

A wise person—I don't remember who—once said, "Change is inevitable. Growth is optional." It takes work and intentionality to continue to grow, to ascend that staircase. In *Beowulf*, this is described as having "wintered into wisdom." Wisdom is there in all of us; we just have to bring it out and fluff it up. But if we don't address our addictions, our stagnation, or our old attitudes, or if our life goal is centered on continuing the past, remaining powerful or good-looking in the mechanistic sense, then age is a downward and very slippery slope. Eventually someone smarter and quicker supplants us at the top, the golf swing gets iffy, the old rituals become empty. While surgery can tighten the face, there's still the giveaway neck and arms, the tendency toward postmenopausal thickening around the middle.

If, however, our goal is to awaken to a new stage, to awaken our consciousness, harvest our wisdom, burnish our perhaps languishing soul so as to go deeper into life's meaning and manifest it with compassion, then age can be a positive process of continued development and growth, moving us toward our goals instead of causing us to leave our goals behind.

Plastic Surgery

I have not hidden the fact that I have succumbed to wanting to look good in the mechanistic sense. Yes, at seventy-two I had plastic surgery on my jawline and under my eyes.

From early girlhood, starting with my father, I was judged by how my face and body looked. This became what I thought determined whether I would be loved. I've tempered my anxiety around these surface issues, but I cannot deny that they still lurk. I sometimes wonder what my life would have been like if those things hadn't mattered as much. Would I have accomplished less because of being less driven to prove myself? I certainly would have had a lot more time to do character-enhancing things instead of obsessive ballet, dieting, suntanning and then tanning beds, and eventually plastic surgery. Oh, well. I finally got tired of looking tired when I wasn't, and I wanted to be able to continue working as an actor in a field where it's hard to work if you've not had any "work" done. (Or so I thought till I worked with Geraldine Chaplin, who hasn't had a speck of "work" done, who works constantly as an actor, and who is absolutely glorious! Ditto the magnificent Vanessa Redgrave!) I still have plenty of cherished lines, however, and

I don't think I look like someone else, but my face is less droopy, and that makes me feel better.

Droopy skin isn't the only manifestation of my age. I choose shoes for comfort now, not style. As Ted Turner's father once said, "What's the good of money if your feet hurt!" My eyesight has diminished. When I began writing this book, I was using font size 14; now I use size 18 and still need glasses. And I rail at restaurants with menus whose print is so small and faint that I need a flashlight! Whatever it is I'm doing, I know now that I have to do it a little slower. I don't leap gracefully out of cars; I don't rush across streets; I use railings and am careful to watch where I step; I pay more attention to posture, partly for looks, but mostly so my back won't hurt. None of these things is a big deal. I know others are less fortunate, including those who face major health problems. I'm not happy about any of my physical problems, but I do not want them to define me. Instead, like many people I have talked to who are in Act III and whose stories are in this book, I just get on with my life, trying to live it, make it useful, and enjoy it as fully as I can. The Positivity and Generativity that I write about in Parts Two and Four are very much at the center of my life.

More on the Longevity Revolution

Opting for mounting the staircase of life rather than staying on the descending arch becomes especially important given that, as already mentioned, longevity has become a new cultural phenomenon. Certainly, there have always been very old people—my mother's father and mother lived into their nineties—but they bore little resemblance to grandparents of today. My grandparents did not seem to enjoy the potential vibrancy we can now expect. They did not come of age with an awareness of the importance of aerobic and weight-bearing exercises for keeping our metabolisms high, our weight in check, and our muscles and bones strong. No one knew, really, about the cost of smoking cigarettes, or about the healing effects of good cognitive therapy, twelve-step programs, or meditation. They didn't have the benefits of joint replacements or organ transplants, or medicines that can eliminate or at least relieve many of the major age-related illnesses or conditions (including Viagra, Cialis, and testosterone therapy).

My maternal grandmother, Sophie Seymour, holding Vanessa as a baby, 1968

With Malcolm, my grandson, when he was about one year old

RICHARD PHIBBS/ ART DEPT

Today, almost 20 percent of the U.S. population is sixty-five or older—25 million men and 31 million women—and every year people live two-tenths of a year longer!

Think about it: At the time of our founding fathers, in the eighteenth century, the average life expectancy was only thirty-five. Since then, science, modern medicine, improved nutrition and lifestyle, sanitation, and lower maternal mortality rates have extended our life expectancy by forty-five years, from thirty-five to *eighty*! As I have said, this represents an entire second adult lifetime. The jump of thirty-four years in just the last century is truly stunning given that during the previous forty-five hundred years, from the middle of the Bronze Age to the twentieth century, human life expectancy increased by only twenty-seven years. This may be one of the most dramatic changes in contemporary times, and we have barely begun to come to terms with what it means for us individually, for the future of our society, and for the planet. From a policy and cultural point of view, we are still functioning as though this extension of life expectancy hasn't happened. That is why Professor Arnheim's staircase is the one we need to climb.

If we are not burdened by a debilitating disease, this is the time when we can begin to assume our essential personhood.

Freed from being so strongly defined by a uterus or penis or a taut body or a job or our relationships to our children, to a partner, to a firm or a profession, we now have at least a third of our life span still to go. In that time, we can explore life's new potentials and deepen what we already are and what we already know.

Becoming Whole

When I wrote *My Life So Far,* I called the section about Act III "Beginning" because that is what it felt like then. Now that I am a decade into this act, I think a more fitting title for this stage would be "Becoming Whole." To see Act III in this way, to see it as continued human development, represents a revolutionary paradigm shift. Ours is the generation to make this shift, to reinvent the last third of life, and we will do it not just for ourselves. It will represent a seismic shift for the world around us, and particularly for our children and young friends. Whether we like it or not, we have become the first role models for the younger generations of how to prepare for the last third of life. Here's to being good role models!

The next chapter is about why doing a review of my life has changed everything for me now.

CHAPTER 2

A Life Review: Looking Back to See the Road Ahead

He is the happiest man who can see the connection between the end and the beginning of his life.

—GOETHE

ONE OF THE SMARTEST THINGS I EVER DID—AND I CAN SAY this unequivocally—was a life review. I examined myself and my life in Acts I and II as carefully and honestly as I could, as a way toward wholeness and to prepare for a good Act III. By doing a life review, I gradually began to see myself, as well as certain events and people in my past, with new eyes. It wasn't the facts of them that changed; it was the meaning they held for me. I was able to see my younger self in a new way—with both more compassion and more objectivity. The quality of my relationships to certain people and events in my past—my mother and father, especially—was also transformed, as was how I feel about myself now. In a way, I discovered the feisty, strong girl I had always been.

The Meaning We Assign to Our Lives

Only recently, while reading *Man's Search for Meaning*, by the psychiatrist Viktor Frankl, did I understand why my personal life review had such an effect on me. Frankl, who spent many years in a Nazi concentration camp, came to the conclusion that everything you have in life can be taken from you except one thing: your freedom

Act I: Me at age three

Act II: Me with Vanessa, speaking at a rally in 1972 when I was pregnant with my son, Troy
© VINCE COMPAGNONE

Act III: At the Golden Globes, 2011
FRAZER HARRISON/
GETTY IMAGES

to choose how you will respond to a situation. That, I now believe, is what determines the quality of the life we have lived—not whether we've been rich or poor, famous or unknown, healthy or ill. What determines our quality of life is *how we relate to these realities:* what kind of meaning we assign them, what kind of attitude we cling to about them, what state of mind they trigger.

Beginning a Life Review

It was the day of my fifty-ninth birthday—December 21, 1996— when it first hit me: *In one year I will turn sixty, and that will be the beginning of my last act—the final three decades of my life.* "Last"s and "final"s had not been featured in my prior vocabulary, and, frankly, as I faced the looming six-oh, I felt a knot in my stomach.

I was leaning against a hay bale in the back of a pickup truck when the realization swept over me. Four cowboys and I were heading back to headquarters after a long day rounding up bison on one of

Me rounding up bison on one of Ted Turner's ranches in southern New Mexico © ANNIE LEIBOVITZ/CONTACT PRESS IMAGES

Ted Turner's spacious ranches in southern New Mexico. Dear reader, I know this is not the first time something in my life has sounded like a scene from a bad western movie script! But that's how it was.

As we drove across the top of a high mesa, the vast, lunar landscape extended as far as I could see—endless, flat mesas, volcanic rimrock, steep canyons where exposed geologic strata gave evidence of upheavals and ancient oceans, created perhaps during Paleolithic times. Surrounded on all sides by stark reminders of the earth's fourteen-billion-year existence, I felt the issue of time—the inexorability of it—pressing in on me. Okay, I know that in the grand scheme of things, three decades are negligible, but this was *my* life. Those three decades to come were *my* decades. What had I done with all the time—the almost six decades—now past? What did I want to do with my remaining time? How could I make the most of these coming years?

In the theater, the Third Act is when everything that has happened in Acts I and II must pay off if the play is to be memorable. "Maybe life is like that," I thought. Maybe, in order to know how to have a good Third Act, I needed to look back at Acts I and II—to do what is called a life review. Maybe in order to answer my own questions, I would have to figure out what my first two acts had been about.

I knew I had to clear a path to my future by clarifying the road from my past until now. As I said in my memoirs, *My Life So Far,* I didn't want to be like Christopher Columbus, who didn't know where he was headed when he left, didn't know where he was when he got there, and didn't know where he'd been when he got back.

As we drove past walls of exposed rock, I saw how the stratifications revealed events, layered one on top of another over long periods of time. Just like life. Experiences are laid down, and for a while, the most recent one is the top, the plateau, the ground on which you walk. But then newer experiences occur and new layers are put down, changing the size and color and slope of what came before.

By the time the cowboys and I had arrived back at ranch headquarters, I had made up my mind that I would spend my fifty-ninth year excavating my life—examining the strata of my years.

I had also decided to make a short video based on my research that I might show, if it was good enough, to guests at my sixtieth-birthday party a year hence. This would give me a concrete narrative project with a deadline that I would have to meet. Maybe from the vantage point of fifty-nine, after surveying, observing, and reflecting upon the events and people of my past, I might gain a new understanding of them. And a new understanding might lead me, loins girded, into a successful last act.

I had a lot of experiences to learn from. We all do. There is a very human tendency to deny the failures and tragedies in our lives, but these are the very things that sometimes deliver us to ourselves—if we can learn from them.

I have known failures of all kinds: career failures, wrong paths taken, time wasted, relationships spoiled—the bumps along the searches and meanders of my life. Those failures that I ran from taught me nothing. Those that I confronted, cozied up to, and understood were the ones that permitted me quantum leaps forward. In another way of looking at it, they became the compost from which new growth emerged.

There are usually no rewards without a price. You can't learn much that is new by playing it safe. Someone once said to me, "God doesn't look for awards and medals, God looks for wounds. God enters us through our wounds." I decided I would look at my wounds, see what they could teach me, let them help me set my compass and rechart a course for the time that remained. What I had to continually bear in mind—and heart and body—was the knowledge that life isn't a dress rehearsal. *This is it.* I may have conceived of life in acts, but this coming period wasn't an act! I had to try to get it right.

I saw some things that I needed to work on in this Third Act: my sense of fun and humor; my capacity for intimacy. I knew I didn't want to die without succeeding in an intimate relationship with a man. I realized that I might have chosen the partners I did in Act II because they, like me, were challenged in the intimacy department.

I saw what I wanted to do in Act III: keep myself as fit and healthy as I could; repair the breaches with those I felt I should be closer to; learn to avoid stress and be more patient; lead with a loving heart; and stay useful and engaged with issues that matter the most to me, such as helping adolescents see a bright future for themselves and ending violence against women and girls.

I saw what I wanted to stop doing: judging people who disagree with me; being impatient.

What would you say about yourself? What do you want to have as goals for your life? What do you want it all to add up to?

A Life Review

When I first began excavating my life, I found myself reviewing events as someone perched on the outside, chronicling what had happened: I did this; then I did that. It helped me get started, but before long I felt it to be an empty exercise. The power of the memory of my experiences was muted by my focusing solely on the fact that they had happened. I was on the outside looking in, as if I were watching a movie.

What I needed to do was to go inside my experiences, to delve deeper—to try to recapture them more fully by bringing myself back into how that little girl and then that adolescent had felt back then. This involved active remembering—that is to say, remembering not just in my head but also in my body. I needed to envision my experiences and bring the accompanying emotions back into my body—which, if we really think about it, is where these memories and feelings existed most pungently and where they exist still; memories reside not only in our linear minds but also in our bodies, our cells, our tissues, and our senses.

My Life Review

Here are some examples of what my life review was like, at pivotal points along the way. Maybe this will help you think about how to get started on your own life review.

FIRST MEMORIES

I was two years old when my brother was born. My first memory is of my father coming back from the hospital with home movies of my mother, beaming, holding Peter in her arms. Watching the film in the living room of our home in Brentwood, California, was traumatic for me, at two. While going through a box of old letters I had saved but never revisited, I found a handwritten one from my maternal grandmother that read, "I shall never forget your reaction to seeing Peter in your mother's arms. The tears streamed down your cheeks but you didn't cry out loud."

I went through an album I have of my baby pictures, and I could find none of me in Mother's arms. Only nurses with masks over their lower faces held me for Dad's camera. I wrote about this in *My Life So Far*—powerful memories have a way of lingering. Mother had wanted a boy and must have been disappointed when I came along sans penis. I must have sensed her disappointment, the way babies can sense things. So when I saw the images of Peter in Mother's arms, I think I felt I'd lost her to him.

As I thought about this in my life review, I began to grasp where my fear of intimacy may have originated, and to realize that I didn't have in either parent a person comfortable with emotional closeness. I could choose to blame my parents and make that my life narrative, or I could try to understand why they were that way, feel empathy for them, and set my sights on charting a different course for myself.

I began putting other pieces of the puzzle of myself together, like a detective. I discovered that my mother had suffered from postpartum depression when Peter was born. Nothing was known about postpartum blues back then. This partly explained her two-month absence from home following Peter's birth. *It had nothing to do with me.* Facts. Facts. But underneath the facts were the feelings, and I began to access those when I took myself back into the

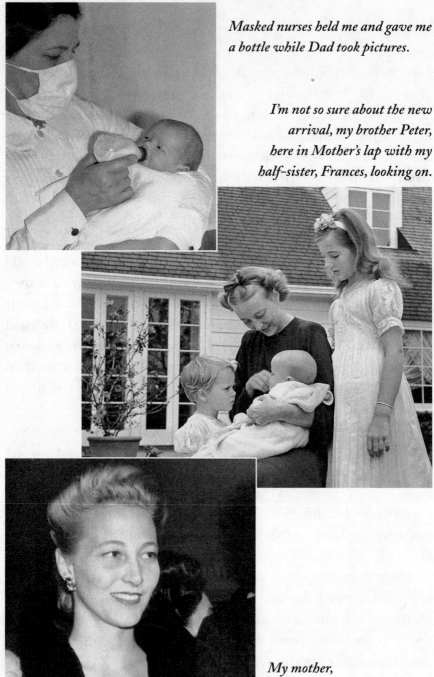

Masked nurses held me and gave me a bottle while Dad took pictures.

I'm not so sure about the new arrival, my brother Peter, here in Mother's lap with my half-sister, Frances, looking on.

My mother, around age 34

little two-year-old girl sitting on the floor next to the 16mm projector, watching home movies of her mother and baby brother. I could hear again the whirring sound of the projector. I refelt my painful feelings of abandonment.

I studied family photographs, honing in on nuances of expression that might provide clues, hoping to recover proof of love in our family, love that was so rarely expressed. Yet I could see it on my father's face as he played with me, at one year old, in our pool. *So he did love me when I was very little!* But how glum I was in childhood photos with my mother, as though deliberately sending a signal for all who cared to pick up on it that hers was not the team I chose to be on. Compassion opened my heart when I noted the desperation in my mother's eyes in the photo of our family posed to look as if we were on a picnic, one year before her suicide. Forgiveness began to creep into my heart, forgiveness of her and also of myself.

I remembered how frightened I was of the noise of a motorcycle. During the Second World War, in the newsreels that would be shown in movie theaters before the main feature, Nazis were often

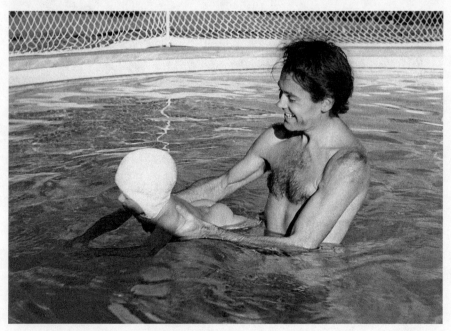

Dad playing with me in our pool

Me around age two, making it clear to the camera that Mother's lap was not where I wanted to be

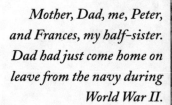

Mother, Dad, me, Peter, and Frances, my half-sister. Dad had just come home on leave from the navy during World War II.

shown riding motorcycles, so every time I heard one I would shout, "Get out of the way! Here comes Hitler!"

I remembered the exhilaration I felt galloping bareback through the avocado groves in Pacific Palisades, California, unafraid, the Lone Ranger!

I tracked down Diana Dunn, my best friend from middle school, whom I had not seen in more than fifty years. She told me stories I'd forgotten, like the one about the time several of us found a dead snake in the road as we walked back from the hockey field. We scooped it up and put it inside the desk of a teacher we didn't like. When she opened her desk drawer and saw the snake, she went into shock. All of us were called into the principal's office and asked who was responsible for the snake. My friend told me that I was the only one who admitted to the prank. She recounted a similar experience when, during a sleepover at a friend's house, we'd knocked over an antique lamp while playing hide-and-seek. Our friend's mother was very upset and wanted to know who was responsible. I fessed up, and because of my telling the truth, the mother didn't punish us.

I recalled the girl at summer camp who beat me up and rubbed my face in the dirt as she shouted, "Don't think you're special just because Henry Fonda is your father!" I refused to cry, but it lodged in my memory as a terrifying experience.

Newly discovered anecdotes like these gave me confidence, made me feel I had some good qualities after all, that I wasn't just the lazy, foolish girl my father seemed to see me as. The faint outlines of a brave, resilient, honest little girl began to emerge, and I realized that I liked her, even if her parents hadn't seemed to be too interested!

PARENTS, GRANDPARENTS, AND FAMILY

Perhaps the most important part of my research on Act I was that which I did on my parents and grandparents. I needed to know who they were behind the parental masks. What did they really care about, and why did they do the things they did? I focused on how my parents were treated by my grandparents, what state of mind my parents might have been in when they married each other and when I was born. I called and met with second and third cousins who knew my parents or grandparents; an aging aunt; and friends of the family who were still alive and reachable. I was like a sleuth, putting together the puzzle of a family, a self, a childhood, piece by piece. I began to see patterns and reasons behind things that had been boarded up in my house of memories.

I knew I was not the sort of person who could have done this life review and this family research much earlier. I needed the challenge of my Third Act to compel me to take the time and be brave enough to face it, to declare a memory open house, to seek the truth about myself and my family. Now I had an added incentive, too: I wanted to get my life right going forward.

Me, around age three

Thus, I learned that there had likely been a long history of undiagnosed depression in the Fonda men, as well as what my cousins described as an almost pathological abhorrence for heavy women, especially those with thick legs. *Ahh.* My dad!

I learned that my father had always avoided any situation that would cause him to be emotional. He'd even refused to attend his mother's funeral, choosing instead to stay in New York, where he was performing in a play. Work always came first for him, perhaps as a way to avoid real-life emotion. He didn't even miss a performance of *Mister Roberts* to be with Peter and me the night our mother killed

*My grandfather William Brace, Aunt Harriet, Dad, Aunt Jayne,
and Herberta, my grandmother*

*Members of the Fonda family, including Sue Fonda, David's wife; Aunt
Harriet; Becky Fonda, Peter's wife; Peter Fonda; Tina Fonda; David
Fonda; me; Cyndi Fonda Dabney; and children, gathered on the porch of
Dad's birth home at the Stuhr Museum in Nebraska*

Family picnic in Omaha, July 1907. Front row, left to right: *My father in the lap of my grandmother Herberta, Ethelyn Hinners Fonda holding my aunt Jayne, my grandfather William Brace holding my aunt Harriet.* Back row: *my great-grandmother "Grammie" Hattie, unknown (could be Hattie's sister), and my great-grandfather, Ten Eyck Hilton Fonda, Sr.*

herself. (I learned that she had not died of a heart attack only when, a year later, I read in a gossip column that it had been suicide.)

ACT II

In my second act, the rap on me was that "there was no there there," that I was only whatever my current husband wanted me to be. In fact, when I asked my daughter, who has made documentary films, to help me with the autobiographical video I was shooting for my sixtieth-birthday party, she said, "Why don't you just get a chameleon and let it crawl across the screen?" I knew that one important thing I needed to find out through my life review was whether this opinion of me was true. I secretly thought that maybe it was.

With Ted at my sixtieth-birthday party

But as I delved deeper, I could see evidence of a new, stronger me starting to emerge. I felt as though I was *owning* myself for the first time. *There is a there there!*

PHYSICAL ABUSE

The most profound event for me during the writing of my memoirs was when I was able to obtain my mother's medical records from the mental institution where she killed herself. In them, the doctors noted that my grandfather had had the symptoms of a paranoid schizophrenic. He'd boarded up windows and kept the front door bolted because he feared that some man would come and steal his beautiful, much younger wife. The records included a fifteen-page autobiography written by my mother, I assume upon admittance, at the request of the doctors.

In her own words, she revealed that she had been sexually

molested at age eight by the piano tuner, the only man my grandfather would unbolt the front door for! All my adult life I had wondered about my mother's childhood. The older I got and the more I understood about the long-term effects of early trauma, the more I intuited that something bad must have happened to her. Maybe that's why I had been drawn to studying childhood sexual abuse over the previous five years. My research enabled me to understand what my mother meant when, in recounting her middle and high school years, she wrote, "Boys, boys, boys." I was able to connect the dots upon reading that she had had six abortions and plastic surgery on her nose and breasts before I was born, in 1937, and that her psychiatric tests at the end were, according to the doctors' reports, "replete with perceptual distortions, many of them emphasizing bodily defects and deformities."

By the time I read my mother's reports I already knew that sexual abuse, be it a one-time trauma or a long-term violation, is not only a physical trauma; its memories carry a powerful emotional and psychic charge and can lead to emotional and psychosomatic illnesses and *difficulties with intimacy.* The ability to connect deeply with others is broken, and it becomes difficult to experience trust, feel competent, have a sense of self. Thus, another piece of the family's intimacy puzzle fell into place.

I also knew that sexual abuse robs a young person of her sense of autonomy. The boundaries of her personhood become porous, and she no longer feels the right to claim her psychic or bodily integrity. For this reason, it is not unusual for survivors to become promiscuous starting in adolescence. The message that abuse delivers to the fragile young one is: "All you have to offer is your sexuality, and you have no right to keep it off-limits." *Boys, boys, boys.*

GUILT

Then there's the issue of guilt. It seems counterintuitive that a child would feel guilty about being abused by an adult whom they

are incapable of fending off. But children, I learned, are develop-
mentally unable to blame adults. They must believe that adults, on
whom they depend for life and nurturing, are trustworthy. Instead,
guilt is internalized and carried in the body, often for a lifetime—
a dark, free-floating anxiety and depression that can cross generations. This can lead to hatred of one's body, excessive plastic
surgery, and self-mutilation.

I had learned, years before I'd read my mother's history of
abuse, that these feelings of guilt and shame, the sense of never
being good enough, and hatred of one's body can cast a long shadow.
These emotions can span generations, carried on what feels like a
cellular level to daughters and even granddaughters. *So that's partly
where they came from, my own body issues, my feeling of not being good enough!*

Reading my mother's typed history, with her little penciled
notes in the margins, filled me with sadness and with compassion
for my mother, as well as gratitude that, fifty years later, her history
would allow me to forgive her—and myself. Again the realization
swept over me: *Her remoteness, her suicide had nothing to do with me. I don't
have to feel guilty.* This was an important lesson, this understanding
that other people have lives and problems you know nothing
about—their behavior is not all about you!

Talking to her few remaining friends and family members, I
discovered that my mother, whom I remembered as a nervous,
fragile, nonsexual victim, was viewed by her contemporaries as a
"rock" on which they could lean in times of need, an icon, an
extremely sophisticated, sexy, ebullient woman who attracted men
"like moths to a flame." It took me a while before I managed to
replace the pathological version of a mother whose genes I share
but had rejected for six decades with this new, powerful vision of
her. Maybe she wasn't able to be the mother my brother and I
needed, but she had so many other fascinating, capable, lovable
parts to her. I was finally able to see more of the totality of her. This
was a mother I wanted to own, and owning her meant that the
love-denying defenses I had erected against her came tumbling

down. I felt a new lightness of being and knew I was finally coming into my own.

I have written about much of this in my memoirs, but I repeat the stories here because they are so important to me. Perhaps my telling them will trigger your own remembrances of formative experiences. Especially important for me was the discovery of my mother's childhood sexual abuse. One out of three girls is an abuse survivor, and there is a real possibility that such a trauma has cast a shadow over your own family. You won't know unless you ask.

In doing my life review, I read books by the famed psychologist Alice Miller; *The Drama of a Gifted Child* was especially useful. It is about people who survived emotionally and physically abusive childhoods with narcissistic parents because they developed adequate defense systems. Also useful was *I Don't Want to Talk About It,* by the therapist Terrence Real, which addresses men's depression and their difficulty in expressing emotion. My goal was to better understand my father. As it turned out, however, these books also helped me understand my three husbands! Terrence Real writes about the many ways men unconsciously disguise depression with addictions, and about how hard it is for them to allow people to see their underlying sadness. It isn't manly! This permitted me to view the significant men in my life with forgiveness and compassion. What a wonderful gift to bring into my Third Act!

FORGIVENESS AND GRATITUDE

Forgiveness is at the center of it all, and gratitude. I was able to see how many people had given me so much, had believed in me even when I hadn't. On a deep, noncerebral level, I could separate who I was from how my parents had behaved toward me.

MY LATE FORTIES AND FIFTIES

When I looked back at Act II, especially my late forties and fifties, I saw that I got stressed out so easily then. I remember feeling like

*With Vadim on our
wedding day*

*Tom Hayden with
Vanessa and Troy*

*With Ted at one
of his ranches in
Montana, in
1977*
© ANNIE LEIBOVITZ/
CONTACT PRESS
IMAGES

Sisyphus trying to roll a boulder up a mountain. I thought that this was just life. I'd wake up in the morning and my first six thoughts would be negative. I realized that my negativity had been increasing as I aged, and I grew concerned.

Today I do not suffer from the "poor me"s; there is no longer a blanket of negativity weighing me down. I no longer react to today's dramas with my own drama, partly because I've replaced stress with detachment. By that I don't mean indifference but, rather, an ability to step back and observe events with greater objectivity, fairness, and perception instead of so much subjectivity. This detachment can be one result of doing a life review. Understanding leads to the realization that *it's not just about you!* I have been able to carry this newly discovered perspective and wholeness with me into my Third Act—proof that it's never too late!

Decommissioning Our Demons

What the experience of doing a life review has taught me is that while we cannot undo what has been, we can change the way we understand and feel about it, and this changes everything. It helps us decommission our demons, frees us from the past, and gives us a boost as we go forward, in new ways, into the rest of our lives.

Self-Confrontation and Transformation

While researching this book, I was surprised to find that a number of psychiatrists advocate the life review process, not for the purpose of wallowing in past problems or pathologies or enshrining our early years in either joy or pain, but as a means of self-confrontation and transformation. We look back, we take responsibility for ourselves, and we move on.

The late Dr. Robert Butler, who was the founding president of the International Longevity Center in New York City, said, "There is a moral dimension to the life review because one looks evaluatively at one's self, one's behavior, one's guilt." He believed that a life review can lead to atonement, redemption, reconciliation, and affirmation and can help one find a new meaning in life. He noted that "if unresolved conflicts and fears are successfully reintegrated, they can give new significance and meaning to an individual's life." I know this can be the case; I have experienced it and the freedom it brings. So, step one in making a whole of your life is spending time on a life review.

As mentioned earlier, Viktor Frankl's idea that you have the freedom to choose how you respond to a given situation influenced me greatly. Approaching the matter from a different vantage point, quantum theorists have reached a similar conclusion, maintaining that "we determine reality by the manner in which we approach it. If we observe from a different perspective, we 'discover' a different reality."[1]

Doing a life review can allow us to discover a different reality lurking within those already-lived years. What exquisite freedom this could give us if it allowed us to rearrange our attitudes about our experiences and the people in our lives—the freedom to choose the *meaning* of our experiences.

Developing New Neural Pathways

If we can learn to assign new meanings to stressful situations, we can actually avoid the biochemical and hormonal reactions that cause damage to our systems, especially with age. Recent cognitive research shows that our ability to change our attitudes and behaviors manifests neurologically, as well. Our brains retain their plasticity well into our Third Acts, and they can be rewired. When we react to a person or the memory of a person or event in a negative way over and over and over, it becomes woven into the fabric of our brain's neural network, like a well-worn footpath that grows deeper over time. The footpaths are not structural; they are patterns made by electrical and chemical signals that are sent via neurotransmitters to parts of the brain's hundreds of billions of cells, or neurons; the neurons get into the habit of interacting in certain patterns. But when we change our reactions through new insight, experiences, cognitive therapy, or mediation, no matter how old we are, a neural-pathway shift can occur; the signals can change direction. If we can manage to maintain the new, positive interpretation of the person or event, this new pathway will win out over the formerly hardwired memory. We may not be able to change what happened, but we can change our feelings about it. This is humankind's ultimate freedom!

The possibility of treading new neural pathways through the landscape of the past is in itself a worthwhile endeavor as a way to grow, to develop your character, to become whole. What a potentially precious gift doing a life review can be, for ourselves! And, perhaps, for our relatives and children (should we choose to write it down and show it to them): not writing a history for the purpose of impressing or pleasing or reassuring, but to tell our own real story. Our truth may help set our children free. And it will surely help us shape a strong Third Act, one built on a foundation of truth—about who we are and have, actually, always been.

CHAPTER 3

Act I: A Time for Gathering

*We shall not cease from exploration
And the end of all our exploring
Will be to arrive where we started
And know the place for the first time.*

—T. S. ELIOT, *Four Quartets*

THE FIRST ACT OF OUR LIVES, AS I SEE IT, BEGINS AT BIRTH AND lasts for twenty-nine years. Originally, I called the First Act "Gathering" because it is the stage when we gather together the ingredients—the tools, the skills, the scars—that make us uniquely *us,* the elements we will spend Acts II and III recovering from but also building on. In terms of the passage above from T. S. Eliot's *Four Quartets,* Act I is the "place" we come back to after all our exploring, and, because we are laden with experience and perhaps forgiveness and wisdom, we see it and understand it for the first time. This is why it is important, in a life review, to visualize and reflect on who we were back then and what that can teach us about who we are now and what we want to focus on going forward. Often, by doing so, we can make our present life better.

Unhappy Childhoods Can Fade Away

Interestingly, I discovered research that indicates that whether our childhoods were happy or miserable is not all that important in later life. Dr. George Vaillant, a psychiatrist and researcher, is the director of the thirty-year-long Harvard Study of Adult Development, one of the most important studies ever done about aging and why people either thrive or fail to. In his book about the study, *Aging Well,* Dr. Vaillant, talking about the men in the study (although women were also participants), says, "Unhappy childhoods become less important with time. When the lives of the men whose childhoods were most bleak . . . were contrasted with men whose childhoods were the most sunny . . . the influence on college adjustment was very important. By early midlife, childhood was still significantly important, but by old age the warmth of childhood was statistically unimportant. A warm childhood, like a rich father, tended to inoculate the men against future pain, but a bleak childhood—such as with a poverty-stricken father—did not condemn either the Harvard or the Inner City men to misery."[1]

The Young Brain

One thing scientists know for sure: at birth, babies' brains have around twenty-five hundred synapses, or points of connection between the neurons that receive and send signals. These continue to multiply during the very early years, and until recently, it was believed that this increase in synapses happened only once—in childhood. Not true! Brain scientists now know that there is a second surge right before adolescence that lasts into the late twenties.

Think about it: Whether you are a boy or a girl, you have all these high-octane hormones flooding through you, but the prefrontal cortex, the part of the brain that will allow you to avoid risks, determine appropriate behavior, decide on priorities, and understand the consequences of your actions is still under construction!

"The skills you practice as a child and pre-teen become much sharper in the teenage years; and those practiced reluctantly, if at all, will diminish on your brain's hard-disk drive," writes Judith Newman, an author and columnist.[2] In other words, when it comes to brain neurons, early on we need to use them or lose them!

Education

This aspect of neural development is the likely reason that education is one of the key ingredients of Act I, an ingredient we need to have gathered when our brain circuitry is being established. Early education is particularly critical in determining cognitive function in old age—at least in Western cultures.

Many important studies show that lifelong learning is one element found in happy, healthy older people. It has even been shown that for every added year of education you receive, your life is likely to last more than a year longer! In her book *A Long Bright Future,* Dr. Laura Carstensen, the founding director of the Stanford Center on Longevity, says, "Although income level and occupational status are influential, when push comes to shove, I think most social scientists would put their money on education as the most important factor in ensuring longer lives."[3] Dr. Carstensen goes on to explain that educated people have better jobs, earn more money, live in safer neighborhoods, lead healthier lives with less stress, and manage their health care better when they do get sick. It may be too late to do much about your education in the developmental sense, but other studies show that learning new things at any age affects one's brain synapses and has a positive health impact. We can try to keep learning, and we can ensure that younger people—our grandchildren, perhaps—receive a good education. Do you think you might want to go back and study some more? Lots of people of all ages are doing so these days, and schools are making it more convenient for us.

Gender Identity

Another central factor in Act I involves how we have internalized our gender identity—what goes into being a girl or a boy. This is more culturally determined than we realize. As the spiritual leader and philosopher Krishnamurti once said, "You think you are thinking your thoughts, you are not; you are thinking the culture's thoughts." When it comes to gender distinctions, early on the culture's thoughts profoundly determine who we become. Starting in Act I, boys and girls internalize messages about gender and society's expectations. If we do not become conscious of these unspoken communications and thus do not address them, they continue to determine our thoughts and behaviors throughout our whole lives, in ways that can rob us of our full humanity. One's gender identity may be a key aspect of Act I, the area where we can sustain the deepest wounds during this stage of gathering.

GIRLS

When you do a life review, think about your adolescence. What was it like, in gender terms? What scenes do you remember? What were you like? What was your mother like? Your aunts? What role models did you have? How did your father and mother respond to your changes and development during puberty?

Doing my life review, I realized the extent to which I changed

Taken at my high school graduation

when I entered adolescence. For me it began to happen around age twelve, when boys entered the picture and my father began to insinuate that I was fat. Prior to that, I had been a tomboy and what had mattered to me about my body was that I was strong and limber and brave enough to climb high trees and wrestle with my boy friends. Once it was expected that the boy friends would become boyfriends, the emphasis shifted to fitting in, being popular, looking right, staying thin. This is when I became disembodied—I can feel it now, in retrospect. I moved out of myself and took up residence next door. The most authentic parts of me took a backseat to the girl (and then the woman) who tried—at least on the surface—to become whatever I thought the boy (or man) I was with wanted. I was beginning my Third Act before I felt I had recovered from this Act I conditioning. This phenomenon, by the way, is not unique to me . . . far from it.

Because of my work with adolescents, I have studied the ways in which this stage of gender-identity development in Act I is different for girls than it is for boys. For many girls, especially Caucasian girls, adolescence is when they try to hide what they know and feel; the code says, "Don't be too strong, too outspoken, too sexual, too aggressive."

A perfect example of this was related to me by Catherine Steiner-Adair, an instructor at Harvard's Department of Psychiatry and the former director of Eating Disorders Education and Prevention at the Klarman Eating Disorders Center. "I was doing research in a middle school," she said. "Sometimes I'd invite the students out for pizza. When I would ask the girls what they wanted on their pizzas, the ten-year-olds would want double cheese with pepperoni, the thirteen-year-olds would say, 'I don't know,' and the fifteen-year-olds would answer, 'Whatever you want.'" In other words, girls lose their relationship with themselves and what they want in order to fit in and to be in a relationship, especially with a boy. Asking for double cheese and pepperoni might make them look like they're pigging out or not "feminine" enough.

Like many girls, I first began to experience anxiety and depression during adolescence. That is also when my twenty-year-long battle with anorexia and bulimia began. As I know all too personally, this doesn't end with adolescence but is a pattern of disembodiment that, unless consciously broken, can make intimate relationships nigh impossible; we are not bringing our whole selves to the table—literally and figuratively! If we manage to break the pattern of anxiety, disembodiment, and addiction, then, in our Third Acts, we will be able, as the psychologist Carol Gilligan says, to find our way back to the spirited ten- and eleven-year-old girls we once were, *before* our voices went underground—only better, wiser.

If you are a woman, think about your own adolescence. Did you feel you had to conform to culturally imposed stereotypes of femininity, or did you have an authentic relationship to your sexuality and to your gender? Did you *own* it? Were you able to embody your sexuality because someone made sure you understood that sexuality isn't just about the act of sex, it's also about sensuality and feelings? Were you made to feel you had to look and behave a certain way if you were to earn love? Were you supposed to be seen and not heard? Did you have someone who made you understand that your feelings and ideas were as valuable as a boy's? That you could be strong and brave as well as caring and giving? What kind of role model was your mother? Did she express her own opinions? Take some time for herself? Did your father rule the roost and your mother always acquiesce? How did your father respond to your adolescence? Did you feel you weren't pretty enough or good enough or thin enough?

This is all so subjective, isn't it? Some of the most beautiful women I know think they are unattractive because of early messages, and some not traditionally attractive women exude confidence and beauty because that's how they were made to feel growing up. Did one or both of your parents act as a buffer to the misogynist media? Did they talk to you about how ridiculous it is that so often advertisements use ultrathin, stereotypically sexy girls and women or macho, super-buff men to sell things? Ads can make women and men feel anxious about how they are (real life) in order to persuade them to buy things that, the implication is, will make them more acceptable—like the models.

BOYS

From my friend Carol Gilligan, a psychologist, a writer, and the mother of three sons, I learned that one of the big differences between girls and boys is that girls' *voices* go underground at adoles-

At around age four with Peter, my brother—two years younger—playing in the sandbox

cence, whereas boys' *hearts* go underground when they are around five or six years old, the age when they begin formal schooling, leave home, and are exposed to the broader culture. If you are a man, did your parents or your teachers make you feel like a sissy if you cried, or a momma's boy if you walked away from a fight? Were you taught that a "real man" would never let anyone get away with shaming him and that shaming had to be met with violence? Did your template for manhood mean having to choose between a non-thinking, nonfeeling macho man and a New Age wimp? Did you have an adult who helped you understand your uniqueness, that you weren't better than girls but wonderfully different? Did they instill in you an admiration for attributes like being present, brave, trustworthy, focused, goal-oriented, or a good team player? These are positive masculine qualities (good for women, too!). As a boy, did you feel it was okay to be wrong? Did you find it hard to ask for support? Did you believe that asking for help showed weakness and vulnerability? Did you feel pressure to prove your manhood and, if so, did you ever wonder why it needed to be proven as opposed to its being assumed as a part of your innate, authentic self? Were you helped to believe that a real man or woman is one who refuses to be casual about sex, who respects his or her own body enough to not be nonchalant about giving it away?

It is at this early age that so many boys are encouraged to bifurcate head and heart so that they will be "real men." They become emotionally illiterate to the point where they often don't even know what they are feeling and they lose their capacity for empathy, the ability to feel what others are feeling. And it happens so early that for men it is just the way things are. They can't remem-

Brother Peter as a young teenager

ber a time when they felt differently. The psychologist Terrence Real, in his wonderful book about men and depression, *I Don't Want to Talk About It,* writes, "Recent research indicates that in this society most males have difficulty not just in expressing but even in identifying their feelings. The psychiatric term for this impairment is alexithymia and psychologist Bon Levant estimates that close to eighty percent of men in our society have a mild to severe form of it."[4] For boys, this can manifest in signs of depression, learning disorders, speech impediments, and out-of-touch and out-of-control behavior.

Obviously, not all boys experience the early trauma of manhood. It seems that a warm, loving, structured home and school environment can act as a vaccine, helping boys stay whole. Were you lucky enough to be surrounded by adults who showed you explicitly or by example that being a man means being a whole human being—strong *and* emotional, brave *and* compassionate?

In today's Western culture, most men are still very vulnerable to shaming, to being seen as not manly enough, and this affects every part of men's lives—and women's, as well.

Consider the economy. In her book *Backlash,* Susan Faludi writes about an opinion poll that asked men and women around the world how they defined "masculinity." Overwhelmingly, the response was "Masculinity is the ability to bring home the bacon, to support their family." So, if this is the main criterion for masculinity everywhere in the world, what happens when the economy goes south, jobs become scarce, and it is women who are bringing home the bacon (albeit for lower wages and benefits)? Violence against women goes up because men feel ashamed.

Or consider issues of war and peace. In his book *War and Gender,* Joshua Goldstein, a professor of international relations at American University, wrote, "As war is gendered masculine, so peace is gendered feminine. Thus the manhood of men who oppose war becomes vulnerable to shaming."

The Pentagon Papers showed us that in the 1960s and '70s, the advisers of four different administrations—Republican and

Democrat—told their presidents that the Vietnam War could not be won short of annihilating the entire country, and yet our leaders kept sending more young men to fight. I wondered about this, and then I read Doris Kearns Goodwin's biography of President Lyndon Johnson. He told her that he feared being called "an unmanly man" if he pulled out of Vietnam. This seems to be an ongoing pattern in the United States—a fear on the part of our male leaders of premature evacuation!

In the 2004 presidential campaign, when Democratic candidate John Kerry spoke in favor of upholding international law and supporting the United Nations, he was called "effete" by Vice President Dick Cheney. There's that masculinity thing again, as though advocating for peace and diplomacy is effeminate.

I cite these examples because gender is such a core issue affecting every one of us—not because all boys and men are potentially violent and hawkish, but because the root of what surfaces in *some* of our boys and men as violence and hawkishness exists in too many of them as lack of empathy, emotional illiteracy, inability to be authentic, and vulnerability to shame. When adults help boys and girls shape their identities without resorting to gender stereotypes, they prepare them to have an optimal chance at future relatedness and intimacy in the stages of life to come.

A noteworthy shift has taken place over the past thirty years. Psychologists have come to believe that the highest form of human development lies not at the extremes of the gender-role spectrum—men as autonomous and dominant, women as dependent and malleable—but in the middle, where true, authentic relationships take place. From Jung forward, most psychologists have recognized that only when partners are able to let go of rigid, hierarchical sex roles can there be intimacy and authenticity.

In a later chapter, I explain the good news that as we enter our Third Acts, a great many of us, women and men, tend to move away from damaging sexual stereotypes and, as a result, find deeper intimacy and more gender parity in our relationships.

As I have learned from Carol Gilligan, gendered adolescent

behaviors are not simply a matter of biology—"boys will be boys" and "girls are just experiencing hormonal surges." Psychological and cultural factors also play a role. In addition, the success of programs that encourage girls' interest and performance in math, science, and sports and the proven benefits of interventions that help young men get in touch with their emotional lives argue against a simple biological determinism.

That's not to say that boys and girls are the same. Today's brain science has revealed beyond a doubt that there are many innate and universal differences in how we think, how we see, and how we react to various circumstances. We need to respect those differences, while also not letting them become exaggerated, overly self-conscious expressions of what "masculine" and "feminine" mean.

For the health of our boys, we need to define the positive qualities of being male. It is hard for a boy to learn to be both tough and tender—and then to learn to integrate the two into appropriate behavior so they can become holistic men who can move toward intimacy and communion and not feel that empathy and emotions mean weakness.

How Much Can We Change?

Like many people, I went through my First Act pretty much on my own in terms of figuring things out. My dad was a naval officer in the Pacific during most of World War II, but when he was home, I learned important things from him, mostly by osmosis (and from the roles he chose to portray in theater and movies)—about fairness, sticking up for underdogs, and the wrongness of racism and anti-Semitism. No one taught me about sex, however—how to know if a relationship was real, that it was okay to say no and to honor my body. Maybe this is why understanding these things (and writing about them) and trying to teach them to young people became important to me toward the end of my Act II. Part of this has to do with understanding in what ways people do and don't change. If in your First Act you did not receive much guidance of the sort I have just written about, how can you get over it? What might be some ways? Frankly, I wouldn't be writing this book if I didn't think change was a real possibility.

ON TEMPERAMENT

Psychologists generally agree that our temperaments are mostly hereditary and that while they can be modified to some slight degree, we are pretty much stuck with them. Temperament is what determines the level of our tested IQ and "the genetic component of our social intelligence"[5]—whether we are introverted or extroverted, sullen or positive, rigid or resilient. I saw clearly, while reviewing my first two acts, that my genetic temperament makes me someone who was dusted with a sprinkling of depression; this became more acute during my adolescence and early twenties. The trait came mostly from my father's genetic line; I consider it blind luck that I didn't inherit my mother's bipolar genes. Time, therapy, and a decade of psychopharmacological assistance during the end of Act II allowed me to mostly banish my depression to a corner; it lurks there still, trying occasionally to send out negative, "who do you think you are" scenarios that I refuse to read. I am also someone who likes solitude for long stretches (my father's genes). But when I've had enough aloneness, I become very sociable, outgoing, and even garrulous (my mother's genes). Maybe this is why the animal I have always identified with is the bear, which hibernates during the long winters and then loves to play and socialize.

I am always alert to people whose genetic inheritance makes them positive, able to turn lemons into lemonade. I try to hang with these types as often as possible, because their attitude rubs off. And, as you will learn in Chapter 9, most of us have a fair chance of becoming such people in our Third Act, even if we didn't start out that way. On the other hand, I try to steer clear of people who walk around with a perpetual dark rain cloud over their heads, like Eeyore, the "woe is me" donkey in *Winnie-the-Pooh*.

Me, fly-fishing with my golden retriever, Roxy, in 2001 © VERONIQUE VIAL

Often such people's conversation focuses on themselves and their problems and how unfair the world is to them. They embody the Victim Motif. When I am with such types, I invariably wonder if they are aware of their negative vibe and if they've ever tried to get help moving out from under their cloud. It was only in the last decade of my Act II that I became aware of my own cloud and realized I had to try to do something about it. That is when I began taking medication, which helped me change gears and allowed me to open up to the benefits of talk therapy, after which I no longer needed the meds. We need some mileage under our belts before we are able to see that it is ourselves rather than others who are responsible for our willingness to accept rain clouds instead of going for the sun.

I know that some of you reading this book don't believe in therapy; maybe you view it as self-indulgent, the way my father did. But, according to author and therapist Terrence Real, "most psychological conditions can be significantly improved with the right care. Treatment for depression, for example, has been shown to be 90 percent effective. Yet only two in five depressed people ever get help."[6]

If temperament is inherited and relatively immutable, why are so many of us able to change how we feel and behave? My interest in the possibility of change stems from a sense I had, starting in my late twenties, that if I was to make my life all that it could be, I would have to change certain things about myself. My belief in the possibility of behavioral change is also what motivated me to found two nonprofits that aim at reducing risky sexual behavior among teenagers—the Georgia Campaign for Adolescent Pregnancy Prevention and the Jane Fonda Center for Adolescent Reproductive Health at Emory University's School of Medicine.

In Georgia, around 1997, with some of the young men and women my nonprofit, the Georgia Campaign for Adolescent Pregnancy Prevention, worked with

ON CHARACTER

Dr. George Vaillant addresses the issue of personal change in his book *Aging Well*. He says that while "temperament to a large extent is set in plaster,"[7] our character does change because it is influenced by environment and by our resilience, assuming we have inherited any. Resilience means that we can commandeer the resources, the good coping mechanisms, to deal with stressful situations. An example would be a forty-year-old woman who, in her young years, was sexually abused by her father. Instead of marrying a fourth abusive husband, she decides to run a shelter for abused women. I like Vaillant's definition of resilience. He says it "reflects individuals who metaphorically resemble a twig with a fresh, green living core. When twisted out of shape, such a twig bends, but it does not break; instead, it springs back and continues growing."[8]

When I reviewed my Act I, I could see that I was blessed with resilience. My mother may have been MIA when it came to parenting, but my radar was constantly scanning the horizon in search of a warm, nurturing person from whom I could receive love and learning. Usually it came from the mothers of my best girlfriends. A child who lacks resilience may be in the presence of love but unable to take it in, to "metabolize" it, as George Vaillant puts it.

ON PERSONALITY

Okay. I have discussed temperament (permanent) and character (able to evolve). Where, then, does personality fit in? According to Dr. Vaillant, personality is the sum of temperament and character. This means that some of our personality is permanent (my needing solitude and my tendency to melancholy, which has been banished to a corner, yes, but hasn't disappeared) and some is changeable (I am less judgmental and negative and more optimistic and loving).

Cognitive therapy has been shown to alter a person's behavior. Working with a talented cognitive therapist, a person can begin to think differently about the past, for instance, and over time this new thinking activates different structures in the brain. This is referred to as "cognitive restructuring." With practice and time, a person can begin to automatically think—and act—differently.

During their First Acts, most people are too young to think much about whether and how their character and personality ought to change. They haven't had enough time to experience the ways in which they affect other people, to become aware of their behavioral patterns. Perhaps that can happen in Act II. As the playwright Nigel Howard once said, "The beautiful thing about learning a theory of your own personality is then you are free to disobey it."

CHAPTER 4

Act II: A Time of Building and of In-Betweenness

Perhaps the practice of crossing the boundaries of work and rest, the habit of navigating transitions, of trying on new roles and personas, should be established earlier, allowing people to become familiar with, and adept at, reinventing themselves.

—Sara Lawrence-Lightfoot

We now have an opportunity to exchange the wish to control life for a willingness to engage in living.

—Zen priest Joan Halifax

In my view, Act II spans ages thirty to fifty-nine, and during those three decades most of us go through a number of very significant transitions. These can be particularly dramatic for women.

Transitions

You may be looking back over this time in a life review, or, if you're young, looking forward to it; in either case, these years typically can include the transition into parenting, then suddenly out of it, when you face the empty-nest syndrome (which can be a wonderful time for a couple, or hard to adjust to); the transition into more power in a job, then perhaps less, or losing a job altogether; and the hormonal shifts that mark the beginning of menopause, which may

In 1969, holding my daughter, Vanessa

make us feel we are losing our minds. I felt this way! Because so many of us have postponed motherhood due to careers—births to women ages forty to forty-four increased 71 percent between 1990 an 1999—many of us go through the menopausal transition while we are still trying to cope with our teenagers' own hormonal turmoil, and these difficult-to-navigate events may coincide with our being laid off from work because of age and our—in the company's

Around 1985, with Vanessa © 2001 SUZANNE TENNER

view—onerous seniority! To add to all this, we may find ourselves
having to care for ailing parents and in-laws. All these things,
together with potential changes in looks, weight, and self-image,
can make us feel that our lives have peaked, that it will all be downhill from here on. That is certainly how I felt at this stage! But trust
me, for many if not most of us, the best may be yet to come.

Try to think of this time as noted ob-gyn Dr. Christiane
Northrup does when she calls it the "springtime of the second half
of life." I will write later about why this can be so!

In *My Life So Far,* I called Act II "Seeking" because, as I looked
back, I could see that, for me, the defining feature of this act was
the search I undertook to find meaning in my life. I'd ended my
First Act playing Barbarella! With the start of my Second Act—and,
with it, the birth of my first child—I left my marriage of eight years,
profoundly changed the way I lived, and began asking, *What am I
here for? What are other people's lives like? Can I be useful?*

For most people, Act II might be called "Building," because this
is when we are building families, careers, our place in society, and

our egos. As a result, during this act we are so vulnerable to the many challenges to our egos: Am I being recognized as much as she is? Am I getting paid what I deserve? Why has his business plan worked and mine hasn't? Why does no one love me? That sort of thing!

Dr. George Vaillant writes, as mentioned previously, that in early midlife, childhood is still significantly important, whereas "unhappy childhoods become less important with time."[1] Those of us with challenging early lives may have a harder time of it as we enter our Second Acts. We're supposed to be becoming *someone,* but we can't quite find our footing and may—involuntarily—still resort to immature coping mechanisms such as acting out, projection (imposing one's own thoughts and feelings onto another), or passive-aggressive behavior. A number of long-term studies over the last forty years have shown that maladaptive coping mechanisms such as these can mature into altruism and sublimation as we age, but while we're in the midst of it, life can be so hard.

It seems to me that those who do the best in their Act III are those who began to manage their egos while they were younger; they became aware of their character traits, how and why others responded to them the way they did, and, if the responses were problematic, asked themselves if perhaps their own behavior, their own thinking, might have been the problem. Often people with immature coping traits blame everyone else for what goes wrong. They have what I call a "the world is full of assholes" attitude. This is especially true of people with addictions. If the same problems keep arising, one should consider getting help, either with individual therapy or group therapy, or with a twelve-step program.

In our parents' time, it was common to graduate from college and go right into a career or, for many women, into the unpaid but challenging jobs of marriage and parenthood. These days, many more—perhaps most—women are working, and for both women and men, changing careers not once but numerous times during the Second Act is not unusual. Nor is starting a career, marrying, divorcing, and reentering the workplace. Maybe Act II should be called "Churn."

Finances

Act II is the optimum time to take a careful and honest look at your financial situation. Your future security may depend on your starting a savings plan now. Midlife is also the ideal time to develop a healthy lifestyle, if you haven't done so already—it will help maximize Third Act potentials. I will discuss this in later chapters.

The Challenge of In-Betweenness

During the middle to latter part of the Second Act, especially between the mid-forties and the mid-fifties, many women feel they're losing control of life and have nothing to hold on to. I certainly felt this way. I call it the challenge of in-betweenness, and it's scary. As Marilyn Ferguson has written, "It's not so much that we're afraid of change or so in love with the old ways, but it's that place in between that we fear. . . . It's like being in between trapezes. It's Linus when his blanket is in the dryer. There's nothing to hold on to." How we handle our time between trapezes can determine much about how well we swing into the rest of our lives.

I THOUGHT I WAS DISAPPEARING

In my late forties, joy seemed to be leaching out of my life. When I look at photos of myself during that period, I see a blankness on my face. It's as if nobody was home. I watch my movies from that time—*Old Gringo* and *Stanley & Iris,* in particular—and I can tell. It felt as if I was uninhabited, going through the motions—sometimes fairly well, but with no hookup to the heart. Those were the last movies I made for a long time. I quit the movie business after them. Fifteen years later I went back, but at the time I thought I was finished with it forever. I felt so empty, so low, that it was just too painful to try to be creative. You see, the only instrument an actor has to bring a character to life is her or his own body and spirit, and if those are shut down, there's nowhere else to turn—no violin, no canvas, no pen and paper. That's not to say that many actors don't continue their work despite personal meltdowns. Work may provide their only escape, or maybe it's their only source of income. I was fortunate in that the Jane Fonda Workout business was bringing in enough money for me to be able to stop acting.

I looked ahead and saw no future beckoning, yet I had to plow onward. I had a family, organizational responsibilities, and myriad other duties. Besides, it's not as though I understood what was going on. What was I going to say to those who depended on me? "I don't know why, but I feel like I'm disappearing, like I'm getting

Me in 1988, as my marriage to Tom was falling apart—and so was I
MARY ELLEN MARK

all blurred around the edges"? They would have thought I was mad, and in a way I was.

I was sure that if the approach of menopause was to blame I'd be experiencing hot flashes and night sweats; since that hadn't happened, I lay the blame for my sadness, confusion, and irritability on my deteriorating second marriage of seventeen years, to Tom Hayden.

In the 1970s—Tom Hayden, our son, Troy, and me, with my daughter, Vanessa, peeking from behind

Despite the fact that I was researching and writing *Women Coming of Age,* it didn't occur to me that what was happening, at least in part, were the effects of perimenopause, that varied stretch of time leading up to menopause when women begin to experience the erratic cycling of hormones, and the estrogen and oxytocin levels in our brains begin to drop. These substances support our mood-elevating serotonin-releasing cells, the ones that make us feel good. According to the neuropsychiatrist Dr. Louann Brizendine, at the University of California, San Francisco, perimenopausal women are fourteen times more at risk of depression than younger and older women. Of course, many women sail through this hormonal

One of the last Christmases Tom and I had together. Troy is behind and Vanessa is on the right.

transition with very little difficulty. But according to the National Survey of Midlife Development in the United States, life can take a downward turn for more than two-thirds of women between the ages of thirty-five and forty-nine. After that, once the hormones have stabilized with the completion of menopause (which happens, on average, at age fifty-one and a half years), life can take a surprisingly upward turn for a great many women.

Hormonal Shifts

Another factor comes into play as we approach and enter menopause, one that can have a complex effect on our interpersonal relations: Our estrogen and oxytocin levels begin to drop below those of the more masculine, goal-oriented testosterone. Those feel-good hormones were what encouraged us to take care of others, smooth things over, and avoid conflict. Now we may find ourselves not caring so much about keeping the peace, and we may express our previously repressed anger more openly. Old Let-Me-Take-Care-of-It-for-You-Honey morphs into I'm-Going-to-Class-See-You-Later-and-the-Cleaning's-Ready-to-Pick-Up. Contrary to what we may think, 65 percent of divorces after age fifty are initiated not by men wanting to leave their wives for younger women but by the wives themselves. They may start to ask themselves, "Have I lived my own life or the life others have wanted me to live, making decisions others wanted me to make rather than my own?"

Had I known what was behind my depression and anxiety as I approached fifty, I might have sought help from a doctor who specialized in hormone therapies. This, I have since learned, is the optimal time for healthy women who are experiencing perimenopausal symptoms to consult their doctors about hormone therapy in low doses. (I will discuss hormone therapy at greater length in Chapter 14.)

Breakdown

Even with pharmacological help, my marriage would have ended sooner or later. I was fifty-one when it happened and, always the late bloomer, still going through perimenopause. All the sadness and despair I had been experiencing over the previous several years crashed in on me. My lifelong, ever-ready carapace fell apart, and I had a nervous breakdown. I couldn't eat or speak above a whisper or move quickly. I was in free fall. Everything I had relied on for self-definition—marriage, career—was stripped away, and I hadn't a clue about who I was or what I was supposed to do with my life.

People told me to stay busy, and this was, in fact, my usual way of dealing with times of uncertainty. "If I just keep moving," I'd always thought, "no one, including me, will notice that I'm stuck . . . maybe." But as Suzanne Braun Levine, who writes extensively about women's issues, has said, "The cure for 'stuck' is 'still.' "[2] I sensed that time wasn't just an empty space asking me to fill it with something. Time just was, and its was-ness was asking me to simply be in it—fully.

I sat alone most days in the company of my golden retriever, reading books such as Riane Eisler's transformational *The Chalice and the Blade,* about Neolithic societies that practiced goddess worship and the rise of patriarchy that crushed it, and psychiatrist M. Scott Peck's *The Road Less Traveled,* about what makes for a fulfilled human being. I knew I was raw and vulnerable, so I stayed close to the wall, and avoided movies that weren't uplifting, people who weren't loving and positive, music that didn't soothe. My survival instinct motivated me to keep a fairly regular exercise routine in order to boost my endorphin levels and remind myself I did actually exist. If I'm sore, I must exist.

The Fertile Void

After a while I sensed changes happening within and around me. It occurred to me that this was similar to what happens to actors as they draw closer to the time when they have to play a new role. They begin to morph into a new character, but who they're morphing into hasn't fully taken shape. This place between who they are and who they will become can be a time of vulnerability, but also one of tremendous creative ferment, when care and attention are called for. Many smart people have delved into the meaning these transitions hold for our lives. The organizational consultant William Bridges calls it the "neutral zone." The philosopher Viktor Frankl called it the "existential vacuum." For Donna Henes, it's "sitting in the shadows." The metaphor I prefer is Braun Levine's "fertile void," a space of "unremitting unknowingness."[3] "Fertile" is good because it emphasizes the potential for growth, and "void" feels emptier and more neutral than "zone" or "vacuum." It is in the fertile void that tendrils of something new can begin to sprout—if you surrender to it and don't numb yourself with busyness.

Turns out, the potentials that lie within the fertile void are par-alleled within the natural world. Several years after my painful midlife transition, an ecologist in southern Georgia told me that it is in the zones where one ecosystem ends and another begins that one finds the richest, most exciting diversity of life. And quantum physics says that "the closer a system can move to the edge of chaos, the more creativity and 'option space' exists." I like that—"option space." That's exactly what the fertile void is: a space where, if you just quiet down and go with the flow, options open themselves.

Maybe the fundamental arrangements of your life have dis-solved through no fault of your own and you have to totally rethink how you live in relation to your life. You may have to scale way back or start from scratch. Maybe there has not been an objective, life-altering crisis, such as a divorce or death, but your children are moving on and age is making you vulnerable to forced retirement and the subsequent loss of the clear, defining structure you've relied on, the office routine and performance reports that for profession-als provide concrete proof of "productivity."

Redefining Productivity

Maybe this is the time to begin redefining what we mean by "pro-ductive." What was productive in youth may now hold us back from entering the "option space" and achieving new and as yet unrecognized potential. Our reproductivity may be over, but who says our productivity went with it? Goethe wrote, "Whoever, in midlife, attempts to realize the wishes and hopes of his early youth invariably deceives himself. Each ten years of a [person's] life has its own fortunes, its own hopes, its own desires." I think every seven years is actually more like it. The play (and later movie) *The Seven Year Itch* may have been a comedy, but the underlying premise was very real. Every seven years—give or take a year on either side—all our cells are renewed, and we are apt go through impor-tant transitions around this time. Many cultures throughout his-tory have recognized seven as a defining, transitional number. In relationships, if the two partners are not transitioning in ways that sympathetically echo each other's, troubles can ensue. I was very aware of this around the seventh or eighth year in each of my three marriages.

But our time in the fertile void can be more than just figuring out new hopes and goals and worrying about what is going to happen to us. This uncomfortable limbo can offer, in the words of the Zen priest Joan Halifax, "an opportunity to exchange the wish to control life for a willingness to engage in living."[4] No act of will can make this happen. We must have the courage to just be, to not feel pressure to set big goals but to let the grounding we used to find in people's praise for our work now come from within us. We may feel we are broken when, in fact, we are being broken open. For women in midlife, the void is fertile because we are becoming midwives to our new selves.

In fact, the fertile void may be an optimum time to do a life review—when you can feel that change is happening, and when parents and even grandparents may still be living and available to be interviewed. Such a review may help you heal from the challenges you experienced in childhood. As William Bridges, who specializes in understanding transitions, wrote, "The past isn't like a landscape or a vase of flowers that is just there. It is more like the raw material awaiting a builder."[5] Maybe, by doing a life review, you will build a ladder out of the void, the way I did a decade later ... when I was sixty, not fifty.

A Rite of Passage to Act III

Painful though this in-between time might be, it can also be a rite of passage into the Third Act. Then all you need do is stay mentally and physically healthy and put up the sails. If our sails are up, in time the wind will come and take us where we will go, where we are meant to be.

I hadn't quite finished hoisting my sails when my third husband, Ted Turner, Captain America himself, sailed boisterously into the harbor. Those who knew him were sure my sails would be luffing forever in his wake, but he needed me and wasn't afraid to show it, and this gave me confidence. Besides, I wasn't ready yet to do life solo. I wanted and needed to try again to be a whole person within the context of a marriage, and we were well suited for each other on many levels. I wanted it to work with him so much that I did what I had not done previously: I went into therapy.

Ted, my stepdaughter Nathalie Vadim, me,
and Vanessa in 1991 at our wedding BARBARA PYLE

We separated after ten years of marriage, when I was sixty-two. It had taken me eight years to grudgingly realize that I would not be able to be healthy and authentic within the confines of that marriage, and then two more years after that to get the courage to say so. Oddly enough, it was the preparation for my sixtieth birthday and the confidence that this brought me that exposed the extent to which I needed to renegotiate the terms of our marriage. Those two post-sixty years were difficult, and I felt myself sinking into numbness. Unlike the malaise I had experienced more than a decade earlier, in my second marriage, this was not a matter of my hormones; this was a matter of my humanity. I saw that as I entered my last act, I'd have less time to squander. Fish or cut bait.

It was terrifying. I had abandoned my professional career ten years earlier, and at sixty-two I knew it was unlikely, given Hollywood's proclivity for young flesh, that I could reclaim it—nor was I interested, just then, in doing so. But who would I be now, and in the years ahead? I had been married—to one man or another—for most of my adult life, and had drawn my identity from men. The very thought of going it alone had always filled me with profound dread.

I vividly remember the moment I realized the marriage to Ted was not going to work. I stood before him and I knew I had a choice: I could opt for safety or try for integrity. I thought of Virginia Woolf, who wrote about the angel in her house, the hovering Victorian angel who would whisper into her ear as she wrote the lines so inspirational to future feminists, words to the effect of "Tsk tsk, Virginia, nice women would never say that." On my right shoulder I heard an angel whisper with great certainty, "Oh, come on, Fonda, lighten up. You know how they always say you have no sense of humor. You're so serious. He's cute and smart and funny and he has all these incredibly beautiful properties and you'll never have to work and . . ." while on the other shoulder, barely audible, was another angel whispering, "Jane, you know what's right. This is your life. You can die married and safe, sure, but you won't die whole, and you'll regret it. You did all that work preparing for your sixtieth birthday so you'd know how to live your last act. Well, this is it, kiddo, and it isn't a dress rehearsal." It felt like letting go of a trapeze without a net under me.

When the parting finally happened, I took my golden retriever and moved in with my daughter, Vanessa, who had a home in what was then a relatively modest part of Atlanta. It was funny, actually. As I wrote in my memoirs, I went "from twenty-three kingdom-sized properties and a private plane that could sleep six to a small guest room with no closet." And that time was wonderful, scary but wonderful, because it felt like I was stripped down to rawness and reality, which is just where I needed to be in order to allow a truer me to emerge. It felt right that the womb of this transition was in the home of my firstborn. It was a bittersweet time, a time of beginnings and endings. Vanessa had just had her first baby, this was her first home, and yet her father, the French film director Roger Vadim, was in Paris dying of cancer. In fact, when I first moved in, she was with him in Paris, and so the silence and aloneness that surrounded me was abrupt and total. I relished it. Here I was in another fertile void. Alongside the mourning over what could have been with Ted, I could feel something happening. I was terrified, but I knew that all the work I had done on myself to try to save the marriage and my preparations for the start of my Third Act had borne fruit. These things hadn't saved the marriage, but they had saved me. Giving birth to ourselves before we die is definitely something to work for. Around that time, I read a quote that stuck with me: "Sooner or later we will come to the edge of all that we cannot control and find life, waiting there for us."

The psychologist Marion Woodman says that within "vulnerability lives the humility that allows flesh to soften into the sounds of the soul."[6] I experienced the truth of this during those aching weeks alone in Vanessa's home. A space began to open, allowing me access to another wavelength beyond consciousness. It wasn't something that came to me through thought. If I had to locate it somewhere, it would be in my body. I could feel myself moving back into myself, becoming whole, awakened. I sensed at the time that this was God.

Being Perfect

All my life I had believed that unless I was perfect I would not be loved. This had engendered a futile struggle, since we aren't meant to be perfect, and it had gotten me into a lot of trouble—like silencing the parts of myself that didn't seem good enough, and developing eating disorders. In fact, I now think it was this long-standing disease to please that had prevented me all along from being whole.

Why inhabit yourself if yourself is yucky? Recently, I was excited to read in William Bridges's *The Way of Transition* that in Matthew 5:48, when Jesus tells his disciples, "You, therefore, must be perfect, as your heavenly Father is perfect," there is a mistranslation of the Greek adjective *teleios,* which actually means "whole, fully formed, fully developed."[7] Jesus wasn't telling his disciples to be perfect, like God; he was telling them to be whole, like God.

I am grateful that this feeling of becoming whole occurred later in life, when I could experience it consciously. Now that we're living longer, being a late bloomer has a lot of advantages. Maybe some people are intact spirits from the beginning, and maybe it happens to others in early life. But it's glorious to be at an age when you are aware that it's happening, that you worked for it, and that you're on the right path. For the first time as an adult, I was without a man in my life yet felt whole, rather than like a half a person waiting to be completed.

I was going through what Gail Sheehy in *Sex and the Seasoned Woman* calls the passage "from pleasing to mastery."[8] This time can be the hallmark of our Third Acts, the mirror opposite of our first major life transition, in adolescence, which sent us careening from mastery to pleasing, turning us from, as I have heard Gloria Steinem say, "a confident child who's been climbing trees and saying, 'It's not fair,' into a self-doubting teenager who prefaces her thoughts with 'It's probably only me but . . .' "

Before now, most of us have been defined by others—our husbands, our children, our parents, our jobs. Now the time comes when we can begin to define ourselves. I knew I was ready, I just didn't know what form the definition would take.

This was not my first fertile void, and I knew what to do: nothing. For a couple of months I raked the leaves in my daughter's yard, and friends came to see me. I found refuge in a black Baptist church (until the press followed me there), where the soulful preaching and stirring gospel singing lifted my spirit. I went to occasional meetings of the organization I had founded seven years earlier, the Georgia Campaign for Adolescent Pregnancy Prevention. I listened to classical music and read books by the psychologists Carol Gilligan and Marion Woodman. I prayed regularly, dabbled in meditation, made a point of breathing deeply, and waited for the wind to take me, this time with my sails fully hoisted.

This time it was Oprah Winfrey who sailed into my harbor. She'd come to interview me for the second issue of her just-launched magazine, O. Clearly, my digs weren't what she'd expected, as she pulled up in a stretch limousine, totally incongruous in that neighborhood. "Gee, didn't Ted buy you a swank condo?" she asked, bewildered, as she walked into the modest living room. "He probably would have if I'd asked, but I didn't. I like it here," I explained, "I'm starting over." In that interview I told Oprah about preparing for my Third Act and what that felt like, and, in verbalizing it, I saw clearly the gendered theme that ran through my life: the need to please, to leave myself behind so as to be loved, the feelings of never being good enough, the difficulty with "no." As I thought about it more in the ensuing days, I was struck by how crystal clear my thinking was. New ideas came to me, but not because I was trying to figure something out; they just appeared.

With Oprah, the day she came and interviewed me in my daughter's Atlanta home, just after Ted Turner and I split up

RICHARD PHIBBS/ART DEPT

True ideas have always seemed to ambush me when I least expect them. Just when I'm meandering along, paying no heed to my flanks and rear, a true idea will float out of the sky, hit me on top of my head, and change the color of my life. And one of those true things was the idea to write *My Life So Far*. There it was. So simple. This is what I would do and how I would figure out my next decades. My life hasn't been a representative one, but I was sure the themes that ran through it were universal enough to resonate with others and that if I could write it deeply, below the surface it could provide a road map for others. This would be for them and for me—a deeper, fuller life review than what I had put together for my sixtieth birthday. One that would help me—not to grow old but to grow into myself, and into Act III.

CHAPTER 5

Eleven Ingredients for Successful Aging

Whether we live to a vigorous old age lies not so much in our stars or our genes as in ourselves.

—George Vaillant[1]

WOODY ALLEN ONCE SAID, "I DON'T WANT TO ACHIEVE IMMORtality through my work. I'd rather achieve it by not dying." Sorry about that, Woody. It doesn't appear that science will ever change that reality of human life. (Though in Appendix I you will learn what is being done in that arena.) What's needed, therefore, when it comes to issues of physical aging, is a shift in thinking, from a focus on life span or life expectancy to a focus on health span or health expectancy . . . getting to the end in better shape, since we cannot change the end itself!

Earlier, I described the old paradigm of physical aging as an arch. Now there is a new metaphor for successful physical aging that focuses less on decline. This is the one that we can strive for. It is life as a rectangle—the top half of a rectangle, that is. We're born; then we live a long, level, and healthy stretch of time. No rise and then a slow, gradual decline. Rather, there is a steep, sudden drop-off at the far end, right before we go.

This rectangular metaphor for physical aging is the new goal.

Dr. Tom Kirkwood came up with a term for this drop-off at the end of the rectangle: the "compression of morbidity." "We want to squeeze the bad things that happen to us at the end of

Long Healthy Lifespan

Compression of Morbidity

Birth   *Death*

life into as short a period as possible while leaving the life span
as it is," says Kirkwood, who is a professor of medicine and the
head of the Department of Gerontology at the University of
Newcastle.[2]

The Eleven Ingredients

There are eleven ingredients that can help us age successfully—
physically, emotionally, and psychologically. All of them are within
our power to do something about. Listed below, they reflect the
findings from a number of important studies and books, most
notably the MacArthur Foundation Study of Successful Aging, the
Harvard Study of Adult Development, and the writings of Dr.
Robert Butler, the late president and CEO of the International
Longevity Center in New York. Some of these ideas were given to
me by the experts I interviewed, and in the following chapters I
discuss each of them, with illustrative stories from the lives of my
friends and from my own life.

I.   NOT ABUSING ALCOHOL

Never having abused alcohol is considered by some gerontologists
to be *the single highest predictor of successful aging.* In his book *Aging Well,*
Dr. George Vaillant defines "alcohol abuse" (rather than simply
"reported alcohol consumption") as "the evidence of multiple
alcohol-related problems (with spouse, family, employer, law, or
health) and/or evidence of alcohol-related dependence."[3] He goes

on to say that "alcohol abuse is a cause rather than a result of increased life stress, of depression."

2.   NOT SMOKING

Never having smoked or stopping at a relatively young age is another major predictor of healthy aging. According to the Harvard Study of Adult Development, "If a man had stopped smoking by about age 45, the effects of smoking (more than a pack a day for 20 years) could at 70 or 80 no longer be discerned."[4]

As critical as these first two points are, I have not elaborated on them because I feel they are self-evident.

3.   GETTING ENOUGH SLEEP

My father always told me that you need less sleep as you get older. Well, Dad, I'm still waiting! On average, I get eight or nine hours of sleep every night and, frankly, I don't do well on less. I rarely feel stress if I've slept enough. Perhaps that's because sleep is one of the best remedies for stress.

Unfortunately, Dad was right in one way: As you get older, your sleep lightens progressively. Many older people say they spend more time in bed but sleep less; when they do sleep, it's what is called "dream sleep," as opposed to deep sleep. Deep sleep is important throughout the life span, but it is essential when we are older, when our tissues need replenishing yet our human growth hormone and testosterone levels are diminished. When we are in a state of deep sleep, there is a surge of growth hormone. This is important for the restoration of our body's tissues, especially the tissues of the heart. Regular exercise, by the way, is a wonderful way to develop your ability to sleep more deeply.

If you are sleep challenged, try not to drink coffee or caffeinated tea or sodas after lunch—duh! Better yet, do away with all of it, except perhaps one cup in the morning. At night, try eating foods that contain natural tryptophan—milk, turkey, and complex carbohydrates.

4. BEING PHYSICALLY ACTIVE

I have a lot to say about this point. Maintaining a healthy weight, a strong heart, and strong bones through regular physical activity is a major ingredient in the recipe for successful aging. And what is truly good news is that even if you first start to incorporate exercise into your life after age sixty, you can reverse many of the problems associated with inactivity, and you will feel so much better. That in itself should be an inspiration to keep you moving! The next chapter, "The Workout," goes into detail about this, as do Appendixes II and III.

ANNA-MAREE HARMAN, AMHPHOTOGRAPHY@YAHOO.COM.AU

5. EATING A HEALTHY DIET

Never has the phrase "You are what you eat" been truer than in the Third Act. As individuals and as a nation we must pay more attention to reducing the amount of sugar and fats we eat, and to increasing our consumption of fresh fruits and vegetables and complex carbohydrates. There'll be more on this in Chapter 7, "Now More than Ever, You Are What You Eat."

6. MAINTAINING A HEALTHY, ACTIVE BRAIN
    THROUGH LEARNING

The current wisdom says that if you regularly do crossword puzzles or Sudoku, your brain will remain healthy. Maybe, if you're not used to doing them! Certainly your brain is active during those activities. But I have chosen to use the word "learning" here rather than "mental activity" because what brain science tells us today is that to maintain healthy cognitive function, we need to do things we aren't accustomed to doing—things that make new demands on our minds, force us to make decisions or choices. Furthermore, this learning has to be sustained over time. There will be more about the brain in Chapter 8.

I took a yoga class at Tara Stiles's Strala Yoga studio in New York taught by this ninety-three-year-old instructor

7. POSITIVITY: ENCOURAGING A POSITIVE ATTITUDE

Almost all the people I have met who are in their nineties or even older seem to have one thing in common: positivity. Scientists at the Stanford Center on Longevity adopted the word "positivity" to express what they, too, have observed. Positivity is an attitude, a way to approach life; it is expressed through humor, gratitude, forgiveness, playfulness, creativeness, and adaptability. I am conscious of this happening to me in my Third Act, which shows that what the experts say is true: We can attain these positive attributes even if we didn't start off with them! This is one of the aspects of aging that fascinates me the most, and so I have a chapter to come on Positivity—Chapter 9.

8. REVIEWING AND REFLECTING ON YOUR LIFE

I was somewhat surprised when I discovered, in the writings of Dr. Robert Butler, that many gerontologists and psychiatrists advocate this for their older patients. In Chapter 2, I wrote about how important doing a life review was for me; in Chapter 10, I talk more about how to do it.

9. LOVING AND STAYING CONNECTED

Humans are hardwired to interact with others. Having friends, loving partners, and strong social supports have long been demonstrated to have a direct positive effect on health, better cognitive functioning, and longevity. I will explore the various aspects of connectedness—to friends and to spouses or to lovers—in Chapters 11 through 15.

10. GENERATIVITY: GIVING OF ONESELF

This term, coined by the social scientist Erik Erikson in his conceptualization of the stages of human development, refers to older people's responsibility to care for younger generations by giving of oneself—one's knowledge, experience, time, resources, and values. This can mean mentoring a child, being a coach, reading to your grandchild's class—and making sure she is in class!—or helping girls and boys in your community or in the developing world. In *Aging Well,* Dr. Vaillant writes that "mastery of Generativity tripled the chances that the decade of the 70s would be for these men and women a time of joy and not of despair."[5] I discuss this subject in Chapter 16, "Generativity: Leaving Footprints."

11.   CARING ABOUT THE BIGGER PICTURE

Moving from a focus on oneself to caring about things greater than oneself makes us whole and strong so we won't be overwhelmed by

Jane Lynch of **Glee** *fame helping me warm up the crowd before Maria Shriver's march to defeat Alzheimer's disease, 2010*
FREDERICK M. BROWN/GETTY IMAGES

the inevitable losses that come in later life. This can mean a focus on your community, your nation, or the planet. You might, building on your experiences, talents, interests . . . your wounds, even . . .

make a difference. For example, a retired CEO helps set up a microfinance project in Kenya; a former schoolteacher volunteers to teach adults to read; a former UPS employee offers to help working mothers by providing carpool services; a chemical engineer teaches corporations how to become green.

Chapter 17, "Ripening the Time," further develops this concept.

The ingredients that keep us vital, happy, and continuing to grow are there for a majority of us. During our last three decades, as we move from being the "young old" to becoming the "old old," we can have some of the best years of our lives, and the best news of all is that it is never too late to start making it so. A lot of it—*most* of it—has to do with lifestyle choices we make and how willing we are to live with real intention, instead of just drifting.

Lifestyle Choices

Genes may predispose us to, say, heart disease or arthritis, but the right lifestyle and the right attitude may help us overcome these infirmities. I know older people who are disabled and even ill but who do not *feel* sick. They experience joy and vitality and, in my opinion, exemplify successful aging. Some of the lifestyle and attitudinal choices we can make are best addressed before we enter our Third Acts. But even if we decide to change our ways after sixty, we can still make a big difference in how we age.

In the chapters that follow, I go into more depth about how I and others have incorporated these ingredients into our own lives, and how you might do the same.

PART TWO

BODY, BRAIN, *and* ATTITUDE

CHAPTER 6

The Workout

> It's not that very old people . . . can exercise because
> they are healthy . . . rather, they achieve a healthy old
> age because they exercise.
>
> —JANE BRODY, *New York Times* HEALTH WRITER

> I've been screaming at the top of my lungs at my family,
> "Work out! Work out! Old age is coming!" At some
> point you will need the strength. Who would have ever
> thought you would get this old?
>
> —CHER

ONE DAY, AT AGE FIFTY-NINE, I WAS DRIVING WITH TED TURNER
to one of his ranches in Patagonia when we came around a corner
and I caught sight of the most magnificent snowcapped mountain
I had ever seen, a perfectly symmetrical extinct volcano named
Mount Lanin, rising straight up from the flat pampas to twelve
thousand feet. Right then I vowed to climb that mountain as a
present to myself for my sixtieth birthday.

My stepson Beau Turner said he'd go with me, along with two
guides. I trained for several months, bought the needed gear to
scale the glacier that composed the top two thousand feet, and off
we went. We camped overnight in a blizzard at about ten thousand feet, getting up before dawn in order to make the rest of the
ascent and get back down before nightfall. I was totally psyched as
we set out in the dark. My heart was pounding with the exertion

of hiking through the thigh-deep snow at that altitude, and I felt great about being out ahead of everyone else. One of the guides shouted, "Don't go too fast, Jane, you'll sweat," but I wanted to prove (to myself, mostly) that a sixty-year-old woman still had her mojo. Stupid me. A thousand feet from the top I had to turn around. Just as the guide had warned, the sweaty, damp inner layer of clothing—evidence of my ego—had gotten cold, and and my plummeting body temperature put me at risk of hypothermia.

On his way down from the top, Beau picked me up at the mid-mountain campsite and regaled me with descriptions of what it had been like to scale the ice at the summit. I felt like such a failure.

You'd have thought I'd learned my lesson. Right? Wrong! For my seventieth birthday, I wanted to climb to sixteen thousand feet (two thousand feet higher than I had ever been). But I learned that you can't get that high without getting very cold, and I don't do cold well.

My boyfriend at the time liked scuba diving and suggested that, instead of going up, I should try going down. Together we went to Ambergris Cay, a small island in the Turks and Caicos chain, where, with a couple of friends, we spent three days training in a pool. We passed the written exam to qualify for scuba diving, and then the time came for the three ocean dives needed for certification. Our guide again stressed the importance of going down slowly and equalizing the air pressure as we went. As I descended, I looked up at my boyfriend, who seemed to be lingering near the surface, and thought, "What a wuss!" I sank down toward the bottom, feeling pretty cocky, until my ears began to hurt; the pain forced me to pass my (much more sensible) boyfriend on my way back up. I lay on the deck of the boat feeling miserable, realizing that for a second time (at least, that I could remember) my need to be competitive had made me go too fast and fail.

I said to myself, "Jane, you're seventy now. How many times do you have to do something wrong before you learn a lesson? Can't you finally understand the value of taking time and being deliberate with your actions rather than driven? Promise that you will never make this mistake again."

I returned to Turks and Caicos four months later for a second try. "Slow down" was my mantra this time, and together with my already-scuba-certified daughter and son, I made two successful dives to eighty-five feet. I descended at a pace that seemed preposterously slow, but I wasn't about to fail again! The sheer joy of swimming with my children along a spectacular coral shelf among reef sharks, stingrays, barracudas, sea turtles, and many colorful fish was the big payoff, and I learned a big life lesson: This is the stage of life where there is less room for ego and more need for humility, balance, and common sense.

In *Women Coming of Age,* I included a photo of a woman in her eighties jogging with her daughter. I was utterly confident that that's how I would be when I got to that age. Well, I'm ten years younger than she was, and I haven't been able to jog for nearly a decade! My replaced hip and knee won't let me. But I've found that that's okay, just so long as I do *something.* It would have been easy to stop exercising after my hip surgery, or because my knees sometimes hurt due to osteoarthritis. For a while I felt sure I'd never be able to do anything close to what I had done before. But when, mostly for vanity reasons, I started up again, I soon discovered that moving, walking, swimming, lifting light weights, and stretching made my muscles and joints feel much better. It was when I was inactive that the arthritis got worse—and so did my mood.

I don't jog anymore or do anything else that overly stresses my joints. Even downhill skiing is out. But I've gotten into snowshoeing, and this slower, more meditative, but equally aerobic sport is, for me, perfectly suited to the Third Act.

Since I'm not in the snow very often, what I do to burn calories and stay aerobically fit is walk briskly (anywhere) or hike (when I'm in the country and the weather's nice) for an hour, five or six days a week. When the weather is too hot or too cold, I go to a gym and get on a recumbent bike or an elliptical trainer (the kind that works the arms as well as the legs). I'll go for thirty minutes, switching every ten minutes from one machine to the other to ease the boredom.

Occasionally I replace walking with swimming for thirty minutes, and when I do, I protect my neck by wearing a well-fitted mask and snorkel, which eliminates the need to turn my head every few strokes to catch a breath. It also makes it easier for me to go into a meditative state without worrying about bumping into the ends of the pool.

Too many people—men, especially—will stop physical activity altogether if they are no longer able to do things the way they did when they were younger. This is a real mistake. It's far better to

Me, hiking a steep hill

keep active, but at a lower level. And if, for some reason, you have been unable to work out for a time, be careful when you start up again. I always make sure to cut back a notch rather than trying to pick up where I left off. Older people hurt themselves trying to go from inactivity to sudden, challenging activity, like deciding to play basketball with the grandchildren one weekend. Instead, you want to try to establish a regular routine of a minimum of twenty minutes of some sort of aerobic activity at least three times a week.

The Exercise Imperative

I have realized over the last decade that the difference between a younger person who is physically active and one who isn't is not particularly dramatic. But the difference between an older person

ANNA-MAREE HARMAN,
AMHPHOTOGRAPHY
@YAHOO.COM.AU

A group of seniors, all part of Tewantin–Noosa R&SL club, made a calendar and sent it to me. This was the cover!

ANNA-MAREE HARMAN, AMHPHOTOGRAPHY@YAHOO.COM.AU

who is active and one who isn't is enormous. "Fitness for the young person is an option," says expert on aging Dr. Walter Bortz, "but for the older person it is an imperative."[1] Younger people's bodies are more resilient and forgiving, whereas older bodies are weakening; unless we deliberately intervene to slow this process down (or, yes, even reverse it), we risk sliding into early decrepitude. It is largely up to us. The human body is fully capable of vigorous use well into the nineties and even longer.

In his book *The Blue Zone: Lessons for Living Longer from the People Who've Lived the Longest,* Dan Buettner visits places in the world where large numbers of people live past one hundred: Sardinia, Okinawa, Costa Rica, and Loma Linda, California. One of the things all of them have in common is daily, low-intensity physical activity such as walking, hiking, and farming. Activity strengthens the heart and bones, improves the circulation, reduces obesity, thickens the skin, and can help with depression because of the endorphins released into the system. I learned from years of watching exercise change women's bodies and minds that it is also empowering: It gives you a sense of being in charge of yourself and your well-being, which is particularly important for older people, who often feel they aren't in charge of much of anything anymore.

"Use it or lose it" is a truism, but what it leaves out is that *if it's lost, we can get it back.* Not only can we recover lost functions but, as Dr. Bortz notes, "in some cases we can actually *increase* function beyond our prior level."[2]

How Active Does "Being Active" Mean?

Don't worry, it doesn't have to be scary. In fact, "Easy does it" is the appropriate mantra. I never thought I would say this, old go-for-the-burn me. But I've learned the hard way to respect that I am no longer the Jane Fonda who created the original Workout. My body will make me suffer if I don't slow down. This is why I created the new Jane Fonda's Prime Time line of exercise DVDs for boomers (people born during the demographic birth boom between 1946

In the early 1980s, I was in my midforties and I had just launched my workout studio. PHOTOS BY HARRY LANGDON

and 1964) and seniors (those born prior to the end of World War II) who, like me, need to take it a little easier.

Let's discuss all the components of a good weekly exercise regimen—aerobics, resistance, balance, and stretching—and why these are especially vital for people over fifty.

Why Is Aerobic Activity Important?

Aerobic activity is important on many levels and, certainly, is critical to one's overall health. But right now, we'll begin with weight loss. Aerobic activity is the only thing that gets rid of fat from all over your body, including the marbled fat deep inside your muscles; dieting alone can't do this. In fact, for permanent body-fat weight loss (as opposed to fluid or muscle weight loss), the combination of reducing calories (from unhealthy food) together with aerobic exercise is the answer.

Aerobics for Your Heart

Heart disease is the primary cause of death in older men and women, killing one in four. How well our cardiorespiratory system functions is one of the best clues to our overall fitness, and something we can have considerable control over, even if we are genetically predisposed to heart disease. In fact, aerobic exercise can influence whether the genes for heart disease, diabetes, or other illnesses are ever activated. Understanding the importance of cardio fitness, including what can go wrong, helps us understand why aerobic exercise is so important.

The cardiorespiratory system is responsible for delivering blood, which carries oxygen and nutrients, to every cell in the body, and for carrying away carbon dioxide and other waste products. This is the system that supplies the muscles with the oxygen essential for burning calories for energy. It determines our "maximum aerobic capacity," or VO_2 max, as it's known in sports circles. This is one of the most critical measures of our body's performance: how much

*I was 72 and was
doing my first
workout DVD for
boomers and seniors
after twenty years
out of the business.*

DARREN CAPIK

oxygen we take in; how much blood is pumped, and with what degree of ease, throughout the body; and how well oxygen is taken up and utilized by the muscles and other cells. These dynamics are a master key to our vitality.

With age, the heart and the circulatory system gradually begin to lose some of their effectiveness. After age thirty, there is an average decline of about 1 percent a year in our Vo_2, or aerobic, capacity. The lungs are less elastic and, because they can accept less air, transfer less oxygen into the blood. The heart muscle and the blood vessels thicken and become more rigid, which means that each stroke of the heart pumps less blood. Inelastic and narrowed arteries cause the heart to work harder to move blood from the chest to the head, arms, and legs. As the heart pushes the blood more forcibly through the circulatory network, our blood pressure tends to rise.

All of this is common and needn't mean a loss of basic health, provided we don't also become sedentary. Inactivity increases the likelihood that fatty plaque will begin to cling to our arterial walls, causing atherosclerosis and chronic hypertension, which can spiral into a heart attack or, if the brain is involved, a stroke. Atherosclerosis, hypertension, heart attack, and stroke combined account for half of all disabling health problems in women and men alike.

So just do it! Stay vigorously and aerobically active!

Aerobics and Your Brain

"Perhaps the most direct route to a fit mind is through a fit body,"[3] says Jane Brody, the wonderful health writer for the *New York Times*. All brain experts will tell you that physical activity will do more for your brain health than the expensive computer-based brain games that are so much the rage these days. (Although Dr. Michael Hewitt, at Canyon Ranch, suggests that doing both might be the smartest move of all!)

Obviously, aerobic fitness helps the brain by reducing the risk of heart attack and stroke. But it also improves cognitive functioning by slowing the age-related shrinkage of the frontal cortex of the brain, which is where "executive functions" like reasoning and problem solving take place.

In a 2007 *New York Times* op-ed piece, Dr. Sandra Aamodt, a freelance science writer and former editor in chief of *Nature Neuroscience,* and Dr. Sam Wang, an associate professor of neuroscience at Princeton University, wrote, "Exercise causes the release of growth factors, proteins that increase the number of connections between neurons, and the birth of neurons in the hippocampus," which is the seat of memory and where Alzheimer's disease starts. Reports show that as many as fifty million older Americans may get Alzheimer's by midcentury. While research is under way to prevent or postpone the disease, scientists already know, as Jane Brody writes, that "people who exercise regularly in midlife are one-third as likely to develop Alzheimer's in their 70s. Even those who start exercising in their 60s cut their risk of dementia in half."[4]

A decline in cognitive functioning has long been seen as a "typical" part of aging, but it is not normal. New brain science now shows that seniors who have remained fit and who continue to exercise continue to have good brain functioning.

Earlier I mentioned how aerobic exercise releases endorphins, brain chemicals that give relief from pain, enhance the immune system, reduce stress, and bring us a sense of well-being. Some people need only ten minutes of moderate exercise to experience the endorphin rush; others might require thirty minutes. The effect is often called a "runner's high," and it is one reason why physical activity is increasingly becoming part of the prescription for the treatment of depression and anxiety—a beautiful side effect of exercise that motivates many of us to keep doing it.

What About Weight-Training Exercise for People over Fifty?

Weight lifting—or resistance training, as it's sometimes called—is great for people over fifty, even essential! While it doesn't increase your endurance the way aerobic exercise does, it does maintain or increase the size and strength of your muscles, and there are several reasons why this is important at any age.

For one thing, increasing your muscle mass helps you lose weight, because muscles are the active tissues in the body. They determine your basal (or resting) metabolism rate, the rate at which your body burns caloric energy. Muscle tissue turns your body into a calorie-burning machine even when you're resting.

We tend to put on weight as we get older. This is due partly to our tendency to be less active while continuing to eat the way we always have. But it is also due to the fact that we lose, on average, 3 to 5 percent of our muscle tissue each decade after age thirty. This means that by the time we reach seventy-five, our resting metabolism (basal metabolism) will have dropped by about 10 percent—unless, of course, we become active enough to maintain our muscles. In either case, we should also consciously eat fewer (but more nutrient-rich) calories.

Here's a dramatic example of what can happen: If you eat just one hundred calories more than you burn up every day, you can expect to gain more than fifty pounds in five years. In order to lose this fat, you have to burn it up as a source of energy. (That is, if the calories you eat are fewer than the number of calories you are burning as energy, then the additional energy you need will have to come from stored fat.) To sum up: Aerobic or fat-burning types of activities will help with weight loss, as will increasing your resting metabolism rate through weight-training or resistance exercise to maintain your muscle mass. According to research done at Tufts University on people fifty to seventy-two years old, muscle mass can actually be increased by more than 200 percent with exercise.

Weight Training and Your Bones

Lifting weights or doing resistance training with elastic resistance straps or tubing will not only maintain or increase your muscle mass, it will also improve the strength of your bones, which, in turn, will reduce your risk of osteopenia and osteoporosis, the loss of bone mineral density.

The Tufts study that reported increased muscle mass in older people through resistance training also reported that bone mass can similarly be increased. This is important because osteopenia and the more advanced condition osteoporosis put us at greater risk of fractures, especially of the hip, wrist, ankle, and spine. There are more than 250,000 hip fractures in the United States every year, 80 percent of them to women, and, in 10 to 15 percent of older people, these fractures can lead to death. Something else that is increasingly important with age is the fact that strong muscles can reduce stress on the joints.

Weight Training and Your Brain

Researchers in British Columbia found that women who did an hour or two of weight training every week had better cognitive function than those who did only balance and toning exercises. After one year, the women who lifted weights scored higher in the ability to make decisions, resolve conflicts, and stay focused.[5] As Dr. Michael Hewitt, the research director for exercise science at Canyon Ranch Health Resort, says, "Looking better and being stronger are wonderful, but functioning better is life-enhancing!"

Some Specifics on How to Do Weight Training

If you want shorter workouts, you can work one set of muscles on one day—say, your upper body—and target a different set the following day—in this example, your lower body. Or instead of spreading your weight workouts over several days, you can do a longer, full-body workout three times a week; even two times is beneficial.

For muscles to become stronger they have to be stressed enough to cause overload or cellular fatigue, after which they need forty-eight hours to recover. This is why you should never work the same muscles on consecutive days. However, because of the nature of abdominal muscles, they can be worked every day!

I recommend doing two sets of twelve to fifteen repetitions for each muscle group: abdominals, chest, shoulders, back, arms, legs, and so forth. (See Appendix II for a chart of the muscle groups.) If you need to use lighter weights because of uncontrolled blood pressure or joint health, make up for it by doing more repetitions.

Keeping our quadriceps muscles (on the fronts of the thighs) strong is so important now because those are the muscles we use (together with our gluteal, or buttocks, muscles) to get up from a chair, or into and out of a car. But muscles come in pairs: the quadriceps (front of the thighs) and the hamstrings (back of the thighs), for instance; the triceps (back of the upper arms) and the biceps (front of the upper arms). To have a balanced body that is less injury-prone, it's important to exercise both sets equally. When we lift weights to strengthen our biceps, we should also work the triceps. Exercising the large quadriceps muscles should be balanced with exercising the hamstring muscles, and so forth.

Posture

It's critical, especially now, to pay attention to your posture when you're working out. If you are in the wrong position, you have a greater risk of injuring yourself than when you were younger. This is why it is a good investment to spend some time with a certified professional trainer—not some gung-ho, push-to-the-limit sort, but one who is knowledgeable about older bodies and knows what to look out for and when to correct you. Be certain that in addition to training and certification, your trainer also has a personality and style compatible with yours.

Key 3: A Three-Step Exercise Program

For those of you with very little time, I have included a short, three-step exercise program called Key 3 (see Figures 1–3), developed by Dr.

Michael Hewitt, who, as I have said, is the research director for exercise science at Canyon Ranch Health Resort. These three exercises, done with handheld dumbbells—wall squats, chest presses, and the single-arm row—will challenge 80 to 85 percent of the body's muscle

Figure 1. Chest Presses: Lie on your back, knees bent. Hold your dumbbells with elbows bent out to the sides, shoulder height, and bring them together up above your chest. KAREN WYLIE

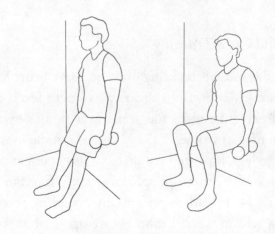

Figure 2. Standing Squats Against a Wall: With feet hip distance apart, hold your dumbbells with arms hanging straight at your sides and squat until your hips are level with your knees—not below your knees! Your feet must be far enough out from the wall that when you squat, your knees are not farther forward than your toes. KAREN WYLIE

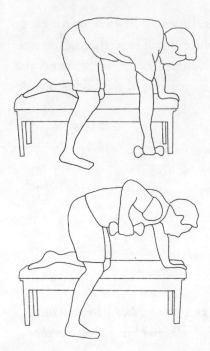

Figure 3. Single-Arm Rows: Place one knee and one hand on a chair or bench. Bend the standing leg. Hold the weight in your other arm and let it hang straight down. Then bring your elbow up close to your side, and control it down. Keep your back flat. Think of sawing a big log as you bring your elbow up and down. Keep your elbow close to your body. Exhale as you lift. Inhale as you lower.

KAREN WYLIE

mass. Dr. Hewitt says that once you get the hang of it, you can complete two sets of the Key 3 exercises in about ten minutes.[6]

When it's this quick and easy, is there any reason not to just do it?

Balance and Core Training

"Without regular muscle-building exercise," says Scott McCredie in his book *Balance: In Search of the Lost Sense,* "strength levels decrease by about 12 to 14 percent per decade, starting at about age sixty in men and about age fifty in women."[7] This loss of muscle mass and tone, especially in the legs, hips, and trunk, has a direct effect on balance.

Every year, one in three people over sixty-five fall. As I have already said, this can lead to potentially crippling fractures, even fatalities. The reason we fall more as we age is that we are more likely to lose our sense of equilibrium. Actually, like muscle loss, balance loss is natural and begins very gradually, as early as in our twenties. As we age, various physiological changes in the inner ear, the bottoms of our feet, and our eyesight challenge our sense of balance. More important, we process these signals more slowly and less accurately than when we were younger. I'm not sure which of these (or maybe it's all of them) is the culprit in my case, but balance is definitely my Achilles' heel. One reason I try to keep my muscles strong is to compensate for this.

I also do exercises specifically designed to improve my balance. Whenever I can, like when I am brushing my teeth or hair or waiting in a line, I practice standing on one foot. At home, to challenge myself even more, I do the one-legged stand with my eyes closed. Once a day, I walk for a dozen or so steps, placing one foot directly in front of the other, as though I'm walking a plank. Balance can be developed just as muscles and aerobic capacity can.

Certain medicines and combinations of medicines can make you dizzy. If you find yourself having trouble with balance, have your doctor or pharmacist take a look at all your medicines (including any over-the-counter ones) to see if that could be a contributing factor.

Physical therapist Karen Perz offers a useful tip: "When someone is off balance, it's better for them to hold on to you, rather than for you to hold on to them . . . and you should offer your elbow, not your hand."[8]

Yoga and tai chi, a Chinese martial art where you do a series of slow, flowing, standing movements, are excellent for developing balance. So are core training and Pilates, which more and more gyms are offering. In core training you do exercises while standing on various surfaces that wobble. In addition to stimulating adaptations in the balance centers of the central nervous system, these exercises deliberately create instability, which recruits the smaller, stabilizing muscles, such as the gluteus medius, in the hip; the vastus medialis oblique, in the knee; and some of the small muscles in the back and the shoulders that aren't normally challenged. My Prime Time Workout also includes exercises to improve your balance.

Physical Therapy

I woke up one morning unable to lift my right arm above breast height. A physical therapist explained that sleeping on my side had aggravated an already-existing rotator cuff problem, and the injury required six months of manual therapy. After that, my back went into spasm, which reminded me of what my friend Bette Davis said: "Aging isn't for sissies."

Chiropractic therapy, if done by a qualified practitioner, can provide quick relief through joint manipulation; it's a lifesaver for many people. But with a trained and talented therapist, physical therapy can get to the underlying causes of your problems by deeply working the muscular, skeletal, and nervous systems. The therapist uses her or his hands and arms to apply sustained pressure where the muscles have become hard and claylike, as opposed to springy. This makes the knot relax and increases circulation to the area. Very often, the knot is caused by a lack of mobility in the joints and/or the related muscles, tendons, and ligaments, which is why the therapist works on all the systems.

In searching for your own manual therapist, what you want to look for are the letters OCS (orthopedic clinical specialist) or SCS (sports clinical specialist) following the person's name. Or you can visit the American Physical Therapy Association website at www.apta.org. They provide lists by region of therapists and their certifications. Once at the APTA website, choose "Find a PT," then select "Musculoskeletal" and fill in your zip code.

Get the therapist to help you understand the underlying causes of your problem: what muscle weaknesses and joint immobility brought you into therapy, and what exercises you can do to address them. Treating the cause of the problem is usually much more effective than treating the symptoms. Many such therapists can be reimbursed through health insurance.

For example, I learned from my manual therapist that my posture had contributed to my back, neck, and shoulder pain. The slight rounding of my shoulders (begun, as with so many women, in adolescence) had gradually gotten worse. The smaller back muscles that pull our shoulders back had weakened, causing pressure on my neck and shoulders. Doing something about it after years of neglect is hard, and correct posture feels awkward at first—at least it did for me. But with practice, it has become (almost) second nature. (My therapist says it takes six weeks on average to reeducate the muscles.) I now check regularly to make sure that while I sit at my computer or at the movies, in a restaurant, or in the car, I always use good posture.

Flexibility

How important it is to keep our muscles, tendons, and ligaments flexible is the final point I want to make about physical fitness in the Third Act. Flexibility can protect us from injury no matter our age, but it is especially critical when all these body parts are beginning to lose their mobility and to stiffen. It is best to stretch *after* working out, and to hold each stretch for at least twenty seconds. It takes that long for the muscle to fully relax and release. Yoga can be an excellent way to maintain flexibility, although you should start with a gentle form. So can Pilates and tai chi.

PILATES

The Pilates method seeks to develop controlled movement from a strong core; it does this using a range of apparatuses to guide and train the body. Each piece of equipment has its own repertoire of exercises, and most of the exercises involve resistance training, since they make use of springs to provide additional resistance.

TAI CHI

The ancient art of tai chi uses gentle, flowing movements to reduce stress, improve balance, and help with a variety of other health conditions. Each posture flows rhythmically into the next without pause, ensuring that your body is in constant motion. The movements are coordinated with your breathing to help you achieve a sense of inner calm. The concentration required for tai chi forces you to live in the present moment, putting aside distressing thoughts.

Tips on Walking

Walking can be as good for weight loss as running. Here's one comparison: Say you are a 145-pound, sixty-year-old woman. If you run for 30 minutes at 5 miles per hour, you will burn about 285 calories. If you walk for 30 minutes at 4 miles per hour, you will burn 165 calories on a level surface, 225 calories on a slight incline, and 360 calories on a 10 percent incline. Don't underestimate the power of a brisk walk!

Posture is key: Your shoulders should be back and down, your head high and directly over your neck. Look straight ahead (to anticipate obstacles) and take long, smooth strides, with your arms swinging freely. Be sure to breathe.

Wear lightweight, breathable, supportive, comfortable shoes with a flexible, cushioned sole to absorb impact. Different shoes work better for different feet.

Warm up for a few minutes before you begin your walk.

Try using walking poles. They help with balance, take a little weight off your joints, and encourage you to use more muscle groups, so you will burn more calories. Good ones have rubber tips and wrist straps. (Go to leki.com, bdel.com, or anwa.us for more information about walking with poles, which is sometimes called "Nordic walking.")

Here-and-There Exercise

It's not simply doing thirty or forty minutes of moderate exercise every day that will keep you healthy. What you do, here and there, during the remaining fifteen or so waking hours of your day matters just as much!

Physiologists have grown perplexed about the rapid increase in obesity in the developed world. How, they ask, can this be so, when the percentage of people who perform the minimum half hour of daily moderate activity has remained relatively stable? This phenomenon has led scientists to define a new health risk called *inactivity physiology*.

It is now believed that even if you devote thirty to forty minutes daily to exercise, if the rest of your day is spent in a sedentary position, you are at risk of poor health. Well, it's no secret that too many of us spend too much of our time sitting. We sit in our cars or on buses to get to work; we sit at desks once we're there; and we sit in front of the television when we get home. The average adult spends 9.3 (61 percent) of their waking hours sitting. Scientists are starting to believe that simply getting up and walking a few steps every hour can mitigate the negative effects of this inactivity.

In airports, I always walk rather than take the "moving sidewalk" and use the stairs rather than the escalator. And if I do have to take an escalator, I walk up it instead of just riding passively. These little decisions can really add up to your becoming more physically active.

Interoception: The Deeper Meaning of Body Awareness

I feel strongly that this is the time in our lives when getting "into" our bodies is less about being into our bodies in the "How do I look?" sense, though that is a part of it. But there can also be a psychic effect of physical activity.

So many of us have, to greater or lesser extents, become numb and cut off from our bodies. This lack of connection often increases as we age. We may be saying to ourselves, "Why deal with our bodies now? We're through having children. We're beyond trying to appeal to someone else. We don't even appeal to ourselves!" Numbness especially occurs with people who have been abused or are burdened with obesity, but it is more widespread than that. We can be alienated from feeling our muscles, our heartbeat, our breath within the body. Obviously we are aware of these things, but it can be only on a superficial, disembodied level.

My friend Joan Halifax, a Zen master, has challenged me to consider a deeper significance of body awareness. "We think the mind is between the two ears and is the expression of the brain," she told me. "But neuroscience shows us that the mind isn't just in the head; it is throughout the entire body, informing the entire organism." When we are cut off from our bodies, our thinking becomes *disembodied.*

I know what that feels like. For years, I suffered from anorexia and bulimia. Food addicts, like all addicts, are inevitably disembodied. By the time I started my Workout business I was not engaging in my food addiction, but I was not healed, either. I guess I was the equivalent of a dry drunk (but for food, not alcohol): one who is sober but has not worked through a twelve-step program. The result was that I spent a lot of time taking up residence next door to myself—disembodied. As I look back over those years of building the Workout business, I think I was instinctively searching for a way to heal myself, to get back into my body. Discovering that I could be in control of my body through exercise, and thereby learning to accept and even love my body, was a first step in making that happen.

I ask you, right now, to put your index and middle fingers on the artery at the side of your throat and feel your pulse. In a moment, I'm going to ask you to stop reading, close your eyes, and sink into your body. When you do, be aware of your breathing, the rise and fall of your chest, your pulse, the sensations inside your body, the feeling of the flesh of your buttocks against the seat, the bottoms of your feet. Don't rush and don't forget to breathe. And, with your breath, bring forgiveness into your body for perhaps not being everything you wish it was. Smile into your body. It's gotten you this far. It deserves your love, respect, and attention. Now close your eyes for a minute and experience your body.

Assuming you did the above, you were, for a moment, present in your body. When we get into the habit of body awareness through meditation, attentive, deliberate exercise, or yoga, we can nurture what Joan Halifax says is our ability to be *interoceptive*—we have the capacity to sense or experience the body, including our ability to sense our body temperature, feel our hunger or sexual urgency, be in touch with the gut, the lungs, the heart, and so forth. Another way of saying this is that we develop an image of our body's internal state. What I find most interesting is that interoception allows *self*-empathy. Empathy means we feel the suffering (or other emotions) of others, which can lead to kindness. We can't feel empathy and kindness for others if we lack it for ourselves. Self-empathy starts with our embodiment—being in our bodies, our muscles, our cells, our breath. You have to love and be kind to your body.

Taking it a step further, Joan Halifax says that while empathy is about feeling for others, "compassion means feeling the suffering of others but with an attendant aspiration to transform the suffering. Compassion is the most important mental quality we can cultivate."[9]

Very different than pity, which masquerades as compassion and drains us and the other person, compassion energizes us and others. It activates an impulse to outward action. This is what I see as the beautiful sequence: from visceral, attentive, nonjudgmental body awareness, to empathy for self, extended out to empathy for others, to compassion for others, and then to universal compassion, an expression of compassion that is unbiased, all-inclusive.

Deep inner to wide outer.

My challenge to you to become physically active and attentive to your body is also a call to become both embodied and compassionate. You have the time—now more than ever—to do this work. You need to *make* time and develop the guts to get into your guts—to feel, accept, love, and be present in your body.

In Conclusion

Even if you have never been active a day in your life, you can start now. The MacArthur Foundation Study of Successful Aging concluded that physical activity is "perhaps the single most important thing an older person can do to remain healthy . . . the crux of successful aging, regardless of other factors."[10]

It's not too late, but the sooner you begin, the better. You have to get up and "just do it." And chances are, once you do, you'll be motivated to keep on doing it, as you start experiencing how much better it makes you feel. You'll actually come to miss exercise when you have to skip it. Now's the time.

CHAPTER 7

Now More than Ever, You Are What You Eat

Had I known I was going to live so long, I would have taken better care of myself.

—Eubie Blake, jazz pianist, at age 102

My doctor told me to stop having intimate dinners for four; unless there are three other people.

—Orson Welles

I MENTOR A FORTY-YEAR-OLD WOMAN, KELLY, WHO HAS HAD A very challenging life. We correspond by email. A while back, she wrote and told me what her usual diet consisted of: Kool-Aid, Doritos, pizza, whatever was cheap. I was horrified! Of course, her "normal" diet was the same as many people's, especially poor people. So I sent her a little money and told her to go to a store and buy chicken, broccoli, and fresh fruit, and I explained how to cook the chicken. After several months of her new diet, she sent me this email:

My situation caused me to become depressed (no job, constant setbacks, etc.). It seemed no matter what I did or tried nothing ever worked. I was isolated, angry, and depressed. Then you wrote me those magic words, "Get out of your head and into your body." You told me to just try eating healthy. I really didn't want to but I did anyway. I began to notice a change. I began to feel better. Then when I finally got my food stamps I was able to afford to buy healthy foods. (Before the food stamps I tried to conserve money by buying cheap food that would last the longest. I was trying to stretch a dollar—but that food was horrible.)

So, running and eating healthy actually changed not only how I feel physically but how I feel mentally—and it goes further than that. It changed how I react to things. I get upset sometimes but I don't STAY upset. My emotional state is stronger and getting stronger. I know it has something to do with the fact that I'm no longer eating sugar, dyes, chemicals, artificial this or that, or preservatives. I am able to sleep better and I feel less fidgety and hyper.

Jogging and eating healthy is not gonna make unemployment, racism, discrimination, poverty, violence, the system, or any of the other stuff disappear from my life but I tell you one thing, working out and eating right is like armor. It makes me feel stronger and better able to deal with the tough stuff.

Well, getting older is "tough stuff," and to handle it and keep our body, our "container," as healthy and strong as possible, we need to pay more attention to how we eat.

Back when I was ten or eleven years old, on the mornings when I expected a school test, I would always eat oatmeal for breakfast (not the instant kind—I don't think that even existed then—but the traditional kind, which takes a while to cook). To this day, I think I scored well on those tests due to the oatmeal, because if I'd forget and eat sugary cereals, I wouldn't do as well. I'd be fidgety and hyper, just like my friend Kelly said. There's a reason for this, which I'll explain in a moment.

As I got older, I stopped eating breakfast altogether because I was always on some diet or other—or in between bouts of bulimia and anorexia. Sometimes I'd go for days—weeks, even—without drinking water or eating anything green or any fruit and never feel affected by it.

Most of us did all sorts of injustices to our bodies earlier in life, out of ignorance and a feeling of immortality. Our bodies were still young and resilient, so, beyond the immediate effects, we didn't really notice. The rate of our body's breakdown and repair on the cellular level were essentially equal. Our cells may have gotten damaged from what we ate or didn't eat, but our repair mechanisms kicked in right away. It felt like a free ride.

But by midlife, our cellular self-restoration processes begin to fall behind, and as we grow older, what we eat determines a lot about who and how we are. Now, for better or worse, we tend to notice it. This is because, with age, the ability of our cells to utilize life-sustaining nutrients and eliminate waste products so as to remain robust is diminished. We become more vulnerable to diseases. Of course, the speed of the breakdown process varies widely, depending on a person's overall health and her or his exposure to external toxins such as cigarette smoke, air pollution, pesticides, poor diet, radioactivity, and anesthetics, as well as excessive stress, time in the sun, and alcohol intake, all of which compound the normal damage.

This chapter is about how the quality of what we eat and *how much* we eat can intervene to slow down the cellular damage and keep us healthy for as long as possible. (Avoiding the external toxins I just mentioned is also very important, so it might be good to reread that list.)

Calories

A moderate calorie-restricted diet is especially good for us now, and not just as a weight-reduction strategy. So try to keep your caloric intake within a range that is appropriate for your age and level of physical activity. According to the Dietary Guidelines for Americans published by the U.S. Departments of Agriculture and of Health and Human Services, a woman over fifty who is sedentary should eat only 1,600 calories a day. If she is moderately active, she can consume 1,800 calories per day, and if she is active, 2,000 to 2,200 a day is appropriate. A sedentary man over fifty can eat 2,000 calories a day; a moderately active man can have 2,200 to 2,400, and an active man can consume 2,400 to 2,800. The more calories you burn up though activity, the more you can consume safely. The main challenge for us now is keeping the calories we consume under control while still meeting our nutrient requirements. This means that every calorie has to count! They have to come from nutritious, fresh foods. We mustn't squander our daily allotment on the wrong foods, such as soft drinks and typical restaurant fare, which can offer little nutritional value and a lot of sugar, fat, and sodium. These days, the old adage "You are what you eat" takes on added significance.

Five Key Things to Watch

Five key things you should cut down on or cut out of your Third Act are:

ADDED SUGARS

Americans today consume 50 percent more sugar than we did in 1910. The sugar industry now produces about 130 pounds of sugar per person each year! This is more than a third of a pound daily for every woman, man, and child. A major Harvard study notes that, besides being devoid of nutrients, excess sugar promotes obesity, heart disease, diabetes, and tooth decay; the study singles out sugary beverages in particular. The label might say corn syrup, dextrose, maltose, glucose, or invert sugar, but, honey, it's all sugar! So don't eat those sugary muffins and cereals for breakfast! Don't snack on candy. Cut back on the sweet desserts. **Try to consume less than 30 grams of sugar a day—but don't worry about the naturally occurring sugars in fruits, vegetables, milk, and yogurt.**

FAT

Fat is an essential nutrient. Without enough fat, the skin deteriorates and vitamin deficiencies flourish. Fat is a carrier of the fat-soluble vitamins A, D, E, and K, and aids in the digestion and absorption of important disease-fighting plant components called phytonutrients (*phyton* is "plant" in Greek). Those substances include carotenoids, lycopene, and lutein, which may help prevent inflammation, cellular oxidation, and ailments such as macular degeneration (the major cause of blindness with aging), cancer, and heart disease.

To many people, the term "healthy fat" seems like an oxymoron. Evolving science is finding that there is a minimum level of fat you must eat to maintain health, but the type of fat you choose is crucial.

Fat is our second most important source of energy after carbohydrates, but there are good fats and bad fats, and the bad ones are a potential dietary time bomb.

Trans Fats

Artificial trans fat (from partially hydrogenated oils) is, gram for gram, the most harmful fat in the food supply. It both raises the "bad" LDL cholesterol and lowers the "good" HDL cholesterol in our blood. Thankfully, the amount of this artificial fat created by the food industry (it's cheap and so very profitable—at our expense!) is now required to be stated on food labels—and most large food manufacturers and restaurants have stopped using it. (In fact, California, New York City, and other jurisdictions have largely banned it from restaurant foods!) The amount of trans fat in the food supply has declined by at least half since 2004, but trans fats are still found in some brands of microwave popcorn, fried foods, pies, cookies, and pastries. Check out the labels carefully (or ask a baker), and you'll see. **Your goal should be to eliminate trans fats from your diet altogether. (Beef and cheese have small amounts of naturally occurring trans fat; you'll avoid most of that if you choose low-fat meat and dairy products.)**

Saturated Fats

The other bad fats, the saturated fats, are the ones that are solid at room temperature—such as butter, lard, and shortening, including shortening made with coconut or palm oil. Saturated fat increases the "bad" (LDL) cholesterol level in the blood and your risk of heart disease. However, it is not nearly as harmful as trans fat because it also tends to raise the "good" (HDL) cholesterol. Try to avoid fried foods, butter, ice cream, full-fat cheeses, cream sauces, processed meats such as cold cuts, sausages, and bacon, and most red meat. By the way, those of us over fifty don't need to worry as much about cholesterol; it doesn't carry as much risk for us as it does for younger people. **Minimize your intake of saturated fats to less than 10 or 20 grams per day.**

Good Fats

There are, however, good fats: the unsaturated kinds, which are liquid at room temperature. These come from vegetable oils such as olive, soy, canola, corn, and safflower and provide essential fatty acids. Typical vegetable oils, including those found in nuts and soybeans, lower LDL cholesterol and reduce the risk of heart disease. Fat in fish provides omega-3 fatty acids, which help protect against heart attacks. While those oils are actually beneficial, they also contain calories, so don't overdo them.

Good fats should account for about 20 or 25 percent of our daily calories, so getting those calories from an oil-and-vinegar salad dressing is a whole lot better than getting calories from 2 percent milk, cheese, or meat.

SALT

Too much sodium is a major cause of high blood pressure and water retention. High blood pressure, of course, is a major cause of heart attacks and strokes. As a nation, if we cut our sodium intake in half, it would likely save at least 100,000 lives per year. Enough said?

Most of the sodium we consume comes from packaged and restaurant foods, so check the "Nutrition Facts" labels carefully and either avoid high-sodium foods entirely or choose lower-sodium versions. The government classifies a food as "low sodium" if it contains less than 140 milligrams of sodium per serving. Eating out can be treacherous. Restaurant meals are generally huge, and often very high in sodium—a meal at a place like IHOP or Denny's may contain three or four times as much as you should eat in an entire day! **Try to make your daily intake of sodium less than 2,300 milligrams—ideally, under 1,500 milligrams—and do not add salt to your food.**

ALCOHOL

Excess alcohol interferes with healthy nutrition for several reasons. It reduces the intake of nutrient-dense foods, and it affects the metabolism and absorption of several key nutrients. In fact, malnutrition—otherwise rare in the United States—is common among alcoholics. Alcohol depletes our levels of vitamin C, vitamin A, the B vitamins folate and thiamine, and such essential minerals as iron, calcium, magnesium, and zinc. I write elsewhere about the damage oxidation does to our cells. Well, too much alcohol is a potent oxidant, and it stresses the digestive and hormonal systems, the kidneys, and the liver. As a result, alcoholics can suffer gastrointestinal distress, immune system disorders, nerve and brain damage, heart inflammation, osteoporosis, and fat malabsorption, contributing to deficiencies of the fat-soluble vitamins (A, D, E, and K). Moreover, one drink adds 100 to 400 nutritionless calories.

However, in moderate amounts (one serving a day for women, two for men) alcohol relaxes the blood vessels and raises the level of good (HDL) cholesterol in the blood by about 5 percent, which helps protect the heart. This is especially true in people who exercise, perhaps because exercise also raises the HDL level. Moderation and drinking *with meals* is the key! **One serving is five ounces of wine, twelve ounces of beer, or one and a half ounces of spirits.**

AND NO SMOKING

Smoking is the major cause of preventable deaths in the United States. Smoking—even exposure to secondhand smoke—harms nearly every organ of the body. Cigarette smoking causes 87 percent of lung cancer deaths. It is also responsible for many other cancers and health problems. These include lung disease, heart and blood vessel disease, stroke, and cataracts. Women who smoke have a greater chance of certain pregnancy problems and of having a baby die from sudden infant death syndrome (SIDS). Your smoke is also bad for other people; those who breathe in your smoke *secondhand* can suffer from many of the same problems that smokers do. *Quitting smoking* can reduce your risk of these problems. The earlier you quit, the greater the health benefit.

Additionally, smoking depletes us of important nutrients. It is also a potent oxidant, accelerating the aging process, causing the cross-linking that can mean wrinkles and the stiffening of blood vessels and other connective tissues. Every study I have read cites smoking as one of the most dangerous health habits of all.

Essential Things to Add

Besides reducing our intake of these five destructive things, here is the number one positive thing to do: **Increase your intake of fruits, vegetables, and whole grains.**

We ought to base the bulk of our diets on fruits; vegetables; nuts; legumes, including lentils, peas, and beans; whole grains, such as brown rice, bulgur, and buckwheat; and whole grain products, such as whole wheat bread, multigrain and bran cereals, and non-instant oatmeal.

These foods should make up **50 to 60 percent or more of our daily**

calories. You don't have to become a vegetarian, but we all ought to move much more in that direction.

Unfortunately, many people eat far too few fruits and vegetables, and the grain foods they choose are usually made with white flour. That's a prescription for gastrointestinal disease, heart disease, diabetes, and maybe cancer, according to a preponderance of scientific research.

Five Basic Food Groups

These five food groups should provide our basic nutrition: 1) breads and cereals; 2) fruits and vegetables; 3) dairy products; 4) proteins; and 5) heart-healthy fats. Getting an appropriate daily amount of each of these is the key.

BREADS AND CEREALS

This category includes all of the whole grains (rice, barley, millet, cracked wheat, corn), whole grain breads and cereals (non-instant oatmeal, bran, etc.), and whole grain crackers, pasta, and tortillas. *This food group should provide the primary daily source of our energy.*

Just to be clear, by whole grains I am talking about foods that contain all the germ and fiber from the grains, not just the starch. Here's why this is important: Before grains are refined, they contain the bran and the germ, which provide a wide range of nutrients, such as vitamin A and the B vitamins (thiamine, niacin, riboflavin, and pantothenic acid); minerals (calcium, magnesium, potassium, phosphorous, sodium, selenium, and iron); protein; essential oils; and phytonutrients, including antioxidants (the free-radical fighters), which appear to promote health. They also contain small amounts of sodium or sugar and a lot of fiber. When flour is refined, however, the nutrient-rich germ and the fiber-rich cell walls, the bran, of the grain are removed—and fed to livestock!

Fiber-Rich Foods

Fiber is found in whole grains, beans, peas, seeds, nuts (raw and unsalted is best!), lentils, fresh fruits and vegetables, and sprouted seeds such as soybeans, mung beans, and alfalfa, which you can sprout yourself at home. Besides being high in fiber, these foods are packed with vitamins, minerals, and phytonutrients. Most plant foods are little factories of nutrients. When these phytochemicals are taken into your body's tissues, they may have health-promoting properties. Almost everyone—including, probably, you—does not consume enough fiber-rich foods and, therefore, dietary fiber.

Not all fibers are the same. According to the excellent *Nutrition Action Healthletter,* soluble fiber from oats, barley, and fresh fruits and vegetables can lower a person's cholesterol and reduce their risk of heart disease.[1] On the other hand, insoluble fiber, like that from whole wheat (especially the bran part), is not broken down by bacteria in the gut and helps with bowel regularity. All high-fiber foods break down into glucose more slowly than simple or refined foods do. This means that they provide more sustained energy over a greater length of time than refined grains like white bread or white rice (or sugars) can. (Which is why my breakfasts of oatmeal helped me perform well on tests as a youngster.) Dietary fiber is also important for people who want to lose weight, because it helps make meals more filling.

Highly refined carbohydrates like white flour are low in fiber; whole wheat bread—the kind that contains the wheat germ and the bran—has three times as much fiber as white bread. The Dietary Guidelines for Americans recommends 14 grams of fiber per 1,000 calories consumed, so that's about 22 to 39 grams of fiber every day, depending on your caloric needs. When you see that most whole grain foods have only have about 2 or 4 grams per serving, you realize that getting enough fiber takes work; you'll need to consume numerous fiber-rich plant foods every day.

Food Labels

You may think you are buying whole grain breads when you see packages that say "whole wheat" or "multigrain," but it's not necessarily so. If you are shopping for bread, pancake mix, or other grain-based foods, you need "whole wheat" or "whole rye," for example, *to be the only grain listed in the ingredients.* When you see the term "made with whole grain," the food is not 100 percent whole grain. Don't waste your money on foods made with "unbleached but *refined* flour." And forget about the ice creams, yogurts, juice drinks, and even waters that claim to contain fiber. These are not the kinds of real fiber you get from whole grains, beans, fruits, and vegetables. There is no solid scientific evidence that the mostly purified, processed, powdered versions of fiber that are being added to foods have the same benefits.

Food labels always list the ingredients in descending order of amount, so if sugar or refined, enriched flour is the first or second ingredient, you know that the food, whatever it is, is best avoided. You should also avoid products that contain such questionable additives as nitrites, saccharin, acesulfame potassium, artificial colorings (such as Red 40 or Yellow 5), and synthetic preservatives such as BHA and BHT.

FRUITS AND VEGETABLES

Fruits and vegetables, which are excellent sources of dietary fiber, should be a major part of our daily supply of energy. In order to ensure that we are getting the necessary vitamins, minerals, and micronutrients we need at this stage of life, our supply of healthy carbs shouldn't all be beige (that is, from the whole grains, nuts, breads, etc.).

Try to eat five to ten servings of different colored fresh fruits and vegetables every day. (Don't freak! As Jane Brody points out, one serving consists of only "half a cup of cut-up or cooked vegetables, one cup of fresh greens, half a cup of cooked dried beans, or, if you must, six ounces of vegetable juice."[2]) Why is color important? Because colorful foods are usually rich in nutrients. Dark leafy vegetables, such as kale, spinach, and broccoli; dark purple fruits, such as blueberries and blackberries; and dark orange fruits and vegetables are among the richest in nutrients and antioxidants. Containing vitamins C and E, beta-carotene, and selenium, these foods are real scavengers of free radicals. Beta-carotene is the precursor of vitamin A, which is critical to healthy eyes and skin and can help fight infection. Since older people should not take vitamin A supplements because vitamin A builds up in the liver and can cause toxicity, it is especially important that we eat plenty of these foods. One study has shown that women who eat large amounts of fruits and vegetables are at lower risk of obesity. Provided they are not loaded with butter or high-calorie dressings and sauces, the dietary bulk of fresh fruits and vegetables can fill your stomach and curb your appetite. They can also reduce your cholesterol level and help curb constipation.

Eating by Color

Look at this list of colors and think about how to get at least four or five of these foods—these colors—into yourself every day. (Please note that the foods themselves are far better, with fewer calories, than fruit juices or dried fruits and vegetables.)

RED: tomatoes, pink grapefruit, watermelon, red peppers, red apples, blood oranges, cranberries, red grapes, cherries, red pears, pomegranates, raspberries, strawberries, red onions, rhubarb, beets, radishes, radicchio

BLUE/PURPLE: purple grapes, purple plums, prunes, blueberries, blackberries, black currants, black olives, eggplant, purple Belgian endive, purple peppers, black salsify

YELLOW/ORANGE: yellow apples, apricots, gooseberries, cantaloupe, carrots, yellow figs, grapefruit, golden kiwifruit, lemons, mangoes, nectarines, oranges, papayas, peaches, yellow pears, persimmons, pineapples, tangerines, yellow watermelon, yellow beets, pumpkin, acorn squash, butternut squash, sweet potatoes, yellow peppers, rutabagas, yellow summer squash, yellow tomatoes, yellow winter squash

GREEN: avocados, green apples, green grapes, green olives, honeydew, kiwifruit, limes, green pears, artichokes, arugula, asparagus, broccoflower, broccoli, broccoli rabe, Brussels sprouts, Chinese cabbage, green beans, green cabbage, celery, chayote squash, cucumbers, endive, kale, spinach, collards, mustard greens, leeks, lettuce, green onions, okra, fresh peas, green peppers, snow peas, sugar snap peas, watercress, zucchini

WHITE: garlic, onions, parsnips, shallots, turnips, cauliflower, ginger, jicama, kohlrabi, mushrooms, bananas, dates, white nectarines and peaches, brown pears

DAIRY OR CALCIUM-FORTIFIED SOY PRODUCTS

One to three cups daily of low-fat or fat-free dairy products such as milk, cheese, or yogurt is the goal. Skim milk contains more calcium for the calories than, say, yogurt. But for an aging intestinal tract, fermented dairy or soy products—such as yogurts or kefir that contain live, active cultures—may promote digestive health.[3]

If you're not consuming dairy, calcium-fortified soy foods, or other calcium-fortified products (like some orange juices and cereals), you may not be getting an adequate amount of calcium—so check with your doctor about taking a supplement (probably one that contains vitamin D). Calcium absorption is most efficient in increments of 500 milligrams or less, taken between meals and as calcium citrate. Your maximum intake of calcium should be no more than 2,500 milligrams a day.

PROTEINS

Approximately 15 percent of your total calories should come from protein. If you are older, protein will help boost your more vulnerable immune system and slow the inevitable bone and muscle loss that comes with aging, according to experts in the field of aging at Tufts University and other respected research centers. Protein is what allows for growth and repair of our bodies, especially our muscles and bones. Without enough protein, our bone health, muscle function, strength, muscle mass, and immune function are all impaired.

There are nine essential amino acids that the human body cannot produce; therefore, we have to get them from the food we eat. Animal foods such as lean meat, chicken, fish, and eggs and dairy products and vegetarian sources such as soybeans and tofu contain all nine essential amino acids in the proportion that we need, and so are called "complete proteins." Many vegetables, grains, dried beans, and nuts contain protein, but with lower proportions of some of the essential amino acids, which is why they are not considered complete proteins. Fortunately, a mixed diet featuring numerous sources of protein provides adequate amounts of all the essential amino acids.

Often older men and women—especially if they're dieting—do not consume enough protein, but protein intake is important. This is especially true for those suffering from infections or recovering from surgery, since protein helps fight disease and heal wounds. **Six to nine ounces of protein-rich foods, making up about 12 percent of our daily calories,** is advised by the Dietary Guidelines for Americans put out by the Department of Agriculture and the Department of Health and Human Services. Meat, fish, poultry, eggs, and dairy are the main protein sources for those who are not vegetarians. Try to eat non-fried fish two to four times weekly, as the American Heart Association recommends. Or, if your doctor approves, take omega-3 fatty acid supplements (preferably from fish oil). Start with a daily dose of 1,000 milligrams of omega-3 fatty acids that include EPA and DHA. Vegetarians should get their omega-3 fatty acids from walnuts, ground flaxseed, flaxseed oil, or canola oil. But if you take an omega-3 fatty acid supplement, this will increase your body's requirement for vitamin E, an important antioxidant, so add a small dose of vitamin E along with your omega-3 capsules.

For vegetarians, tofu, which is made from soybeans, is an excellent source of high-quality, complete protein, healthy soybean oil, and calcium, while also being low in calories and carbohydrates, with no cholesterol. Legumes such as garbanzo beans (chickpeas), black beans, navy beans, lentils, black-eyed peas, and other mature, dried beans contain good amounts of protein, but they still need to be combined with a grain to be equivalent to a complete, high-quality soy or animal protein.

Vitamins and Minerals

Vitamins—unlike protein, carbohydrates, and fat—are not a source of energy. They are catalysts for the biochemical reactions that take place in the body. Since vitamins are not manufactured by the human body, we must eat foods that supply them, or take vitamin supplements.

Like vitamins, minerals are needed for many bodily functions, especially as building blocks for tissue and as regulators of metabolic processes. We need different kinds of minerals for good health and growth, some in relatively large quantities and some, known as trace minerals, in minute amounts.

The minerals that are needed in higher amounts are calcium, potassium, sodium, magnesium, and phosphorus. The trace minerals include iron, copper, zinc, manganese, chromium, selenium, vanadium, and molybdenum.

If we all ate the recommended amounts of fruits, vegetables, and other nutrient-rich foods, we probably would not need most vitamin and mineral supplements. The Dietary Guidelines for Americans advise us to get our vitamins and minerals directly from foods because foods also contain more than nine hundred naturally occurring substances—such as fiber, carotenoids, flavonoids, polyphenols, anthocyanins, isoflavones, resveratrol, and protease inhibitors, the phytonutrients described earlier—that may protect us from chronic health problems.

That said, most of us don't eat such healthful diets, and as we age and our appetites diminish, we can find it hard to consume enough food to provide the necessary nutrients. On top of that, most of the fruits and vegetables sold in supermarkets are transported long distances and stored before being put on sale. That gap from field to table results in nutrient loss and, in some instances, may require that we take a multivitamin and/or mineral supplement and consume certain fortified foods.

Vitamins are either water-soluble or fat-soluble. The water-soluble vitamins—C and the B family—are not stored in the body, so we must eat foods that provide them every day. The fat-soluble vitamins—A, D, E, and K—are stored in the fatty tissues and are absorbed and used by the body only if we eat appropriate amounts of fat with our meals.

Because of their low intake of protein and because they don't absorb it well, many older people suffer from a deficiency of B_{12}, which causes anemia and neurologic disorders. The Dietary Guidelines recommend that people over fifty consume foods to which vitamin B_{12} has been added, such as fortified cereals, or take the crystalline form of vitamin B_{12} supplements.

By age eighty, 35 percent of men and women suffer from a wearing out of the intestinal lining. This causes lower levels of acid secretion, leading to a decreased absorption of folic acid, iron, calcium, and vitamins B_6 and B_{12}. To counter this, obtain folic acid by eating uncooked leafy vegetables, yeast, and fruits daily, supplemented with 400 micrograms of folic acid.

VITAMIN A

Liver, fish oils, eggs, and whole milk are sources of vitamin A, but the best sources (free of cholesterol and saturated fat) are carrots, sweet potatoes, and dark leafy green vegetables. Plants don't actually contain vitamin A itself but, rather, carotenoid precursors that the body can turn into vitamin A. Vitamin A is important for good eyesight and a strong immune system, **but people should not take supplements that contain vitamin A itself because it can build up to a toxic level in the liver. On the other hand, beta-carotene and other carotenoids are safe at any dose.**

VITAMIN D

Vitamin D is necessary for our bodies to absorb calcium from food, to strengthen bones, and to prevent fractures. Recent research shows that 50 percent of women over fifty in the United States are deficient in vitamin D. That is dangerous for a host of reasons.

We are designed to get vitamin D from the sun. In fact, anyone living north of a line drawn between Los Angeles and Atlanta is almost certainly not getting enough vitamin D from sunlight during much of the year. Modern lifestyle changes—including more indoor activities and sunscreen usage—have reduced or eliminated sun exposure for just about everyone, especially older people, causing unprecedented vitamin D deficiency, rickets, and bone breaks in children and adults alike. Compounding the problem of reduced sun exposure is the fact the there are so few food sources for vitamin D. An adequate intake simply cannot be obtained from food. Hence, a supplement is necessary for most people, especially since we know that too much sun exposure—normally the main source of vitamin D—is correlated with skin cancer.

Poor bone health is not the only consequence of inadequate Vitamin D. Evidence is starting to show that vitamin D may be important for every cell and every organ in your body, and that a deficiency may contribute to a host of diseases, from the common cold and the flu to cancer, hypertension, insulin-dependent diabetes, and even multiple sclerosis.

How much vitamin D is enough? That's debatable, as even the scientists cannot decide!

Foods with vitamin D are fortified milk and oily fish from the sea (such as salmon and mackerel), egg yolks, liver, and fish liver oil. It is difficult to get enough vitamin D from food sources alone, so people up to age seventy should supplement with *at least* 600 IU daily. For those over seventy, 800 units daily is recommended, with a safe upper limit of 4,000 units. To find out what *you* should be taking, get your vitamin D blood levels tested at your next doctor's appointment. Blood levels of at least 32 to 40 nanograms per milliliter or higher are recommended. When choosing a supplement, look for vitamin D_3 (cholecalciferol), not D_2 (ergocalciferol). You can usually get vitamin D as part of a calcium supplement.

CALCIUM

Sources of calcium are dairy products, broccoli, kale, and collards, as well as calcium-fortified foods like orange juice, soy milk, breakfast cereals, and tofu. Assuming we are getting about 700 milligrams of calcium from our daily diet—a big assumption for most people—doctors recommend that in order to help protect our bones, we should supplement this with 500 milligrams of calcium. The new guidelines from the Institute of Medicine recommend a total of 1,200 milligrams of calcium for women fifty-one and older and men seventy-one and older. Too much calcium can result in kidney stones and heart disease; the institute says that the upper limit of safety for men and women over fifty-one is 2,000 milligrams. Calcium supplements need to be taken along with 800 to 1,000 IU of vitamin D—or more—to help with absorption and to reduce bone loss and prevent fractures. (More on calcium in Appendix IV.)

I used to think that vitamin E, vitamin C, and selenium were the antioxidant supplement superstars. I was wrong! There are, in fact, no well-controlled trials showing that supplementing our diets with vitamin E or selenium does any good . . . and it may do harm.

VITAMIN C

Vitamin C is an important antioxidant, synthesizes collagen, helps boost iron absorption, and plays a role in our hormonal and nervous systems. The recommended dietary allowance is 75 milligrams per day for adult women and 90 milligrams per day for men. When a person eats up to 120 milligrams daily, 80 to 90 percent is absorbed. As supplemental vitamin C intake goes up, absorption declines. There is no evidence that older people need megadoses, and everyone should avoid doses greater than 2,000 milligrams daily, which may cause diarrhea, nausea, abdominal cramps, and nosebleeds.

Food sources include citrus fruits, peaches, strawberries, peppers, broccoli, Brussels sprouts, papayas, kohlrabi, mangoes, pineapple, kiwifruit, peppers, cauliflower, cabbage, kale, potatoes, asparagus, and raspberries.

Both vitamin and mineral supplements (with the exception of calcium) should be taken with meals. This way they are absorbed into the system more efficiently and are digested more easily.

Water

Water is the largest single constituent of the human body and makes up two-thirds of our body weight. It is required for almost every function, from digestion to regulating our temperature to transporting nutrients to removing bodily wastes. It's good for mental function, aerobic power, endurance, physical work capacity, the heart, and the bowels. Many older men and women complain about constipation; much of the time, it's because they don't drink enough water. Too little water may also increase the risk of painful kidney stones.

Drink plenty of fluids. The National Academy of Sciences' most recent report stated that most adults naturally, based on thirst, consume enough fluid from a combination of foods, such as fruits, vegetables, and grains (from which we get about one-third of our water), and beverages, so most people don't need to focus on a particular amount. Though the scientists made no specific water recommendation, they concluded that the elderly may experience a diminished sense of thirst. Their recommendations for an adequate daily intake is nine cups for women over fifty and thirteen cups for men; this refers to *total beverages,* including water, milk, juice, coffee, and tea.

While drinking water may or may not curb the appetite, it's good for you! And there is plenty of evidence that eating water-containing *foods,* such as fruits, vegetables, and soups (low-calorie and broth-based, of course), *will* curb your appetite, reducing what you eat at meals, and thus your overall calorie intake. So, if you're trying to lose weight, eat a piece of fruit—for instance, an apple or some berries—or a salad or broth-based veggie soup before a meal to curb your appetite. Or turn your meals into soups or salads by adding veggies or broth. You'll feel full with fewer calories, and studies show that it may save you from eating 100 excess calories—and that could keep you from gaining several pounds in one year.

We need to learn to eat smaller meals and snack only when necessary. Our blood sugar tends to drop at certain times of the day. To avoid grabbing the nearest cookie or doughnut to satisfy our craving and keep us from feeling dizzy, we should always eat a balanced breakfast and lunch, each composed of, ideally, about one-fourth to one-third of our day's caloric needs. Also, be prepared to have midmorning and afternoon snacks on hand, such as red grapes, an apple, a low-fat piece of string cheese, yogurt, some unsalted nuts, or raisins. Apples vary greatly in flavor, so try different ones until you find varieties whose flavors appeal to you. I'm partial to the Honeycrisp, Stayman, Gala, and Fuji varieties. Foods grown locally and in season, picked at peak ripeness, have more flavor and nutrition, making them more enjoyable and healthier. Choosing them also means you're using fewer natural resources, and helping to save the environment.

When I'm away from home, I carry tasty and filling snack foods with me. The natural sugar in the fruits and proteins will raise my blood sugar level, appease my hunger the natural way, and give me energy without the high jolt of refined sugar and the precipitous drop that follows.

When to Eat

It's a good idea to distribute your meals, calories, and nutrients evenly through the day. This way, you fuel your body in a way that improves your nutrient absorption (particularly protein) and your concentration; stabilizes your blood sugar, your mood, and your energy; and reduces cravings. For most people, that means: Don't skip breakfast! Studies show that people who eat more food earlier in the day end up consuming fewer overall calories, and vice versa; people who eat more of their food later in the day tend to consume more overall calories, which may explain why people who skip breakfast are often fatter, according to the studies. As a bonus, people who eat breakfast take in more essential nutrients than people who don't, and people who lose and maintain weight never skip breakfast! If you don't feed yourself properly during the day, you'll be more prone to overeating later, and to impulsively choosing less healthy foods. So eat a good, balanced breakfast and lunch, have planned healthy snacks in between, and snack only lightly in the evening . . . at least three hours before you go to bed. Don't snack after dinner if you can avoid it, and if you must, choose something light, such as herbal tea, a serving of veggies or fruit, or a cup of yogurt or hot cocoa made with skim or soy milk.

One final word of advice: Never go to a restaurant or shop for food when you're hungry. Instead, try eating an apple and drinking a glass of water before you go, and always shop with a list so you won't find yourself improvising in the fatty-food aisles.

You will find more details about a healthy diet in Appendix IV.

CHAPTER 8

You and Your Brain: Use It or Lose It

"Can't you give me brains?" asked the Scarecrow.

"You don't need them," said the Wizard. "You are learning something every day. A baby has brains, but it doesn't know much. Experience is the only thing that brings knowledge and the longer you are on earth the more experience you are sure to get."

—*The Wonderful Wizard of Oz*

THERE WAS THE DAY I WAS SUPPOSED TO BE AT A TELEVISION station to be interviewed about the First Annual World Fitness Day in Atlanta. I was seventy-two at the time, and I felt a huge weight of responsibility on my shoulders. What if the event wasn't successful? I hadn't slept well for quite a while, worrying about all the terrible things that could go wrong. I was halfway to Culver City for the interview when I called my office to get the address of the station only to discover that I was supposed to be in Burbank—over the mountain and in the valley, in the exact opposite direction! I knew I was supposed to be in Burbank! My office had told me that several times! Why was I headed the wrong way? Because I forgot, that's why!

That same day I sat on my glasses, destroying them; I forgot the name of the doctor I was supposed to see that afternoon; and, to top it off, I lost my MasterCard. Had I not been deeply into brain research for this book, I would have sworn I was developing Alzheimer's disease.

But I knew better. All these mishaps were the result of stress on an aging brain. When I was younger, I probably could have managed it fairly well. Sleep deprivation might have caused me to head in the wrong direction even in my thirties, but I probably would have remembered the doctor's name and not lost the credit card—and I wouldn't have needed glasses! I'd been feeling stressed for a while, and I knew that stress causes the adrenal glands to produce high levels of cortisol, which dulls the effects of the brain's hippocampus, where memory is stored and retrieved. The neurons that transmit messages are destroyed. I swear I could feel my neurons disappearing by the minute!

No wonder I experienced one mishap after another. Once the stressful Fitness Day was over—and, as it turned out, very successful—and once I got back to working out and sleeping well, such problems no longer occurred. They will again, I'm sure. But because of what I've learned about maintaining a healthy brain, I make a concerted effort to minimize stress in my life through exercise and meditation. If nothing else, perhaps the desire to protect your brain will motivate you to do the same. (See Appendix V, "Guide to Mindful Meditation.")

Stress isn't the only thing that's bad for the brain. So are hypertension, heart disease, diabetes, high cholesterol, mini-strokes, exposure to environmental toxins, severe head injuries, smoking, drinking too much, using recreational drugs, eating an unhealthy diet, and inactivity. While we may be genetically predisposed to heart disease and high cholesterol, for example, choosing a healthier lifestyle that includes body and brain workouts can do much to improve our cognitive function. "Cognitive function" means thinking—reasoning, remembering, processing what we see and feel, planning, and sending signals out to our limbs.

The good news is that clear evidence from functional imaging shows that the brain has great reserves of plasticity. It is capable of adaptation and reorganization, acquiring new skills, absorbing new data, and changing its circuitry in response to the cognitive demands placed on it. Moreover, where there has been a lessening of certain cognitive functions, such as inductive reasoning, spatial orientation, and short-term memory, these functions can be restored with training.

As we age, our brain volume declines, but some parts are more susceptible to loss of volume than others. I learned from the late Dr. Robert Butler, at the International Longevity Center, that there are many pathways for processing thought. "The circuitry in your brain is interconnected in multiple ways," he told me, "resulting in what neurologists call 'neural redundancy.' Think backup systems: When one goes down, another is at hand to help carry the load." As certain neural networks are broken, the brain searches for new networks. If cognitive functions that have been handled by certain regions of, say, the left frontal lobe are impaired, the right frontal lobe may be recruited to help its neighbor. In stroke victims, for instance, other parts of the brain take over the recovered functions from the parts that are damaged. This is known as "compensatory recruitment." And it's good news, because it provides evidence for the elasticity and adaptation of the brain.

While younger people use one side of their brain for a given functional task—the right frontal cortex, for example—older folks will often use both sides to perform the same task. Their cognitive processes may be slower, but that doesn't mean they have functional impairment. Are you one of those people who panics every time you call your son by your brother's name, or your grandson by your son's name, or when you can't think of something you should know well—like your stepson's name—and see it as a sign that you're about to get Alzheimer's? Don't worry, things like forgetting names are not predictive of Alzheimer's. When I forget a name or a fact, rather than furrow my brow and try to force myself to remember, I let it go—and often as not, it comes to me later. When I think I've lost something, rather than panic, I go about my business, and sure enough, it'll turn up in the purse I carried yesterday, or in the backseat of my car, where I put it two days ago. I've learned to relax into memory, if you will.

Brain-imaging technology shows "that not only is normal brain shrinkage less than we feared, but much of what is lost may be judicious 'pruning,' " says Dr. George Vaillant, director of the Harvard Study of Adult Development. He likens this to an attic that has filled up carelessly over the decades but now, with age, we clean it out and select only the most cherished, meaningful items to keep. Dr. Denise Park, director of the Center for Vital Longevity at the University of Texas at Dallas, puts it this way: "You may lose a bit of horsepower, but you are highly efficient as you rely on your knowledge and experience instead. Maybe this is the Prius model of cognitive aging."[1]

Exercise and the Brain

Science shows us that seniors who have remained fit and who continue to exercise continue to have good brain functioning. Cardiovascular fitness is perhaps one of the best things we can do to maintain our brain health. Even when older people who have never been particularly active engage in moderate exercise, they see their cognitive functioning improve. This is because physical exercise causes an increase in a chemical nerve growth factor that allows brain cells to grow, stimulates the connections between them, and helps in memory function.

Because of the increased obesity and inactivity in the United States these days, it is possible that we will lose, as a country, all the health gains of the last fifty years. Some economists suggest that we could lose it in a single generation. This is frightening when you consider, for instance, that physical health is related to dementia. We might see an increase in the rates of dementia and Alzheimer's disease. Right now, a conservative estimate is that a quarter of the population over eighty will get Alzheimer's. Reports show that by midcentury as many as fifty million older Americans may get the disease. While research is under way to prevent or postpone Alzheimer's, scientists already know that people in their sixties can reduce their risk of Alzheimer's—by half!—through exercise. This is why, when I work out, I am not just thinking about my body; I'm also thinking about my brain. I want to do everything I can to maintain it, so that if I am one of the fifty million Americans who will get Alzheimer's, it won't happen until I am ninety or older, as opposed to when I am eighty-two.

Challenge the Brain

Dr. Denise Park says that "if you are living a life with a high degree of engagement in activities that are cognitively demanding, it may delay the onset of Alzheimer's a little bit—delay it, not change it. You might still be diagnosed, but putting it off by a couple of years extends your quality of life and benefits you, your family, and even our health care system."

When it comes to cognitive function—or brain health—education plays a strong role. This is partly because early education positively affects brain circuitry. Also, a well-educated person will tend to engage more in mentally stimulating activities such as reading, chess, and ongoing learning. Higher incomes and mentally challenging types of work also contribute to maintaining one's cognitive ability.

At a seminar on longevity, Dr. Park explained,

tasks will improve cognition if they continually challenge the cognitive system by making sustained demands on executive function over a prolonged period of time and are relatively novel for the individual performing the task. Just like the person who has had a stroke has to use a different hand to perform tasks to develop new neural networks, it is plausible that performing other novel tasks will do the same for a healthy aging brain. As an example, we think learning to quilt could be stimulating for someone who never sewed before. If you are already an expert quilter, I would suggest learning a musical instrument or some other skill that you find both challenging and fun. It is critical to keep learning and adapting new sequences of complex behaviors. Have fun and try a new domain that broadly stimulates some new neural networks.

"The other thing that people underestimate," continued Dr. Park,

is the unique demands of social interactions. In a social situation, it's really inappropriate not to remember someone's name, or what they told you the day before about their grandchildren, and there is thus actually quite a bit of cognitive demand. I would put social interaction as an important element of stimulation. To enhance cognition, you need to be productively engaged in activities that demonstrate sustained activation of your working memory, reasoning, and other higher-order cognitive functions. These are all primarily frontal cortex functions—the most flexible, plastic area of the brain you have to be using those areas of the brain. Think of a guy who is multitasking at work. He's on the phone; he's at the computer; he is planning for his upcoming meeting. This would be very demanding of neural function, and I would venture to guess that this productive engagement would enhance cognition (as long as the stress level did not become destructively high). The couple that's familiar with each other, sitting around and having a great time at the beach, chatting and telling old stories, are probably not facilitating their cognition very much.

Here are some examples of brain exercises you might consider:

- learn anything new: a new language, a new hobby, a musical instrument;
- meet new people who involve you in conversation;
- memorize poetry;
- learn new words every day;

... and, as I have said, get physically active. All of these activities can be successfully begun anytime, including later in life.

One more thing: Estrogen therapy, if begun while a perimenopausal woman is in her late forties or early fifties, can improve and protect the brain. Hormone replacement is so controversial, and its effects vary with the individual, so it's best to consult a doctor. Still, Cynthia Gorney wrote in the *New York Times Magazine,* "It makes new cells grow. It increases what's called 'plasticity,' the brain's ability to change and respond to stimulation. It builds up the dendrites and number of dendritic spines, the barbs that stick out along the long tails of brain cells, like thorns on a blackberry stem, and hook up with other neurons to transmit information back and forth. The thinning of those spines is a classic sign of Alzheimer's."[2]

In the next chapter, I will tell you some really good and interesting news about aging.

CHAPTER 9

Positivity: The Good News Is You're Getting Older!

We are all happier in many ways when we are old than when we are young. The young sow wild oats. The old grow sage.

—WINSTON CHURCHILL

GUESS WHAT? YOU CAN PRETTY MUCH EXPECT TO BE HAPPIER at eighty than you were at twenty! Regardless of whether you are male or female, married or single, employed or not, or have your children living with you! Regardless, in other words, of events in your life. Surprising, huh? Especially given all the things that can start to go south with age—for example, buttocks, joints, valves, skin, hairlines, and social networks!

Nonetheless, a 2008 Gallup poll showed this result after interviewing 340,000 Americans aged eighteen to eighty-five. Dr. Arthur A. Stone, a professor of psychology at the State University of New York at Stony Brook, who led the study based on the poll, isn't sure why this uptick in well-being occurs.[1] Could it be psychological changes? Alterations in brain chemistry or endocrine changes? No one really knows. What appears to be certain is that between the ages of eighteen and fifty, those interviewed tended to feel more sadness, stress, worry, and anger—and then, *vavoom*, beginning at fifty, life seemed to take an upward turn.

This has been my personal experience as well, although I became more aware of it at age sixty than at fifty. As I said in an earlier chapter, one of my main character traits as a younger person was a tendency to melancholy. On top of that, I was wound pretty tight. The ten years I spent with Ted Turner (from ages fifty-two to sixty-two) taught me more about laughter and letting go than almost anything ever had before. In fact, I'll tell you a secret: I wouldn't have been able to be as funny playing Jennifer Lopez's mother-in-law in *Monster-in-Law* had I not had that time with Ted, who made it possible for me to learn to laugh at the outrageous and to see that over-the-top can be endearing.

But it has been more than ten years now that Ted and I have been apart—from ages sixty-two to seventy-two—and I continue to notice how much more positive I have become . . . joyful, even. Most things that would have run me up the wall with anxiety or sent me to bed with depression roll right off my back now. Very few things really stress me anymore. Well, children and grandchildren can still cause stress! As they say, "You are only as happy as your

Laughing with my friend Robin Morgan in 2004. She was interviewing me for Ms. *magazine.*
PHOTO COURTESY OF
HAROLD DANIELS

least happy child." But for me, it's not anywhere near what it used to be, and when stress comes, it doesn't linger.

Dr. Ken Matheny, Regents Professor in Georgia State University's Department of Counseling and Psychological Services, which he founded in 1966, told me that one of the premier sources of information about centenarians in the country is the Institute of Gerontology, at the University of Georgia in Athens. "There are now about fifty-six thousand Americans who are centenarians," he said, "and when they study these folks, they find that on the whole they report more happiness than the average person. Which is startling, isn't it?"

Come to think of it, the oldest people I have interviewed for this book have one striking thing in common: a sense of humor. For instance, ninety-five-year-old Karl. When I asked him for his age, he said, "I don't know how old I am, but I was around when the Dead Sea was only sick." When 104-year-old Cal Evans was asked by a Denver reporter, "Have you lived in Denver all your life?" Cal laughed and answered, "Not yet, sonny." And there was Jeanne Louise Calment of Arles, France, the longest-lived person on record. Born in 1875, she died at 122 years and four months. She is reported to have quipped at age 119, "I have only one wrinkle, and I am sitting on it." At one of Jeanne's last birthday parties, in Paris, a journalist said with great hesitancy in his voice, "Well, I guess I will see you next year," to which she responded, "I don't see why not; you look to be in pretty good health to me."

The Zen priest Joan Halifax and I were discussing the various ways in which our bodies are starting to weaken. "Yes," she said at age sixty-five, "on some level, certain aspects of my life are shrinking. But as they shrink, something else expands, and there seems to be this compensation."

"Give me an example," I said.

"Well, my sense of humor has expanded. My robustness has expanded. My tolerance and patience have expanded. My love of people and of my work and of the earth has expanded. Younger people tend to get more obsessed over little details," Joan ex-

At the Upaya Zen Center with Roshi Joan Halifax   TERI THOMSON RANDALL

plained, "whereas older people tend to just find out what is important."

"They don't sweat the small stuff," I said.

"That's right. And on the other side of the equation, I think
aging has stripped away a lot of my fear."

I had heard the same thing from the writer Erica Jong. "I am
much more relaxed now," Erica told me over lunch in her art-filled
New York apartment. "I am much less uptight. I know that things
are not personal. If somebody criticizes something I have written,
if somebody says something vicious about me, I think it is funny
and I think it's about them, not about me. I hadn't gotten there

earlier. After *Fear of Flying* I nearly dried up and stopped writing because the attacks were so vicious."

At a breakfast meeting in Ann Arbor, Michigan, I told Dr. Marion Perlmutter about my own growing sense of peace and detachment. "I hate to even use that word, 'detachment,' " I said, "because it can be interpreted as noncaring when, in fact, I do care about most things just as much as ever."

Dr. Perlmutter, who is with the Department of Psychology at the the University of Michigan, answered me: "I understand. As a scientist, I not only know more things about the brain, but I appreciate more all of the things I *do not know.* It is that, perhaps, the appreciation of the limitations of our knowledge, that has us detach a little bit and maybe moves us to something spiritual. Knowing what you don't know is the first stage of knowing. But I think that only in late life does that part of understanding kick in. And this, I think, helps us detach."

Dr. George Vaillant, director of the Harvard Study of Adult Development, discovered that older people develop "mature defenses." By this he means the ability to turn lemons into lemonade and to not turn molehills into mountains.[2]

Dr. Laura Carstensen, founding director of the Stanford Center on Longevity, says that while there are some older people who don't show a "Positivity effect" at all, and some younger people who do, generally Positivity represents an important developmental shift, a way to approach life that is expressed through humor, gratitude, forgiveness, playfulness, creativeness, and flexibility. "Goals change as people age," she told me. "There are so many what-ifs in the lives of younger people, whereas we are armed with a long backward look—'this has happened before.' "

Dr. Perlmutter agrees that Positivity may be due to "the accumulation of perspective. The first time that something happens, like financial loss, for instance, it is horrible. But after you have seen cycles of something like that happening, you have some perspective that this doesn't mean the end of life. It just means a new challenge that we will get through." All of these psychologists seem to agree that the "this too shall pass" view of life is a hard one for young people—and many in midlife as well—to fully accept; less so, for folks in Act III.

During a meeting in Atlanta, Dr. Matheny told me, "Life has shown you that you survived before, you'll survive again. And since you now are no longer competing like you were earlier, there is not as much hypervigilance, there are more acceptances, letting things develop. You can't possibly oppose every force that comes up, every little problem that you've got, and so learning to accept and, I think, accommodate and adjust is every bit as important as mastery because you can't master that many things. So it is like martial arts—if the force comes, you don't oppose it, you just try to guide it. And I think there is something of that that happens with age."

Dr. Carstensen concurs. "Elders tend to know what they want and need to make their lives richer and deeper, and they are able to discard what they no longer need," she told me.

> We are less apt to be thrown by outside events. When people are very young they have long and nebulous futures ahead of them and all sorts of information might be useful even though it might not be useful immediately. It is very informative to know where the tiger is hiding in the brush. But once you know that, you don't have to keep going back to visit the brush. You don't need to spend so much time preparing, you just know. So as the future becomes shorter, you know what information is relevant to your goals and what isn't because your goals are clearer; you know what you are focused on; you know what is important and what is not; you can separate the wheat from the chaff, so to speak. What is relevant to your goals you will learn quickly and you'll let the rest go. I've spent the last thirty years investigating the psychology of aging and my research consistently shows that, in terms of emotions, the best years come late in life. . . . Older people as a group suffer less from depression, anxiety, and substance abuse than their younger counterparts. In everyday life, they experience fewer negative emotions but just as

many positive ones as people in their twenties and thirties—
the people we stereotypically think of as the most happy.[3]

Carstensen also notes that seniors are less apt to bear grudges and
that they pick their fights carefully, which is why we make good
mediators and facilitators.

Many psychologists have identified the Positivity of aging.
According to John Gabrieli, a professor of cognitive neuroscience
at the Massachusetts Institute of Technology, "As people get older,
they seem to be willing to accept things that, when we're young, we
would find disturbing and vexing." Betrayal, for instance, is so hard
to accept when we are young. But Dr. Gabrieli believes that seniors
may be more able to see things from the other person's perspective
and thus don't view certain actions as betrayal. He says, "It paves
the way for you to be sympathetic to the situation from his perspective, to be less disturbed from her perspective." He calls this
"compassionate detachment," which doesn't mean not caring or
that we've become bankrupt of certitudes. It means having no personal agenda, no ego stake in outcomes. This means that with age,
we can be more trustworthy—it's easier for us to see all sides and
give advice that comes more from our heart than from our ego.

As I learned about the Positivity that seems to come with age, it
began to feel more and more like wisdom. Experts on such things
have never quite come to an agreement on what constitutes wisdom or whether we get wiser with age, but the descriptions of it
that resonate with me include:

- The ability to step outside oneself and assess
  troublesome situations with calm reflection.
- The ability to regulate our emotions.
- Knowing what is nonessential and letting it go. The
  philosopher and psychologist William James observed,
  "The art of being wise is the art of knowing what
  to overlook."
- The willingness to embrace uncertainty.

Though I know young people who demonstrate some or all of these qualities, I cannot help but feel that these are attributes that tend to come to the fore as we age and gain experience. Mary Catherine Bateson says, "Experience doesn't make people wise. It is reflection on experience that makes us wise." Many of us don't take time to reflect until age provides us the time to do it. Doing a life review forces us to reflect on our experiences; thus, I believe, it can help lead us to wisdom.

I asked Dr. Matheny why he thought some seniors can adjust and adapt to the challenges of age with humor when others can't. Is it possible, I asked, to get better at that if it hasn't been your character style?

"Look, an awful lot of people suffer terribly in old age, so I'm not judging anybody," he replied. "I am sure that being positive is not all just a matter of willpower. In other words, there is a whole history of conditioning experiences people have—in childhood and throughout their entire lives. So it'd be cruel to say that you should just be able to be positive. But I think this is where you want to get to if you can, and apparently a lot of centenarians have."

After listening to all these experts, I realized that my being able to experience Positivity is, in part, simply because I am older. But I have also worked at it. Doing my life review helped a lot. There is something wonderful about self-examination—looking, devoting enough time and energy, interest, and psychological openness to understand what your trajectory was that made you who you are today. The next step is taking responsibility for it, owning it. Physical exercise, which releases feel-good endorphins, helps with Positivity, and so, for me, does meditation.

I talked to Dr. Matheny about this. He said, "It is sort of like, well, in the Buddhist tradition, they refer to it as 'the witness.' We probably all had the experience where we've been dreaming and very upset and then—it's almost like a nourishing parent part of us comes in and says, 'Don't worry. This is just a dream. You are going to wake up.' That voice, that very wise part of us that Jung referred to as 'the soul,' a depository of wisdom that goes far beyond consciousness—older people have an advantage there. One key goal of mindful meditation is to allow us to become more conscious of what we are doing while we are doing it, and not merely after the fact. We observe ourselves and maybe stop acting out our roles, getting caught up in our own dramas and our conditioning, and only thinking about what we did later. We are always in acting roles, and they are important to us, but if we are not careful we forget who we are and we just become a role enactor. And if the role is not working out well, then we are very, very unhappy and stressed."

I have subsequently thought about how much unconscious acting out of roles I did in my earlier life and how much stress it caused me and others. Stress is definitely what we want to minimize in the Third Act, when, more than ever, it can take a toll on our bodies, even damaging our brains—as I talked about in Chapter 8. I am grateful to have discovered meditation at age seventy. I know meditation can actually develop new neural pathways in your brain that can help lead you away from depression and anxiety. Meditation is a human override of the production of stress hormones. I encourage you to explore the practice of mindful meditation, and in Appendix V you will find a guide for doing so.

Guess what else you can do to develop new neural pathways that will lead you out of sourpussness? Smile! That's right. By smiling, you actually change the pattern of information going from the muscles in your body—in this case, the muscles around your mouth and eyes—to your brain. This has a big impact on health and well-being, both short-term and long-term. Dr. Norman Cousins believed he cured himself of bone cancer and other diseases by watching funny movies and laughing and smiling, which mobilized his endorphins and the healing keys of his immune system, like T cells, lymphocytes, leucocytes, and phagocytes, into action to fight the disease.

I interviewed 104-year-old Rachel Lehman for this book; she told me about creating "an epidemic of love" by smiling at everyone who came her way, especially the sourpusses. Remembering this, I started experimenting with a smile. It began with yoga. I would put on a slight, Mona Lisa–type smile as I held the poses. I would try to maintain the smile while I meditated. And sure enough, it would make me feel better, lighter. Even if I didn't feel like smiling, I would put a smile on my face, and it would make me feel more buoyant. I found this to be similar to the effects of good posture. When I pull my shoulders back and make sure my head is right on top of my neck and not jutting forward, I feel stronger, more powerful. And, just as with smiling, I look better, too.

I've since discovered interesting research showing that the physiology of smiling creates a biochemical response, activating neurotransmitters, hormones, and endorphins, and releases nitric oxide that makes you feel better.

Dr. Rollin McCraty, executive vice president and director of research at the Institute of HeartMath, says,

> Research shows that the brain functions as a complex pattern-matching system. The messages it receives from the heart, facial muscles, and other bodily organs are some of the many input patterns that the brain is constantly processing. An important point is that as recurring patterns of input to the brain become familiar, the brain attempts to maintain these familiar patterns as a stable baseline, or norm. This occurs even if a familiar pattern is one that is ultimately detrimental to our health and well-being, such as living with constant stress. This mechanism actually provides a psycho-physiological basis for understanding why chronic stress can be so difficult to change: The brain learns to recognize the stressful patterns as familiar, and thus attempts to maintain and reinforce them, even though they are unhealthy.
>
> However, just like resetting a thermostat, it is also possible to introduce a new set of patterns, which, by repetition, become familiar to the brain and become established as a new baseline. So, if we consciously make efforts to smile and activate positive emotions, eventually the brain will recognize these coherent, "feeling-good" patterns as familiar and

will reinforce them and they become much more a part of our natural state.

Dr. McCraty adds that having this new, more positive baseline pattern makes it easier for us to bounce back when we do experience stress or challenges.

Elan Sun Star, a photographer, writer, and teacher at Global Creative Networking Media, has written extensively about the power of the smile. He says, "So, what do you do when you don't feel like smiling and you don't even feel like faking it? Well, you can be grateful that you are not being forced to smile, and that may make you smile. Of course we must realize that there are authentic smiles and inauthentic smiles, but we can also realize there is an authentic try at being happy, and an authentic try at smiling."

In 1862, the French neurologist Guillaume Duchenne mapped one hundred facial muscles. He demonstrated that false or even halfhearted smiles involve only muscles of the mouth, but that authentic, deep-from-the-heart smiles activate the muscles around the eyes as well, causing the skin around the eyes to crinkle, the eyelids to drop a little, the cheeks and corners of the mouth to lift.

Mr. Sun Star suggests standing in front of a mirror and practicing putting on a Duchenne smile that crinkles up your eyes and turns up your mouth. Think of it as a new workout, and work those smile muscles! Breathe while you do it and stand up tall. Happy, erect posture adds credibility to the smile. I don't associate a happy, empowered, smiling person with someone slumped over.

I have become a much more inviting and optimistic person since I entered my Third Act. Whenever someone tries to make me feel dopey about it, I remind myself of the findings of a 2002 study, the Ohio Longitudinal Study of Aging and Retirement, which revealed that older people with a more positive attitude toward old age lived seven and a half years longer!

CHAPTER 10

Actually Doing a Life Review

It's never too late to be what you might have been.

—GEORGE ELIOT

The compensation of growing old, Peter Walsh thought, coming out of Regent's Park, and holding his hat in hand, was simply this: that the passions remain as strong as ever, but one had gained—at last!—the power which adds the supreme flavour to existence—the power of taking hold of experience, of turning it round, slowly, in the light.

—VIRGINIA WOOLF, *Mrs. Dalloway*

HAVE INCLUDED DOING A LIFE REVIEW AMONG THE INGREDIENTS of successful aging because, in my experience (and to paraphrase George Eliot), doing so may help you become what you might have been. You may discover your essential self . . . that you are not who you think you are.

We all needed our parents to have loved and respected us independent of how we did or didn't perform in the world. A good number of us didn't have this. Some of us look back and feel as if our lives are failures, or less than they might have been. Perhaps we still feel the pain of an early disabling psychic wound or we haven't had closure in our relationships, and so we don't feel entirely finished. As the psychologist Terrence Real has written, "Our areas of immaturity always represent unfinished business, incomplete conversations, with one or both parents, because it was they who should have steered us toward the relational maturity we now lack as adults."[1]

One way of finishing up the task of finishing ourselves is to go back over our earlier lives and, if it is called for, work to change our relationship to the realities—the people and the events—that composed them. A life review, as discussed in Chapter 2, assists us in doing this. The author and psychologist Stephen Levine calls it a "going-out-of-unfinished business sale." It is easier for us when we have some mileage, some experience, under our belts, when the conflicts and traumas are less affect-laden, and time and adulthood have rounded some of the sharp edges.

Simone Scharff is an attractive, petite, seventy-eight-year-old Frenchwoman I knew during the 1960s, when I was married to my first husband, the French film director Roger Vadim, and we all hung out together on the beach in Malibu. I ran into her again after almost fifty years at WISE & Healthy Aging, a senior center in Santa Monica, where she is a member of a group of twelve women who meet weekly to share their writings. Ethel Schatz, now a dynamic woman of ninety-three, started the group twenty years ago as a way to encourage older women to write about themselves and then discuss what they'd written with the group.

Simone said that her first reaction to the idea of joining the writing group was that she couldn't write. She'd grown up in France during the Nazi occupation and had received only what she called "street schooling." "Not being good enough was a theme of my life. It was always so strong in me," she said in her lovely French accent. "But writing my life, all the things I have been through, gave me a certain kind of respect for myself. You know, 'Wow, I did that, and I did that, and that and that!' But I would have never done it if it wasn't for the light that Ethel gave me, the permission to just express it, to write it, to think about it, not to be embarrassed. It gave me a freedom, made me flexible. My whole attitude has changed." Simone had always been too shy and embarrassed to tell her children about her life, but now she is giving them what she's writing and they are interested, as are her grandchildren, and she feels it is helping them.

While being in a writing group isn't exactly the same as writing a life review, it can jump-start the process, as it did for Simone.

I don't believe that you need, necessarily, to show your writing to anyone else. Just the act of writing for yourself, in an open-hearted, thoughtful, and detailed way, can be transforming. Nevertheless, there may come a time when your children or family members will find great benefit in reading what you write, the way I benefited from reading what my mother wrote when she was admitted to a mental institution before she died.

My friend Nathaniel Bickford, now sixty-five years old, began writing a book about his life right after he retired from corporate law. Two traumas had happened to him during high school that had haunted him all his life. First, a teacher who had been Nat's hero turned on him for no apparent reason and emotionally tortured him until he was forced to change schools. Then, in his new school, his best friend turned out to be homosexual and made a pass at him—this was in the mid-1950s, and it traumatized Nat. Not knowing what else to do, he told the headmaster, and his friend committed suicide.

"I was sure if I had handled it better, he would still be alive," Nat told me one day in his New York apartment. "Therefore, I felt I was a direct cause of his death. Not having been able to talk to anyone about it for so long a time, I wanted to write the book to try and figure it all out, including trying to understand the psychology of the teacher who so tortured me. What did I do that made him so mad?" I asked Nat if writing the book had helped him understand that the teacher's behavior had nothing to do with him.

"It is amazing," Nat answered. "You can say you are not responsible, that the man obviously had some other problems. Intellectually, you can do that until the cows come home. But you really can't get rid of the residue of whatever emotional damage it's caused—scar tissue, whatever—unless and until you really almost relive the whole damn thing. So I had to write what my friend was actually saying when he was embracing me, and it was just horrible, but it was the only way. I had to go through it again in order to then be able to understand my young self. A curious thing happens when you go back: The little you becomes a third person, and you can forgive that little guy. That little guy was really not responsible for what happened. He doesn't have to go through all that now. And that works. It does. It is really amazing."

I told Nat how moved I was hearing him recount this because I, too, had not been able to expunge certain demons from my life until, in writing my life review, I saw that I had to go into enough detail for things to become embodied experiences—I had to *feel* them again.

Nat's book, *Late Bloomer,* was published in 2008 by Tidepool Press. Now Nat is free of his ghosts and is moving on into happy retirement with his wife of forty-six years.

So, I challenge you to be like Simone and Nat, to gather all that you have done, have been, all that you have had—things on the outside and internal things—to claim them, gather them all together into your center so as to possess who you are. All this is not to revisit what others have said you are, what others want or need you to be; the point is to get at who you feel you are in the deepest recesses of your soul. What things happened to you when you were little? What experiences were bad and scary? What was beautiful? How did you feel when you walked into your first school? How did the other kids make you feel? Did you do any-thing you were ashamed of or don't like to think about now? Did you have a teacher who made you feel wonderful and curious? A teacher who made you feel dumb? Did your parents make you feel safe? Proud of yourself? Accepting of yourself? Take hold of your experiences. Feel them. Go into them in your body and then make notes about them so you will remember. Don't edit; just let the ideas flow. Turn them around, slowly, in the light, and try to see past the surfaces. If you are like me, experiencing the transition into elderhood will be far more meaningful and enjoyable if you see it in the context of the full arc of your life, with some of your old business dealt with and tidied up.

Use doing a life review to poultice the wounds of youth with the forgiveness of age.

Understanding comes first, before forgiveness is possible. Before letting go is possible. Understanding requires honesty, and honesty requires courage. So with honesty and courage, in the spirit of forgiveness, as you feel your way through each stage of your life, think not only of the difficult experiences, but of the people who touched you and guided you with kindness and love. Acknowledge them and thank them, in your heart, your body, your writing.

Remember the ones who hurt you, the way Nat did when writing his book. This will not be easy, and you may find yourself forgetting to breathe. Breathing keeps your body open, your muscles relaxed, so that understanding can come. When your body is tight, new realizations and developmental breakthroughs will be harder.

This is why meditation can be so helpful. While you're doing some deep breathing, try, without forcing it, to imagine the pain that those who hurt you must have experienced in their own lives, the self-hatred that may have led them to hurt you. Try—again, without forcing it—to open your heart and send forgiveness their way. And then commit yourself to never doing these same hurtful things to others—or to yourself. Be the one to break the cycle!

In his book *A Year to Live,* the poet and teacher Stephen Levine wrote, "Even an unsuccessful attempt at forgiveness has the considerable power of its intention. We cannot force forgiveness because force closes the heart, but we can explore its possibilities, its capacity to heal the forgiver, and sometimes the forgiven." Levine also said that forgiveness "is mercy in action in the same way that compassion is wisdom in action."[2]

The author James Baldwin wrote, "I imagine one of the reasons people cling to their hate so stubbornly is because they sense, once the hate is gone, they will be forced to deal with pain." Some people also cling to their pain. It defines them. Who am I if not a victim? Such people do not do well in their Third Acts.

A life review can be a way to shed both hate and victimhood, to let the pain out, and to uncover one's true identity.

Zalman Schachter-Shalomi vividly describes what it does to us when we are unable or unwilling to forgive:

> For example, when I refuse to forgive someone who has wronged me, I mobilize my own inner criminal justice system to punish the offender. As judge and jury, I sentence the person to a long prison term without pardon and incarcerate him in a prison that I construct from the bricks and mortar of a hardened heart. Now as jailor and warden, I must spend as much time in prison as the prisoner I am guarding. All the energy that I put into maintaining the prison system comes out of my "energy budget." From this point of view, bearing a grudge is very "costly," because long-held feelings of anger, resentment, and fear drain my energy and imprison my vitality and creativity.[3]

If one or both of your parents are alive, sit down with a tape recorder and notepad (don't rely on just one or the other) and interview them—separately. If they are together, they may tell you what's comfortable, the standard, bought-into script of their lives that they are both familiar with. Your goal is to gently nudge them beyond their comfort zones. They may actually welcome this interest on your part, and they are at an age when there's little to lose and much to gain from finally revealing (to themselves, as well) memories that hold the key to who they became.

Ask them about their parents: Did their parents love each other? Were they loving or cold and strict with their children—that is, with your parents? Try to tease out painful things your parents may have buried, such as abuse, rape, emotional distance, failures, deaths, addictions, depression, or guilt. All these things may have affected how you were treated, how you felt growing up. And, if you are like most people, you probably thought it was your fault. Now is the time to separate who your parents were—or who they wanted you to be—from the person you are.

A man might explore what he was like before and after he started formal schooling. Remember what I said in Chapter 3 about how this is the stage when boys tend to shut off emotionally so as to "fit in," to not be called a "sissy" or "momma's boy"? Try to remember how you felt at that age, what messages were sent to you either implicitly or explicitly about how you were supposed to act. Many psychologists today feel that societal pressures on little boys to fit a macho stereotype cause a bifurcation between head and heart that does damage to their emotional development. Research seems to show that the Third Act of a man's life is when the nurturing, empathetic, sensitive aspects of his psyche can make a comeback, allowing his final decades to be happier and his relationships healthier.

Unlike boys, girls begin to feel pressure to conform to gender norms at the onset of adolescence. A woman will want to closely explore those early teen years, when she may have become disembodied, when her true self might have gone underground, her voice become muted.

As I said earlier, I have found that when you make yourself write things out, whether in longhand or on a computer (which is how I write), you are forced to be more intentional and you learn more deeply than if you simply *think* about your life.

Getting your story published—or even read—is not the goal. Just write. Commit yourself to paper—with all the truth and courage you can muster. Try to interview the key elderly people in your life now, while they are still alive. But even if your parents and grandparents are no longer living, there are probably relatives and friends of the family who remember things. If your life remains too busy for you to actually write, at least gather the information that is most at risk of being lost, as friends and parents die, so you'll have it later when your pace slows down and you can address these things.

Try to identify the times in your life when you went through real developmental changes—when something inside you began shifting and you saw the world and your place in it differently. Adolescence was probably such a time, because that is when we begin to discover our identities independent from our parents.

The onset of the women's movement may have been an important catalyst for many of us. Menopause can also be formative. Developmental changes can be purely internal transformations resulting from our realizing that how we've been leading our lives isn't making sense anymore. Maybe we feel we haven't been "leading" them, that they've been leading us, and so we commit to doing something significant about it. It may have been that external events triggered developmental changes—your parents got divorced, someone close passed away, you were fired from your job, you gave birth to your first child, your spouse left you. How you reacted and adjusted to these kinds of external events would have determined whether or not they caused developmental change and propelled you on to a new life course.

Don't worry about allotting big blocks of time. Just start with Act I. Set aside an hour to begin the process. Get a notebook and a pen you like or, if it allows your ideas to flow more easily, use a tape recorder.

Think about the main events, the scenes that stand out for you. As you make progress, perhaps things will emerge in more detail.

Search out old family albums, scrapbooks, family trees. Study them carefully for clues. Spend quiet time visiting old haunts, like the houses and neighborhoods where you grew up, and try to conjure up how you felt back then. Attend school reunions, interview your old classmates, and explain what you're doing. Who knows, it might inspire them to do their own life reviews! Play the old songs from your past. Music is an evocative way to call up forgotten images. A single stimulus may bring forth buried memories. In his masterpiece *Remembrance of Things Past,* Marcel Proust illustrated this beautifully: The protagonist eats a small cake he enjoyed as a child and memories come flooding back.

It's good to carry a pad with you so that if a thought comes to you, you'll be able to jot it down.

Maybe, like me, as you remember yourself as a child, an adolescent, a young women or man, and so forth, you will discover that to a significant degree, your developmental changes revolved around issues of gender. In my case, I rediscovered the trying to please; the needing to be authenticated by a man; the self-hatred, especially of my body; the responses to my mother; my remote, objectifying father; and the eventual emergence of my own voice. For me, the evolving metaphor for my life thus became that of a gender-role journey. I believe that many women and men doing a life review will find this to be true, too; or in any case, it may be a helpful metaphor for their own journey.

Other metaphors might be the challenges of poverty or violence or always needing to be the best at everything—competitiveness. If you come from a family where alcoholism played an important role, your metaphor may have involved being the hero or the clown—two common roles for children of alcoholics that may follow us into adulthood.

Discovering a metaphor for the story of your life can open you to internal growth, renewal, expanded self-definition, surprising energy, and healing, because your story will then resonate with the universal story.

It wasn't until I was able to see my own life as a gender-role journey that I felt ready to begin writing my memoirs at sixty-two.

PART THREE

FRIENDSHIP, LOVE, and SEX

CHAPTER 11

The Importance of Friendship

. . . Alone, you can fight,
you can refuse, you can
take what revenge you can
but they roll over you.

But two people fighting
back to back can cut through
a mob, a snake-dancing file
can break a cordon, an army
can meet an army.

Two people can keep each other
sane, can give support, conviction,
love, massage, hope, sex.
Three people are a delegation,
a committee, a wedge. With four
you can play bridge and start
an organization. With six
you can rent a whole house,
eat pie for dinner with no seconds,
and hold a fund raising party.
A dozen make a demonstration.
A hundred fill a hall.
A thousand have solidarity and your own newsletter;
ten thousand, power and your own paper;
a hundred thousand, your own media;
ten hundred thousand, your own country.

It goes on one at a time,
It starts when you care
to act, it starts when you do
it again after they said no,
It starts when you say We
and know who you mean, and each
day you mean one more.

—MARGE PIERCY, *excerpted from "The low road"*
in The Moon Is Always Female

Saying "We" and Knowing Who We Mean

It is May 2008. We are in my Atlanta loft having dinner. My brother, Peter, is next to me. He's flown in from Los Angeles, as have my son, Troy, and daughter-in-law, Simone, along with Bridget Fonda, Peter's daughter, and her three-year-old son, Oliver, who is sitting on the floor playing with my grandchildren's toys while they—nine-year-old Malcolm and five-year-old Viva—throw pillows down from the second-floor balcony to build a fort. Their mother, my daughter, Vanessa, is at the table, calm as usual in the midst of raucous children. Odd as it may appear to some, Ted Turner is sitting at the far end of the table with Elizabeth, one of his girlfriends, whom I like. This evening represents a long overdue coming together for my family, and I cannot help but be emotional as I make a toast to love, friendship, and continuity.

The hook that got us all here is the thirteenth annual fund-raiser for my nonprofit, the Georgia Campaign for Adolescent Pregnancy Prevention; the theme this year is "Three Generations of Fondas in Film." Tomorrow the family will be interviewed onstage about our careers by Robert Osborne, the host of Turner Classic Movies, and the evening will end with an homage to Henry Fonda, our father and grandfather.

But the payoff for me is this gathering of the clan, some mem-

Malcolm and Viva, all dressed up to go out. Clearly Viva is happier about the dress-up part than Malcolm.

Reading to my grandchildren, Malcolm and Viva, around 2005

Me with brother Peter, niece Bridget, and son Troy at the
Fonda Family Film Festival in Atlanta in 2007

bers of which, because of festering family "issues," have not been in meaningful contact for more than two years. It was my seventieth birthday last year that launched me into shuttle diplomacy and a commitment to change the situation. I wanted to say "we" and know who I meant. I was tired of not being sure that it included kin. I hated that I hadn't met Peter's daughter's son, my grand-nephew, that he didn't know his second cousins, my grandchildren, that I'd never had a meaningful conversation with Bridget about her five-year absence from film or tried to get to the bottom of what had been going on with Peter. It felt right that a clan gather-ing include Ted. Over the decade that he and I were together, his children and my children had grown close despite the odd-coupling of the two culturally disparate families—mine inclined to tolerance for tattoos, hip-hop, and a discreet earring, his to "yes ma'am, no sir" manners and following military academy rules. Since our divorce, Ted and I have shared the desire to keep it all as connected as possible. So he was excited when he heard we were coming together and asked to be invited, just as he was invited to my son's wedding.

I had experienced the pain of losing family before there had been forgiveness and closure. Not wanting this to happen again motivated me to circle the wagons of love while there was still time. When the event that brought us together was over and I sent the West Coasters on their way, we all knew that we would stay connected—and we have.

I've come a long way since the days when the Lone Ranger was my role model. This isn't surprising, considering that the template for the governing ethic of my world growing up was the rugged individualism of my father. It was partly a generational thing, partly his midwestern staunchness; but mostly, my father was reflecting core western values: A fully mature human being is independent and autonomous. *Don't need anybody. Be tough and self-reliant. Needing is a weakness.*

This cultural scaffolding has posed a dilemma for women. We tend not to be rugged individualists. We build networks of friends upon whom we rely for relational sustenance, to boost our spirits, and to keep our secrets. Because of this, women had been considered less mature, irrational, and even pathological in comparison with men.

Wanting to avoid these labels, I tried to be more like men, not recognizing my emotional needs, much less expressing them, and always holding a part of myself in reserve. Men seemed to be where the action was, and being insular like them felt safer. A friend of the French film director Roger Vadim, my first husband, once said of me, "She's great. Not like most women, more like us." At the time, I viewed this as a compliment. This independence made me very strong. It also made me very weak, although it took me some sixty years to understand the nature of the dichotomy.

The strength part allowed me to embody that old family motto: *Perseverate.* It let me keep moving despite everything, and experience three marriages to challenging men without getting run over.

The weakness part prevented me from experiencing that deep pocket of intimate love—surely the most precious one—which exposes a person to vulnerability. All of which brings me to the Marge Piercy poem that opens this chapter.

I love this poem. It takes me back to the early 1970s, when I first became an activist. I was newly into my Second Act, freshly arrived back home from France, wanting to throw myself into the movement to end the Vietnam War and, on a deeper, barely perceived level, feel that there was meaning to my existence.

At the time, I noticed how different the women activists were from any people I could ever remember meeting. Just being in their presence felt like a haven. I didn't know I was missing community until I met up with it for the first time. These were the early years of the new women's movement, and the feminists I spent time with in the trenches were intentional in living their values of noncompetitiveness and sisterhood—and it was powerful.

I remember vividly when I first witnessed this in action. It happened at a GI coffeehouse in 1971. Run by antiwar activists, these coffeehouses were meeting places that were springing up outside major military bases around the country. A few of the men on the staff had gone ahead on their own and passed out leaflets to GIs without consulting the women staffers. One of the women found out and protested. The men put her down for making a fuss, since they knew the contents of the leaflets would have been approved anyway. The other women on staff stood by her: "If we're trying to model democracy within the staff, then process matters. You're not entitled to take us for granted." I'd always sided with the men—the winning side, or so I'd thought—so this brought me up short.

By now I've grown accustomed to these acts of solidarity among women, but witnessing the power and beauty of it when it was still so startlingly new to me burned away my individualistic dross and allowed the pure gold of friendships to enrich and cushion me. Today, as the separate skeins of my life weave themselves into its final fabric, I want, above all else, for there to be many threads of love shimmering through. I often think how different, how frightening, aging would be for me had this not happened. I know that I can lose everything but that my friendships with women, together with my family, will always be there, no matter what.

Most of my friends are younger than I am, some by more than twenty years. They are creative people, spiritual people, business-people, and activists for social change. We have one another's backs. When I am down I can talk to them, and their understanding, advice, and encouragement lift me. I try to do the same in return.

When I had hip replacement surgery several years ago, Eve Ensler was at my bedside, massaging my feet, as I surfaced through the haze of anesthesia. "Why are you here?" I asked, unused to being tended to and knowing all too well how unimaginably busy Eve was. "Because I'm your friend," she laughed. "Of course I'm here. I want to take care of you." I allowed myself to relax into this caring, but it wasn't easy. To paraphrase Ursula Le Guin, I am a slow unlearner, but oh my, how I love my unteachers.[1]

Eve Ensler in 2011
PAUL ALLEN

*With my friends
Jodie Evans and
Pat Mitchell at a
fund-raiser for The
Women's Center*
REBEKAH SPICUGLIA,
WOMEN'S MEDIA CENTER

*With Lily Tomlin
when she did her
one-woman show
in Atlanta*

*Left to right: Diana
Dunn, me, and Sue
Sally Jones in 2004*

*My best friend, Diana
Dunn (middle), and
me (far right), age 11*

It's good to have younger friends. At least that way not everyone you know will die before you do! As Dr. Ken Methany, Regents Professor in the Department of Counseling and Psychological Services at Georgia State University, told me, "Someone said, 'The worst thing about getting old is that there is nobody around anymore to remember when you were young.' But there is compensation for this. Older people tend to have more intense relationships. So there are fewer people in the network, but the relationships are more intense, more deep. You can't maintain all the acquaintances you had when you were thirty-five, you don't have the energy to do all of that anymore, so people tend to invest themselves with a bit more authenticity, more disclosure."

I agree with this. I think it's also nice to have different kinds of friends. My friends have values, passions, and even early traumas in

In 2011, with my friends Sally Field and Elizabeth Lesser, at then First Lady Maria Shriver's California Women's Conference, where we all spoke

*Me with my new haircut and Vera Wang dress at the 2000 Oscars,
two months after Ted and I split up*

ERIC CHORBONNEAU/BE IMAGES

common, but they're not all alike. With a few I can talk about face-lifts and curtains. A few are immeasurably intense and make me feel downright sluggish in comparison, but they inspire me to expand my horizons and my heart. Three of my friends have rich spiritual lives. One is a Zen priest, one a reverend *and* a sexologist (a useful combination to have in a friend!). Paula Weinstein is my film-producing friend of more than thirty years who always housed me when I was single and in Los Angeles. Whenever anything is physically wrong with me, she will do the research to find the right doctor and actually go with me to the appointment to make sure I ask the right questions. I'm her daughter's godmother; she's a surrogate mom to my two offspring, the one they can go to for an unending supply of advice and a wise referee when the family needs one. She's the one who made me cut my hair and get Vera Wang to design a special dress for my reappearance as a presenter at the 2000 Academy Awards when I was under a bushel from the Ted separation, too down to think about hair and ready to wear an old number from ten

With pal Wanda Sykes at the opening of **Monster-in-Law**

years before. Many moons can pass without my seeing Paula, but when we do reconnect, right off the bat we drill down to an intense, subterranean level, as though no time has elapsed. Actually, that is true of all my women friends. I've had this with a few men, and I know it's possible because two of my friends say they have emotionally intimate friendships with men. It's far rarer, though.

For intimacy, men tend to rely on their significant other, which is why married men seem to do better and live longer, healthier lives than their unmarried counterparts. Because women form broader networks of friends, they do better following divorce or widowhood than men do.

The late Dr. Robert Butler, founding director of the International Longevity Center, told me, "We may have the old boys' network that helps us get jobs, but we don't have the same capacity for intimacy, for dealing with grief or dealing with the kinds of issues women are much more gifted at dealing with."

All people come into the world as relational beings, but from early on, many if not most men are conditioned to split off from their feelings and find their identity in dominance and independence rather than nurturing and community. I read somewhere that "men especially fear that becoming 'we' will erase his 'I,' his sense of self." For most women, their "I" has always been a little porous, whereas women's "we" has been their saving grace.

What psychologists have discovered since the 1970s is that love and nurturing relationships are at the core of human development. In *Toward a New Psychology of Women,* Dr. Jean Baker Miller writes: "All of living and all of development takes place only within relationships."[2] The psychologist Carol Gilligan has said that relationships are the "oxygen of the psyche." Babies die in the absence of attachment. Adults cannot remain stable without outside human contact. All the longitudinal studies on aging show that a key ingredient to doing it successfully is the mutually meaningful giving and receiving of care and nurturing.

In his book *Love and Survival,* Dean Ornish reports that people without loving family, friends, or community are three to five times more likely to die prematurely. Dr. Gene Cohen writes, "Loneliness . . . is associated with a range of adverse health effects, including slower recovery from coronary artery bypass surgery, more office visits to physicians, poorer dental health, and a greater likelihood of nursing home admission. Thus the positive impact of social networks on the health of the mind, body, and brain in late life can be profound."[3] A University of Michigan study reports that feeling close to someone increases one's level of the hormone progesterone, which helps boost the sense of well-being and reduces stress and anxiety. This hormone is also linked to a desire to help others, even at one's own expense.

Kissing my grandson, Malcolm

DONNA FERRATO

The social neuroscientist John Cacioppo is a distinguished service professor at the University of Chicago. He studies the stress of loneliness on our bodies and on our minds. As a guest on NPR's *The Diane Rehm Show,* Mr. Cacioppo said, "Loneliness is the perception that you are isolated from others. It's not the reality of being isolated. In fact, studies have shown it is not the frequency of contact with other people, it is not whether you are alone or not; we actually did such a study and found lonely and non-lonely individuals spent the same amount of time with other people. . . . It's a perception that you're isolated. People can be isolated in a marriage, with friends, being the last one chosen on a team. You're a member of that team and yet somehow you don't feel a part of it. So loneliness is this perception."[4]

This made me think about the many months I spent essentially alone writing *My Life So Far,* and my solitude right now as I write this book. I've never felt alone at such times, and I think it is because I write to communicate with people, and so I am always thinking about those people out there who will read my book, and this makes my aloneness a very non-isolated time. Solitude is not loneliness. I have also found that praying or meditating can alleviate feelings of loneliness because they are a form of being connected to something greater than ourselves.

Loneliness can become more of a problem in the Third Act. Friends and family may have died; disability may prevent us from going out and interacting the way we used to. The physiological impact of loneliness—stress, lowered immune system, anxiety, and depression, along with the challenges I already mentioned—make it important for older people to summon the effort to reach out by phone, over the Internet, by joining a club or going to a senior center. Try putting yourself into situations where you're likely to find people who share your interests, your values—or your challenges. I have talked to a number of women who met new friends while attending a grief management program for women who had lost their husbands. In his book about longevity, *The Blue Zone,* Dan Buettner suggests joining a spiritual community; if you aren't of a particular denomination, you might try humanistic communities like the American Ethical Union or Unitarian Universalism. Volunteering is a win-win: You simultaneously meet new people while doing good. One important thing I've learned over the decades is that when seeking a relationship, it can be more important to be interested than to be interesting.

As Mr. Cacioppo says, "One doesn't have to connect with ten thousand friends. Just connecting in a minor way with someone who you are not going to interact with again, perhaps a taxi driver; just a moment of being nice to another person and having them be nice in return can be the beginning of reconnection. . . . But you want to extend yourself in a safe environment, because underlying the misery of loneliness is this feeling of threatened fear. And so you want to be in a safe place. Don't try to hit a home run with the first social contact. Be satisfied with little steps initially."

Now, dogs are great for companionship; don't get me wrong. In fact, their unconditional love boosts our oxytocin levels and can even cause us to live longer. Reports have shown that "dog-owning cardiac patients die at one-quarter to one-sixth the rate of those who forgo canine companionship." Shirley MacLaine says, "Older people should have dogs. It helps us to go into hyperlove, and love is what ageing is all about."[5]

Dogs are easy. People less so. But all our developmental stumbling blocks stem from relationships with *people*. Turning the stumbling blocks into building blocks of *people* relationships—these are the crucibles in which we can grow.

Two centenarians I met in Atlanta were perfect examples of the kind of attitude that feeds relationships as well as longevity. Ben Burke was 101 years old in 2008 when I met him and "still percolating," as he put it. He takes care of himself and cooks all his own meals, and, I'm told, everyone in his ten-floor, three-hundred-unit condominium building knows him, and he's making an effort to get to know all of them on a first-name basis. Ben also has a passion for making music with his banjo—not just playing it but sharing it with people in his building. "Just brightening them up," he says. "Upstairs is an assisted living department where I go with a couple of musicians, whoever is available, and we play 'golden oldies.'" I discovered that Ben has a woman friend up there, which gives him added incentive—but more about that in the chapter on sex!

Ben didn't start playing the banjo until he was seventy-two. That was when he persuaded his son to resurrect the Tuneagers, a band he'd started as a teenager, so they could play together. "Making music and brightening up people are the lifeline to my living," Ben tells me. "There's gotta be more to life than food and shelter and being a beach bum."

Ben's wife of fifty-eight and a half years died from complica-

tions from Alzheimer's disease on Christmas Day in 1997. "I fig-
ured I had to do something to keep me living, and that was music,"
he says. "So you see what music has meant to me. You had mentioned that the later part of your life can be the best part of it. You
got that right! Not for everybody, but for me, fortunately."

Like Ben, 104-year-old Rachel Lehman devotes her life to
keeping busy and brightening people's lives. A friend who's
known Rachel for a long time told me this about her. It's a recipe
for a long, healthy life: "One of the things so remarkable about
Rachel is that she's rarely self-absorbed. I have yet to see her
when she's not asking about me and my family. That quality has
made her a magnet. She draws people to her, and they love her. It
keeps her connected to lots of different kinds of people of different ages."

The day I met Rachel she walked slowly into the reception
room of an assisted living complex using a walker, helped by her
daughter and the friend, but she had a twinkle in her eye. "You
know, Jane, we met before, at your Workout Studio in Beverly Hills
in the 1970s." "We did!" I exclaimed. "How old were you?" "Musta
been in my seventies. My niece Didi Conn brought me. We did one
of those classes together."

Around that same time, Rachel had moved to Atlanta and
answered a newspaper ad for a volunteer position with the Atlanta
Opera. She got the job and still works there every week as a
fund-raiser. She also has a singing group called the Georgia Classic
Club. "You have to be sixty to join," she pointed out with a wink.

"What do you sing?" I asked.

" 'Second Hand Rose' is my specialty number," she replied and
promptly got up and, using a cane, did a slow soft-shoe while singing a few verses.

When Rachel was 101, she read in the sports section of the *Atlanta
Journal-Constitution* about a bowler named Bill Hargrove who was
102. She called the paper, got his phone number, and called him.
They subsequently became friends, and for her 102nd-birthday
party he brought her three long-stemmed red roses. She confided

to the Atlanta paper that he'd said to her, "I came in here looking for an old lady, but I can't find one." When the paper called to let her know Bill had died (he was about to turn 107), she reminisced with the reporter about the fun times they'd had. "He would tell me, 'When I go to bed at night I see you in my dreams!' How can you top that?" She'd brought Bill a bottle of wine for his 106th-birthday party, in 2007. "I mean at our age, why not?" she told the paper. "We always had so much fun together. I just wish we could have started a little earlier. But I'm so happy I got to meet him. He was so handsome!" She planned to attend his memorial service bearing three long-stemmed roses.

I asked Rachel the secret to her joie de vivre. "There is no secret, really," she replied, "but I find that if you smile at somebody who comes home with a sourpuss, if you just put a big smile on your face, you know, it manufactures into the next person. It causes an epidemic of love."

Maybe we can't all cause an epidemic of love, but putting on a smile and showing an interest in others is bound to draw them to us. Making an effort to play the hand of friendship in our Third Acts will serve us well.

CHAPTER 12

Love in the Third Act

**The one thing that can't be taken from us, even by
death, is the love we give away before we go.**

—REVEREND FORREST CHURCH,
Love and Death: My Journey Through the Valley of the Shadow

FROM EVERYTHING I'VE READ AND WHAT I'VE HEARD FROM
most of the gerontology experts I've talked to, it seems clear that
Third Acts have the potential to be a prime time for deepening
already existing love relationships or forging new and amazingly
rich ones—if one has a desire for such a relationship, and if there is
a partner! Our joints may ache and our eyesight dim, but our hearts
and minds may be primed for deeper intimacy and mutuality than
we've ever experienced before.

Intimacy: Suzanna's Story

One woman whose experience exemplifies the later-life discovery
of intimacy is seventy-year-old Suzanna Graves. A lovely, slender
woman who adorns herself with teasingly sheer, lush, textured fab-
rics that gleam and shimmer when she moves, she was an actor and
is now a therapist. We met in her small, perfume-scented New
York apartment for hours, drank tea, and talked about age and art
and love. I asked how she felt about being older.

"Right now I am in a state of shock," she blurted out. "Every
year in my sixties was better than the year before. I mean, it has
been the best decade of my life. I just can't tell you."

"Why, do you suppose?" I asked

"Well, we know what Freud said: love and work. I have come to the therapy work that I adore, and I have love. It started when I was finally able to get free of my obsession with romantic love—the thinking that the answer to my life was going to be Mr. Right. I was married for seven years and have two daughters and I've been single for forty years. I had many lovers . . . handsome men, famous even. But I finally had enough of all that charisma, with me a mouse in the corner. It always felt so unequal. Then too, I was frigid until well into my thirties. I was pretty. I got it. I knew what I was supposed to do: please men. But I was frigid. I went through it all because I wanted to please men, but my sexuality? What was that? Then, with a lot of therapy, I came out the other side and stopped looking for a man to save me."

Suzanna also attended workshops run by the famous sex therapist Betty Dodson, who taught women to not be afraid of pleasuring themselves—with their hands, with vibrators. Dodson made sexual pleasure understandable and okay for thousands of lucky women, and Suzanna was one of them.

"Five or so years ago," Suzanna continued, "I ran into an actor friend whom I hadn't seen in many years. We'd been in a co-counseling group together. We knew each other's stuff. It was great to see him—chat, chat, and that was that. And the next thing that happened was that my daughter was about to get married and she asked me why I hadn't been in a long-term relationship and I told her, 'It's a lot of trouble and I have no libido.' So guess what she did? She turned me on to a gynecologist who prescribed testosterone pills. This doctor told me there's no reason women in their sixties shouldn't have the sexual responses of women in their thirties. Within a month or so I began to notice that men were looking at me differently. I went to Zabar's deli—remember Zabar's?—and I was standing looking at the food display and the woman said, 'Okay, honey. What will it be?' I said, 'I don't know. I am looking for inspiration.' And this cool actor guy—you know what I mean: little stubble, good-looking, buff—came up to me and said, 'Aren't we all?'

And I said, 'Well, yes.' But there was a palpable difference. I was putting out something. And I thought, 'Hmmm, I'd like a boyfriend.' "

"How old were you then?"

"Sixty-five, I think. I knew I didn't want any of the old stuff.
Now I want somebody I can feel safe with. I want somebody I can
talk with. So I called up my actor friend and I said, 'Would you care
to move to the flirting stage?' and he—bless his soul—I mean, not
a beat, he said, 'I've only been waiting since 1982.' Oh! So I thought
that was pretty good. He is ten years younger than I am."

I asked if this age difference made her self-conscious, but she
waved off that suggestion, adding, "None of it is what I imagined at
this age. Anyway, one weekend my actor friend and I both had to go
out of town to meet with people we had worked with in the past and
to see a play. He carried my suitcase to our hotel and one thing led to
another, but since we did have to go to a meeting and then the theater that night, I had the foresight to set the alarm clock." Suzanna
paused, and a lovely sensuality softened her face. "This man was the
most divine kisser in the world. He had the most perfect touch. He
was— I was beside myself. I had the most ecstatic experience. And I
don't know how to say this, but he had the most wonderful, big, dry,
warm hands. I have cold, clammy hands. I have little Waspy hands.
There was something so utterly perfect. Anyway, at one point the
alarm clock went off. He reached across me, turned the alarm around,
and said, 'No, Suzanna. Wouldn't you like to come again? There is
always time for that other.' And he said it in a tone of voice that was
just—it was just somehow—gruff—the voice came from such a deep
place and, well, there are lovely things in life and, you know, there *is*
always time for that other. And, I don't know how to say it—there
was something about it that was just . . ."

"Irresistible?"

"Irresistible, yes. And that he has this attitude about sex that is, to
me, the most straightforward, the most—'healthy' sounds revolting,
but—healthy, rational, kind, generous, good, whatever, that I have
come across in any man. So, to me, there is this just amazing thing.
And he does it often. There was a time when I had an urgent prob-

lem with my eye. I was scared. It was Sunday, but I called my doctor and made an appointment for the next morning at eight A.M. My lover walked out into the sunshine with me that Sunday afternoon and turned to me and said, 'Well, that's good. We have a plan. We'll go home. I will run you a bath. You'll feel better. I can lick you. You will be calm. No exertion on your part. You will sleep well. Then we will go to the doctor early in the morning.' There is something about his attitude toward sex, to me, that is just amazing. That said, do we have problems? Big problems. We do. So that is the story behind how I am the poster child for testosterone, because I still have a libido at this point. Now, I don't know if I will have it if I stop taking the pills, but at this point the habit is so ingrained that when I see my lover I know that should I wish it, good times will ensue. I don't know whether it's become a habit, Pavlov's dog, or whether it is the testosterone that is keeping me libidinous. But who cares?"

I asked if they lived apart, and she was adamant on that point.

"I'm with clients all day in my practice on a very intense level, and apart from that I'm used to solitude. My default position is 'How can I help? How can I be a good girl?' You called it the 'dis-ease to please' in your memoirs. So now, I need time to reintegrate, to come back into my skin so I won't fall into those old patterns." We gave each other a high five on that one.

"Meanwhile," I said, " you are in a satisfying, loving relationship, having good sex, and you are strong enough now to know what you want and need and what you don't care for. And, through therapy and your daughter's nudging and the hormonal tinkering, you went and got yourself ready for some loving. Staying ready for it but not incomplete if it doesn't come—that's the challenge now, right? That's the road I've been on myself for some years. And it came for me, too. In my seventies!" Another high five.

Individuation and Androgenization

Suzanna and I are examples of women who, later in life, have come to embody two things that allowed us to open to the potential for love and sensuality, elements that tend to be more evident in older women of our generation: individuation and androgenization, which I will explain in a second, but I know, I know! They don't sound very romantic! Nevertheless, possessing them makes romance deeper than ever. For some, this comes naturally . . . and earlier. For us, as for many others, it took work and desire and time. Let me explain.

The psychologist Carl Jung used the term "individuation," which is very different from individualism in that it allows one to maintain healthy boundaries—to not lose oneself—while being in an emotionally and physically intimate relationship. Suzanna's healthy boundaries have allowed her to know that she needs to live alone, have time to herself, and avoid getting caught up in her partner's "stuff." Like Suzanna, I found standing on my own two feet more than iffy in my earlier years, when I lacked confidence and an independent identity. I could become what a man wanted me to be, what I thought was required so as to be lovable. I'm probably the only person in the world who thought Woody Allen's movie Zelig must have been based on a true story. The title character, who literally becomes whomever he is talking to, seemed perfectly plausible to old "I'll be whatever you want me to be" me. Talk about poor boundaries! But real intimacy, however, requires self-revelation, and that's problematic if you're not sure what the "self" is or are scared that your revealed self will be discovered as a fraud and rejected. We speak of falling in love. Maybe that was the problem. Suzanna and I fell because we weren't standing on our own two feet. Individuation, on the other hand, means you "own" yourself, you are a free-standing, self-validated adult, as opposed to entwined and needy, and this tends to happen to women in their fifties and beyond, enabling them, in their intimate relationships, to "stay in connection without being consumed by the other person," as Dr. David Schnarch puts it.[1] The psychologist Terrence Real says, "There is no aphrodisiac stronger than authentic connection."[2]

Carl Jung also believed that with individuation, people's maleness and femaleness come into balance. Dr. Jane Loevinger and many other psychologists today agree that the potential to let go of rigid sex roles for both men and women in the last third of life represents the peak of maturity and points the way to achieving individuation, autonomy and "communion."[3] Betty Friedan's research on aging showed her that "couples facing age with lowest morale and least sense of intimacy are those where the husband *still defines himself as family chief and provider,* and where the woman *still sees her identity only as a housewife/mother.*"[4]

The social gerontologist and anthropologist David Gutmann has written, "Whereas adult males start from a grounding in Active Mastery and move toward Passive Mastery, women are first grounded in Passive Mastery, characterized by dependence on and even deference to the husband, but surge in later life toward Active Mastery. . . . Across cultures, and with age, they seem to become more authoritative, more effective, and less willing to trade submission for security."[5] Scientists I interviewed at the Stanford Center on Longevity say there is no empirical scientific evidence to prove that this recalibration of gender roles is the norm, as Gutmann and others claim. But it seems natural that the hormonal changes associated with aging, along with the man's retirement, would lead to a leveling out of gender differences. And it makes sense that the balancing out of what previously were narrow, socially proscribed gender roles would lead to greater integrity, wholeness, and authenticity for both men and women. Most of the women I have interviewed and read about have experienced this "gender balancing"—with men potentially regaining the humanness they lost in early boyhood and women potentially regaining, with age, the agency and assertiveness they had prior to adolescence. If this androgenization represents the peak of maturity and communion for both genders, why not strive for it?

Interestingly, my age cohort and the boomer generation immediately following may be the last to experience this late-life androgenization. It appears (and I pray this is true) that sex roles for Generation X women and men are already undergoing the kind of relaxation that may, if psychologists are correct, augur happier partnerships earlier in life. A 2007 *Time* magazine article said that "the number of stay-at-home fathers has tripled in the past ten years" and that these "new Dads" "are challenging old definitions of masculinity." "Masculinity has traditionally been associated with work and work-related success, with competition, power, prestige, dominance over women, restrictive emotionality—that's a big one," says Aaron Rochlen, an associate professor of psychology at the University of Texas, who studies fatherhood and masculinity. "Other research shows that fathers who stop being men of the old mold have better adjusted children, better marriages and better work lives—better mental and physical health, even. Basically," Rochlen concludes, "masculinity is bad for you."[6]

In an article in the *New York Times,* Tara Parker-Pope reported the results of a study done in 2000 in Vermont after same-sex civil unions were legalized in the state. She noted that "same sex relationships, whether between men or women, were far more egalitarian than heterosexual ones.... While gay and lesbian couples had about the same rate of conflict as the heterosexual ones, they appeared to have more relationship satisfaction, suggesting that the inequality of opposite-sex relationships can take a toll." Apparently, same-sex couples resolve their conflicts better. In the same article, Robert W. Levenson, a professor of psychology at the University of California, Berkeley, is quoted as saying, "When they got into these really negative interactions, gay and lesbian couples were able to do things like use humor and affection instead of just exploding."[7] These findings seem to confirm what I have been saying: that democracy within a relationship is key to the long-term happiness of the couple.

Individuation and androgenization were present in the long-term relationships whose partners I interviewed. You may think, judging from previous chapters, that I am cavalier on the subject of long-term commitment, whether in marriage or in loving partnerships. I am actually a true believer. I regret that I've not stayed married to one man for the long haul, but I've made some fairly deep transitions over the course of my life so far, and the men I was with either didn't want to transition with me, or couldn't, or were transitioning in a different direction. As Lillian Hellman once said, "People change and forget to tell each other."

Then again, on my side, I think that up until my sixties I was challenged in the intimacy department because I lacked the individuation and androgenization factors. I knew that I risked dying without ever really experiencing the kind of deeply intimate relationship with a man that I have experienced with women. That

Richard and me in 2009

would be my big regret. (I am speaking not of sex but of emotional intimacy!) So I've worked on myself. Writing my memoirs was part of it. I am in a relationship now that has the potential I seek. I cannot know for sure. It's only been sixteen months, as of this writing. I am with a man who is not at all in a spiritual transition. We are actually very different. But he isn't afraid of intimacy, and I have become a freestanding adult, and maybe, just maybe, this relationship can be a crucible in which I get to heal myself even further.[8] He's younger than I by five years, but old enough to feel the need, as I do, of doing all he can to forge something real and—well, not long-lasting; it's not like there's all that much time left! Something real and meaningful is what we're after. We've both had a lot of experience with relationships. We've both either chosen inappropriately or lacked the know-how to work through what was wrong and get it to work. Time is running out . . . there's twenty years or a bit more at best.

It takes being intentional to keep passionate intimacy alive and well. For example, romantic time needs to be scheduled. So does talking things through. In the past, I would often stuff down my feelings about things my partner did that I didn't like, because I was scared he'd leave, and then where would I be? Now when something my partner has done upsets me, I schedule a sit-down to talk about it . . . or he forces us to talk about it when he feels something's not right. Invariably we come away from these talks stronger than before. I've told him what I like about him and what I have problems with. I am realistic enough to know that there are things he can't change and things I'm too old to want to fix. Like Suzanna, I'm tired of trying to fix a mate. (Not that I don't bite my tongue sometimes!) But I feel that at this point, if he wants this to work enough, he will make an effort to do certain things differently if they are deal breakers for me, and I am prepared to do the same for him.

I sometimes feel guilty because I want so much in a relationship. In my grandparents' day, couples seemed to accept that after a while romance would be replaced by companionship. But back then companionship didn't get that old, because *people* didn't get that old. They died. Instead of getting bored and divorcing, people died and the remaining spouse remarried—or not. Terrence Real, in his wonderful book *The New Rules of Marriage,* suggests that the change in the nature of what was desired in long-term relationships really began in the 1970s with the women's movement. Women entered the workplace, became more financially independent, attended consciousness-raising groups, gained a modicum of political power, and discovered in the process that when they brought their innate gifts of empathy and intimacy into their workplaces and relationships, healing would happen, problems would be solved—differently, more easily—and it felt good. Who doesn't want to feel good? Real says, "We have grafted onto the companionship marriage of the previous century the expectations and mores of a lover relationship—the kind of passion, attention, and emotional closeness that we most commonly associate with youth, and with the early stages of a relationship."[9] The five tactics he suggests for cultivating this kind of relationship are:

1. Reclaim romantic space. (This is easier to do now, when the children have left home and there is more time and job flexibility.)
2. Tell the truth. (This is easier for a woman to do if she has confidence and individuation.)
3. Cultivate sharing. (Intellectually, emotionally, physically, sexually, and spiritually.)
4. Cherish your partner. (Develop your "lover energy"— the energy that goes into loving. Don't just feel it; act on it.)
5. Become partners in health. (Share a commitment to relational practice. As I have said, an intimate, passionate, long-term relationship doesn't happen spontaneously. It requires commitment to engaging in relational practice.)[10]

Sociologists say that marriage seems to encourage stability, a sense of obligation to the other, a barrier to loneliness, more financial security because of pooled resources, and better health. "Married people are less likely to get pneumonia, have surgery, develop cancer or have heart attacks. A group of Swedish researchers has found that being married or co-habitating at midlife is associated with lower risk for dementia," notes Tara Parker-Pope, who writes the *Well* blog for the *New York Times*. Parker-Pope goes on to say, however, that a bad, stressful marriage can leave a person far worse off than if they'd never married at all. In fact, it can be "as bad for the heart as a regular smoking habit."[11]

Obviously, though, marriage is not for everyone. If you have found that there is no room in your marriage for a fully awakened, authentic you, it may be far healthier to leave than to swallow your unhappiness and shrink yourself back into a half life. If along the way you've stopped facing your real feelings and needs, stopped being truthful to yourself, you will inevitably go numb—the best, most potentially vital parts of you will shut off. You will also be angry, although this, too, may be covered over. Studies show that a bad marriage, with its potentially toxic stress, is especially bad for the wife's health. A fifteen-year Oregon study cited by Suzanne Braun Levine in *Inventing the Rest of Our Lives* found that "having unequal decision-making power was associated with higher health risks for women, but not for men, perhaps," Levine conjectures, "because women don't have the other opportunities to exercise power that men traditionally do. Powerlessness is a major contributor to stress and depression."[12] Marriage brings more benefits to men than it does to women, since women do the lion's share of the emotional nurturing, child rearing, housekeeping, and meal cooking—which, perhaps, is why married men live longer than single men and divorced women do better than divorced men. Despite the emotional, financial, and social hardships that divorce can entail, "increasingly," Suzanne Brown Levine notes, "women are initiating divorce and regretting it less."[13]

If a woman does decide later in life to take another chance at love, it is commonly with someone she knew previously. I met my current mate, Richard Perry, thirty-seven years ago, when he helped arrange for the musical group The Manhattan Transfer, which he was producing, to perform a fund-raising concert for my then-husband, Tom Hayden, who was campaigning for U.S. Senate. Here we all are in his recording studio in 1975. Richard is kneeling next to my son, Troy, and me. Tom is standing between Janis Siegel and Laurel Massey.

Me, Troy, Richard, and Tom (back row, center) with Tim Hauser, Janis Siegel, Laurel Massey, and Alan Paul of The Manhattan Transfer

Long-Term Relationships

I have long been fascinated by how couples in long-term marriages have managed to adjust to the dramatic shifts that occur over the years, especially in the final third. It was one thing when our life span was twenty years shorter; I find it truly miraculous when a man who was "Mr. Right" during the years of building a family and raising children is still the right partner thirty, forty, or fifty years later. I am in awe, frankly.

One such story is that of Bill and Kathy Stayton, who have been married for fifty-five years and have four children. Bill, seventy-six when I interviewed him, is an impish, courageous Baptist minister and sex therapist. I first met him a number of years ago, when I asked him to speak at a workshop on gender, sexuality, and religion at an annual conference of the Georgia Campaign for Adolescent Pregnancy Prevention.

Kathy Stayton, seventy-four, was an athlete in her younger days, and a school leader, and has kept her trim figure and natural beauty. Sitting next to Bill, quiet and attentive, she seemed the image of an old-fashioned, take-the-backseat homemaker. During our three hours together, however, I discovered a woman who, inspired by the peace activism of her family of origin, has, from girlhood, had her own firm voice.

I interviewed Kathy and Bill in their bright, one-story home in a newish development in Atlanta's growing suburbs.

For eleven years, Bill had been a Baptist minister in Massachusetts. He found himself unprepared for the sexuality issues that came to him from his parishioners and from people in the community. He told me, "Sexual orientation, gender identity and expression, sexual dysfunction, multiple relationships, polyamory, and open marriage were life's experiences presented to me— stories of things I didn't even know existed and I was not prepared to help with. I'd go home and say, 'Kathy, do you know people who do this?' " They both laughed at the memory. "I became really passionate about clergy being trained in human sexuality, no matter what," Bill said. "So, I started taking courses in sexuality myself, became a doctor of theology in the field of psychology. I helped to found the Center for Sexuality and Religion. In 1997, the faculty and students voted to move the human sexuality program to Widener University, in Chester, Pennsylvania, where I served as professor and director. In 2006, I became the executive director of the Center for Sexuality and Religion, eventually at the University of Pennsylvania."

In 2008, former U.S. surgeon general Dr. David Satcher invited Bill to come to Atlanta and merge the Center for Sexuality and Religion with the Satcher Health Leadership Institute at Morehouse School of Medicine. Bill recently retired from being a professor at the medical school and assistant director of its Center of Excellence for Sexual Health.

*Reverend Bill
Stayton and his
bride, Kathy*

"Tell me about your relationship," I prompted.

"Well, first of all, I fell in love the minute I saw her," Bill answered with relish. "It was at freshman orientation; I was a sophomore and Kathy was a freshman. I was entertaining at a church youth group at the school and I saw her. It took several weeks to find out who she was so I could ask her out."

After their first date, Bill said, "I wrote my parents and said, 'I have met the person.' "

"How long did it take you to fall in love with Bill, Kathy?"

"Oh, gosh. Six months?" They both laughed.

"She went home to meet my parents at Christmas," Bill recalled. "Then we got engaged in February and married in September of the next year. So, we knew each other just a year. We often say we got married to have sex." They had both been virgins.

Kathy added, "That's not really the right reason. . . . You know, though, it worked out for us."

The Long Haul

I wanted to know what they credited their longevity as a couple to. "Fifty-five years!" I exclaimed, "It's hard to find one person who is not only good for the early, family-building stage but is still good in the post-children stage."

"I always knew, right from the beginning," Kathy said, "that people didn't expect young people's marriages to last. So I was determined I wasn't going to be like what people expected."

"We had some tears in there, and conflicts," Bill interjected, wanting me to know that it hadn't all been an easy run.

"Yes," said Kathy, "but we knew our love for each other was strong, even though, at times, we may not have liked each other. When we had differences I could always say to myself, 'This too shall pass,' and not worry that our love was threatened. Besides, we have shared values, we enjoy the same types of entertainment—theater, classical music, art museums, film—and we've never harbored jealousy of the friends of the opposite sex each of us have."

Bill smiled at his wife. "I have never, ever thought of separation or divorce. It has never been a part of me." He added that one hard time "was during the feminist period where Kathy felt she had been with her parents and then with me and she had never been her own person."

"I went from one dependency to another," Kathy explained. "At first, when Bill was in seminary, I worked—we both worked. That was survival. But after the first child, I did not work for a number of years. Or, rather, I should say I didn't get paid for a number of years."

"Ah yes," I interjected. "Unpaid labor? You mean you became a homemaker?"

"You got it! But in the seventies, when Bill began his postdoctoral work and his career at the University of Pennsylvania, I went back to work as an administrative assistant and a middle school music teacher. Yet my responsibilities at home didn't lessen. We were not in a financial position to hire housekeeping or landscaping help, and I was the one who negotiated help from our children. I made a decent salary to help pay for one of our kids to go to college. But it got swept up into other expenses of our household.

"Probably," Kathy continued, "our biggest clash of value has been over how to spend money. Because I've always grown up with the belief that 'where your money is, that's where your heart is.' And my heart was in a different place than Bill's heart. But as a woman of my generation, I fell into the 'dependent' role of the wife, wanting to please my spouse, not believing that my voice, if in opposition to Bill's, particularly around issues of large financial expenditures, was equal to his, and I would give in to his desires around those matters and then harbor resentment. Not smart!"

Bill then told me that they had considered separating for a year, to give Kathy a sense of independence, as a way of strengthening both her and their marriage. When that was too complicated because of the children, their therapist suggested that they work on separateness in their own home, by having separate financial accounts.

Bill recalled, "And so for a year—and this was so painful for me—you bought your own Christmas presents for the children and I bought my Christmas presents for the children. Before that everything had always been from Mom and Dad—even though she bought the presents," he told me. "And for a year she decided not to go to church anymore. I would go on Sundays and people would say, 'Where's Kathy?' "

Kathy frowned. "I don't remember that it was for a whole year."

Achieving Individuation

"When did this begin," I asked Kathy, "this feeling that you needed to stand on your own two feet?"

"In the early seventies, when we lived in Pennsylvania, I resonated with the words that Gloria Steinem was saying. I just said, 'That's true! She speaks for me.' "

"Do you remember what it was she said that so resonated with you?" I asked.

"It had to do with roles. When you are feeling imprisoned by what is expected of women, when you don't feel the expectations suit you."

"Because you didn't feel you could be a full person within those expectations?"

"Yes. You feel like, 'Is this what I should be doing?' That kind of stuff."

Privately, I asked Kathy if Bill had been threatened by all this change.

"Yes," she said. "I think the whole feminist movement has had an impact on all the men as well as women, and I think at that time, in his head, Bill was a feminist, but in actions it was life as usual."

"I was that way myself for a few years," I admitted. "A theoretical feminist but not an embodied one."

"It's hard to unlearn those things," Kathy mused. "I didn't really get into feminism a lot. I was kind of on the periphery but watch-

Bill and Kathy Stayton TIM SCOTT, SPENCER STUDIOS

ing to see what was out there. I have more courage in my head maybe than in my body at times."

"Perhaps, but you did go out and begin to create your own space, right?"

"Well, actually, I always have used my leadership skills throughout my life, even while being a full-time homemaker. But I did move into new territory—in terms of my own 'space'—in the early seventies."

Finding Identity in Community

"It was around that time that I started doing community things that Bill didn't do and we just had different lives," Kathy recalled. "One of those things was the symphony orchestra. I played the violin, and when I was part of the orchestra no one asked, 'What does your husband do?' You really are your own person. You just learn your part and are a part of the group. And rehearsals were every week, so Bill had to take the kids. I wasn't going to give it up. And that really did help even before I was aware that that's what it was doing for me.

"Also, in the early nineties," she said, "the board of our denomination, the American Baptist Churches of the USA, issued a new policy, a one-sentence resolution that caught us all by surprise: 'The practice of homosexuality is incompatible with Christian teaching.' Period. Our church was up in arms about this and we began our activism and, within a year, we had a lesbian, gay, bisexual, and transgendered (LGBT) allied group within the church. That was where I became very involved. It was not hard to do because, with Bill being in the field of sexuality, we already knew people who were transgender, transsexual, gay, lesbian, crossdressers, the whole spectrum of human expressions in sex and gender." Kathy talked about the process they had to go through before their congregation finally agreed to become a member of the Association of Welcoming and Affirming Baptists.

Kathy explained that the work she and so many others have done for decades now on LGBT issues has blossomed. "I have a network of people I know all through Philadelphia, and they are very meaningful to me," she said. "Some are clergy, some are lay; they are all out, in their churches and, I presume, in their jobs, but who knows? They became really my second church because what was important about our church was not necessarily the theology or anything; it was the community of people who will support us even though they may not be active in our group. They will support us, and then they talk about it. In fact, some people said they went back to their retirement communities and they would talk about these issues at their dinner table and it kind of grew."

Having found her own voice, her own way to make a difference, Kathy now works within her new church community in Atlanta, on the board of directors for the Association of Welcoming and Affirming Baptists and the Marriage Equality team, which is a group that advocates for marriage equality for same-sex marriage in Atlanta. "We will start up in Atlanta—we'll see if we can ever get the state of Georgia," she told me with a smile.

But Kathy didn't end the discussion there. She wanted me to understand another part of why their marriage has survived for so long, in addition to her finding her own space. "We have always been a part of a community of people who are supportive," she said, "and that has happened in the churches we have been in, with people who have lived a long time and seemed to be happy in their old age and they were still active—and so, you know, we had role models."

"So, there was a community rooting for you and dependent on the two of you to stay together as a couple?"

"Well, I don't know if they depended on us, but it was my expectation that we would stay together, I think. I would have let myself down."

I have thought a lot about these words of Kathy's, this thing about what's expected out of marriage, what we expect from ourselves. It saddens me that we just don't have these same expectations anymore. Quite the contrary. The expectation these days is that one *won't* stay together, and so when the going gets rough, many tend to move on. And yet . . . maybe that is becoming inevitable in the face of our newly gained longevity and our desire for 360-degree relationships, intimate and passionate all the way. Margaret Mead felt that every woman needed three husbands: one for the youthful sexy stage, one for bringing security to the family-building stage, and one for Third Act companionship.

Right now, looking back at the beginnings and endings of my own relational scenarios, I feel that if our loves must be segmented into more doable phases, what becomes critical is to take the time and make the effort to learn the lessons each phase offers so that at least we deepen and grow in our ability to be a loving, intimate partner. Who was it who said, "If you keep doing the same things the same way, you keep getting the same results"?

Intentionality

"I think one of the things that has really been important for us," Bill remarked, "and we had to become intentional about this, was spending time for just us. I've learned a lot working with people, and one of the things that happens all too often is that when people get married you spend all your time on maintenance: the kids, fixing up the home, doing the work around the house. Whereas when people start getting together, you're nurturing the relationship. Then they get married and all that nurturance tends to turn over into maintenance, and when I work with couples it's putting play back into their relationship. Just going to do something with the kids is not nurturance of the relationship. It might be nurturance of the family, but it is also maintenance."

"So, when does this start to happen between couples?" I asked.

"Kathy and I became intentional when our kids were becoming teenagers. We set time aside just to be together because kids take up all your time at home. So, we became really intentional. Like we set ten o'clock at night, something like that—the kids couldn't break in on us. It was time when we could talk about planning a party, or we could—"

"Have sex?" I queried.

With Jewelle Bickford on a hike at Rancho La Puerta in 2008

"Oh yeah. We've always had a good sex life."

"I think that is the glue," I interjected. "Isn't it the thing that helps in the forgiveness, in smoothing over the rough passages?"

"Yeah, absolutely," Bill replied.

The story of Kathy and Bill's successful marriage underscores for me the importance of having healthy boundaries, a life outside the relationship, and a willingness to work at it at all stages along the way—that and good sex!

Another long-term relationship that exemplifies these things is the forty-six-year marriage of Nat and Jewelle Bickford. Nat's the chap you met in Chapter 10 who wrote his life story and purged his ghosts. He was sixty-six when I interviewed him and Jewelle was sixty-four. I first met her at a Women in the Global South seminar at the Council on Foreign Relations. Somewhat cowed by the fact that her background is in assets securitization and that she was, at the time of our meeting, the highest-ranking woman at Rothschild bank, I didn't anticipate getting to know her and her family and still can't quite believe that I have a friend who has been a banker. One thing I hadn't known about Jewelle until the interview was

*Just-married Nat
and Jewelle Bickford*

*Below: Jewelle and
Nat with their
daughters, Laura
and Emily*

that when her daughters were young she was a stay-at-home wife
and mother, doing all the cooking and housework. Only when the
girls turned sixteen and nineteen did she, at age thirty-eight, go
back to college—Sarah Lawrence.

"Nat was the one who said, 'You are too smart not to be
college-educated,' " Jewelle told me with evident appreciation in
her voice. "At that time it was really hard for him to pay for the two
kids in private school and my college education, but he felt it was

absolutely essential." My admiration for the two of them grew immensely at the idea that her amazing career didn't start till midlife and that he wasn't at all threatened by her morphing from mom to career woman.

The longevity of their marriage is proof that people with love-less childhoods can beat the odds and have a happy marriage. Nat and Jewelle focused on spending time together, on sensuality, and on compromise. Jewelle thinks one reason why they married so young was that it provided a way out of their parents' homes. I find their compatibility surprising because they are so utterly different: It's Ferdinand the Bull married to the Little Engine That Could in high gear. Jewelle put it this way: "Nat's the rudder and I'm the engine." He said, "We are the reverse sides of a coin. She's got a tremendous amount of energy, I have a medium amount. She is, let's see, self-directed, proactive, spontaneous, intuitive. These are not words I use to describe myself. I am more reflective, less spon-taneous. I just need time to think about things."

Although they are temperamentally polar opposites, several things are clear about Nat and Jewelle right off the bat. For one, their marriage has been a priority for them. "We always made time for each other," Nat said, "even when we had the kids. We couldn't go away a lot, so we took advantage of the fact that we had two sets of grandparents, both of which were willing to take the kids. So we had some rest from the grind on weekends. And we've always liked talking to each other."

It's also apparent that there is a lot of physical chemistry between them; it's been that way, according to Nat, from the start. He recalled, "I had a date for a football weekend at Harvard and my date was bringing a chaperone, so I arranged a date for the chaper-one and, to bribe him, I got him tickets to the game. Well, Jewelle was the chaperone, and when I laid eyes on her I told my friend, 'Forget the tickets, you won't see her. I am going to take her home for seventy-two hours and you won't see her again.' "

I asked Jewelle how they kept the sensuality going all these years. "People don't have good long-term sexual relationships who don't have good psychological relationships," she said. "Consistently good lovemaking to the same person doesn't come from exciting techniques but from mental stimulation and excitement." She described to me the beauty of getting sexually turned on by and making love with someone whom you've shared so much life with. "You can't imagine, Jane, how fantastically special it is. There's a different kind of richness to it that's way deeper than when you're young and it's new." I can only catch a whiff of what that must feel like, and this is a big regret for me. For me, it will never be "the long haul."

I asked Nat if they've had major differences over the years, and what's changed now that they are in their Third Acts. "One of our major differences was the children," he said. "I am much more laissez-faire than she is. She is a believer in setting boundaries far beyond me, and that produced a lot of friction from time to time."

"It was terrible, just terrible" was Jewelle's description of it. "He thought girls didn't get into trouble. Isn't that amazing? And he wanted to be their friend and not their disciplinarian, so we fought a lot over it." What this meant, though, is that unlike couples who suffer when the children leave home, Nat and Jewelle found that the empty nest meant that a source of tension was removed. Though they love their daughters immensely, that's when, they say, they started really enjoying themselves, sharing a common interest in all the cultural riches New York has to offer.

In 2004 Nat retired from his law practice while Jewelle continued working. I asked her if this caused problems, the way it has for some couples. "Yes!" she exclaimed. "In the first place, he totally took over my kitchen. I like to cook, and it was just a mess. There were stacks of books and papers, and he had an office and never went to it."

Although he was retired, Nat's law firm had given him an office and a secretary for his use—hoping, perhaps, that he would stay involved with clients on some level.

"I know it was annoying to Jewelle," Nat told me. "Why didn't I use it? Why did I have to hang out in the kitchen? There were times when I felt sort of sheepish about not going to the office. I felt this tremendous internal barrier—I just didn't want to go back there. I knew I would get involved in something. When I left that firm for the last day, I was just happy to go."

These seemingly small issues have brought storms to many a calm sea. One retired husband I read about thought he was doing his wife a big favor when he reorganized all her kitchen cupboards while she was away on business. Needless to say, she pitched a fit. What Jewelle did was get them to see a couples counselor and, according to Jewelle, this woman helped both of them. Nat was able to see that invading Jewelle's space and avoiding making a decision about where to do his work and put his stuff was a passive-aggressive act. "After that," said Jewelle, "a lightbulb went off, he came home and, in two days, totally filed everything, and I had my kitchen back."

The therapist helped Jewelle see ways that she, too, can avoid problems. "As you know," Jewelle said, "Nat and I are very different, and now that he's home more, certain things bother me. I've been wanting him to not depend so much on me for social life and for intimacy. I think he should have lunch with more of his friends, but the therapist said, 'That is not your business, Jewelle. Lay off. Quite frankly, you have to pick the things that matter most to you.' So, I started thinking about the things that really did not matter to me and I have been laying off."

"Has this relieved the tension?" I asked.

"Yes, it has," Jewelle replied with relief.

Like most women I have talked to, menopause was freeing for Jewelle. "In some weird way I got much more self-confidence," she told me. "I don't know whether it was hormonal or just age. But my fifties were the beginning of when I started feeling good about myself."

When I told her that the writer Suzanne Braun Levine calls that decade the "Fuck-You Fifties," Jewelle said, "Absolutely! I stopped caring so much how they view me."

" 'They' as in the men you work with at the bank?"

"Yes. That doesn't mean that I don't want to get along with them at work. You have to get along in whatever environment you are in. But you can choose which environments you want to be in. That was a real eye-opener for me."

Nat and Jewell's marriage is a demonstration of how individuation and androgenization—gender balancing—can deepen a couple's bonds. Generativity and passionate involvement have also had a role to play. Jewelle retired from banking in 2009. She is now working with GenSpring, a firm that focuses on wealth management, but is, nonetheless, able to spend more time with her family and grandchildren and to work with the international nonprofit organization Women for Women International, which links women in the developed world to individual women in the Global South and helps them become economically self-sufficient, primarily through microenterprise.[14]

"There's no question that for marital longevity, there needs to be romance. Nat and I work to keep our romance alive," Jewelle told me. While Jewelle has narrowed her professional life and looks to bring her skills and energy to her work with international women's organizations, Nat has unleashed his long-hidden passion for music. He always wanted to be a composer but, knowing that his strict, emotionally remote father would never support that ambition, he set it aside for the law.

"All my life what I have done is play the piano for myself and make up things," Nat confided, and I could hear the timbre of his voice change and the desire bleed through. "Music is my passion."

Option to Renew

In Chapter 16 I will talk about my friends Eva and Yoel Haller, both seventy-seven years old when I interviewed them and married for twenty years. It's his third marriage and her fifth. She calls her first three go-rounds her "training bra" marriages. Between them they have ten children and fifteen grandchildren.

They were each fifty-seven years old when they met in the back of a bus going from the famous Rancho La Puerto spa in Tecate, Mexico, to San Diego. "By the time I got off the bus," Yoel told me, "I knew I was going to marry her."

Eva hadn't really wanted to get married again, feeling that it was too much of a commitment, but he pressed her and they married six months later. Now, as she looks back, she's glad they did. She noted, "There is something about that deeper commitment—that we will spend the rest of our living days together."

She told me that as a widow, what she missed most about being married was the "conspiracy." When I asked her to explain, she said, "I missed a partner with whom I could share the conspiracy, the delicious nonverbal conspiracy. You know, in the midst of a party, the quiet look between us which assures us that we are together. This, for me, is the essence of togetherness, of love."

Both Yoel and Eva evidence another characteristic of successful aging—what George Vaillant calls "future orientation: the ability to anticipate, plan and hope."[15] Yoel explained, "We sold our big home in Santa Barbara. We want to scale down. We don't want to think about stuff." But they have invested in a retirement home there that includes total care, for when that time comes. "We may never go there," Eva said, "but we have it just in case. I never thought I'd live to be eighty, but then I realized that's only two and a half years from now, so I've revised the formula. I now want to think of five years—a five-year plan."

To which Yoel added, "We have a thirty-year marriage contract with an option to renew." So that means that in ten years, at eighty-seven, they'll draw up a new contract. My guess is they'll have a big party—and I'll be there!

CHAPTER 13

The Changing Landscape of Sex When You're Over the Hill

On seeing a beautiful woman, a ninety-something Oliver Wendell Holmes is said to have commented, "Oh, to be seventy again!"

I DON'T THINK THAT 101-YEAR-OLD, BANJO-PLAYING BEN BURKE, whom I wrote about in Chapter 11, lamented over not being seventy anymore. When I interviewed him at an attractive condominium for seniors in Atlanta, Georgia, he told me about his girlfriend, Jocelyn.

"She's got to be ninety-five and a half years old," Ben said. "We were friends while she was living independent, like me, but one day she fell and wound up upstairs in the assisted living department of my condominium."

"Ahh. I knew there was another reason you were going up there besides playing music," I said, gently poking him in the ribs.

"You bet. I've known this lady for, I guess, over three years. As soon as I saw her, I thought, I know my beautiful (late) wife will forgive me, but I got to have a little friendship and she looks like she might supply it. I got her phone number up there and called her. I asked, 'Do you mind if I come by again and share some animal crackers with milk and have a wild time?' She was a little hesitant, but she said, 'Okay, you can come on up.' First time we met, I was a totally perfect gentleman. I cut a banana, two-thirds for me, one-third for her, and we just talked about our background, our life. Her background was Columbia, Alabama. My background was the ghetto of Manhattan. It is like a million miles apart. But it shows you if folks care about each other's company, it don't matter where you come from."

Ben and I had been talking about sex, so I asked him if they had a physical relationship.

"After I had seen her a few times up there, I say, 'You know, Jocelyn, I wonder if we could get a little more intimate.' Was that the right thing to say, Jane?"

"Sure."

"Instead of undressing her like a madman?"

"I'm real proud of you, Ben. That was the right move."

"You know what she says? 'I think it is a little too late.' So I say, 'Well, let's give it a shot.' Now, this is the God's honest truth. The next time I came by to visit her, she was in her pajamas. I said, 'Ask no more.' We got kind of friendly. I says, 'So you're wearing your pajamas?' She was kind of shy. I just started to undress her inch by inch. The first thing is we wound up in the bedroom. We got into bed as is. Like you mentioned before, you can have a great time without penetration. It was like cementing us together as good friends."

"That is so beautiful, Ben." I'd been talking with him about what a shame that all the emphasis is on penetration when there are so many other ways to give and receive pleasure later in life.

"Yeah. She liked it, just the whole experience."

"Skin on skin," I added.

"Yeah."

Ben's not alone in experiencing late-life sensuality. Evelyn Freeman was a licensed therapist, artist, and jewelry maker when, in 1980, she started the Peer Counselor Program at the Senior Health and Peer Counseling Center for Healthy Aging. In 2007, the center merged with WISE Services to become WISE & Healthy

Aging, an agency that provides a variety of support services for people fifty-five years and older.

Retired at eighty-nine, Evelyn was a remarkably beautiful ninety-one when I interviewed her.

"I never expected to be ninety-one," she told me. "So many things I didn't expect. I never expected to be turned on at this age. My husband walks in now, from the pool, nude, and I get sexually turned on. That's such a bonus."

"And can he respond?" I ask.

"Well, not in the way we responded fifty years ago, but he responds with feelings and we touch a lot. But we're not able to be as fully sexual as we were."

I loved hearing these stories from Ben and Evelyn. They fill me with the hope that with any luck, a modicum of health, and a will-

Interviewing Evelyn Freeman at the WISE & Healthy Aging center

MARLENA ROSS, WISE & HEALTHY AGING

ingness to remain open to its potential, the deliciousness of sensual intimacy can continue right to the end.

Collecting Dividends

Dr. Johnnetta Cole, president emerita of Spelman College and Bennett College for Women, the two historical black colleges for women, was seventy-one when I interviewed her in her Atlanta home, and she vibrated with joy and energy. She married her third husband, James David Staton, Jr., at seventy; he is seventeen years younger than she. "In the Third Act sex can be very special," she told me. "While it will probably not be as energetic, as experimental, or as frequent as in the Second Act, it has the possibility of being an important and satisfying part of life now."

"Why?" I asked.

"You can collect dividends from what you've learned in the First and Second Acts to use in the Third. A woman may well know her

Dr. Johnnetta Cole

body better, and she may be at greater peace with her body. In fact, in the Third Act, a woman may become more assertive about sex because she knows what she needs, she knows what she wants, and she is not shy about asking for it. And if a woman in Act III is fortunate enough to have a partner who is also at ease with his or her body, then intimacy, if not sex, can be very special. In my case, how fortunate I am to have a husband who has a deep, nurturing way about him. The way he is no doubt comes from years of being a caretaker for his younger siblings and from being a single parent. I was listening to an NPR story the other day," Johnnetta continued, "and it was talking about aging and sex and how difficult it is for children to imagine their parents in a sexual act. The older the parents are, the more trouble children have with this. The person doing this particular story talked about a woman who was in her late eighties, not in good health, and when asked who should be contacted in a circumstance where somebody needed to be there and be there quickly, she lied. What she really wanted to say was the name of her lover. But she was afraid that her children would find this disgusting, immoral, or bizarre. I think it's really unfortunate that we have so distorted the aging process that we insist on separating growing old from sex . . . something wonderful that many folks in the Third Act can and do enjoy."

I know, of course, that many Third Acters have chosen to pack it in sexually a while ago—for some women, maybe after menopause. For women with low libidos, sex was never an important part of their lives. Chances are, that won't change in this last act. In fact, some women are undoubtedly relieved when, either because of widowhood or a lessening of their own or their partners' sexual drive, they can close the book on that chapter of their lives. In such cases, the man's decision to use sex-enhancing drugs just when his partner thought she'd seen the last of that demanding protuberance can cause anger and resentment. The painful ending of a love affair can also make us want to close up shop. Many widows who had loving, satisfying marriages feel no need or desire to crank it all up again with someone new. There's the story of the elderly couple who had begun dating, really enjoyed each other, and decided it was time to move in together. They discussed finances, their adult children, their living arrangements, and finally the man asked, "How do you feel about sex?" She responded, "Well, I'd have to say I like it infrequently." He paused and then, ever hopeful, said, "Was that one word or two?"

Clearly, a life of stimulating friends, interesting travel, work (paid or volunteer), grandchildren, and hobbies can be wonderful—with or without sex; and none of us should feel we're copping out if this is our choice. This chapter, however, is mainly for those who are still sexually active or would like to be. If you've loved before, you can love again, and the same is true for sex. If there was a time in your life when you enjoyed sex, you can recover that pleasure—if you want to—because Cupid's bow is undeterred by age. In fact, it may fly truer and land deeper. How many times in the last decade have I said that I was through with lovers, wasn't even thinking about relationships anymore? "That part's over for me," I would announce. My women friends would invariably smile and say, "Yeah, okay, Jane, but 'never' is a big word." I was so certain—and then along would come love, and let me tell you (though you can probably imagine), love and good sex are the best rejuvenators, better than any face-lift. And don't think for a minute that older folks aren't getting it on. According to the most comprehensive national survey ever done of sexual behavior among older adults, a lot of us are still doing it. As reported in the *New England Journal of Medicine* in 2007, 84 percent of men from ages fifty-seven to sixty-four reported having had some sexual contact with another person in the last year, compared with 62 percent of women in the same age group. The numbers dropped to 38 percent and 17 percent, respectively, in people seventy-five years and older. But among those seniors who were sexually active, about two-thirds had sex at least twice a month into their seventies, and more than half continued at that pace into their eighties.

There are, however, definite age-related changes. Nearly half of those in the study who were sexually active reported at least one sexual problem, with 43 percent of women reporting diminished desire and 39 percent vaginal dryness; 37 percent of men reported erectile difficulties.

In this chapter I hope to address these changes and perhaps help you manage them. Knowing what to expect of your own body and what to expect of your partner's can make all the difference. Some of the changes are positive, and almost all can be dealt with by giving yourself more time to have sex. Other things that can help include patience, communication between partners, appropriate use of sexuality-enhancing drugs, and some basic knowledge.

Men and Health

There is nothing about aging in and of itself that gets in the way of our having sex. Health problems and medications are the key impediments—more so in men than in women. Only 10 percent of women report that their cessation of sex was due to their own illness or lack of interest. Mainly it is due to scarcity of appropriate partners (for every fifty-one men aged seventy-five and older, there are one hundred women!), illness of the spouse, or inability of the spouse to have intercourse. Dr. Michael Perelman, a clinical associate professor of psychiatry, reproductive medicine, and urology at Weill Cornell Medical College and codirector of the Human Sexuality Program at New York Presbyterian Hospital, told me that the health of the male partner is probably the strongest determinant in whether or not a couple continues to have sex. His failure to perform as he has in the past can become so bothersome to him emotionally that he will develop a pattern of avoidance that is as damaging as the lack of erectile function itself. Avoidance can become a habit and cause the man to pull back from giving or receiving *any* form of affection, for fear that he will be expected to follow up by performing sexually.

In *New Passages,* Gail Sheehy cites the Massachusetts Male Aging

Study: "51% of normal, healthy males aged 40 to 70 experience some degree of impotence," caused by medications, heart problems, diabetes, or anything that impedes blood flow to the penis. The effects of these health issues on sexual performance vary greatly from man to man, but generally they result in:

- Taking longer to get erections and requiring more direct manual stimulation.
- Erections are less firm and harder to maintain because of changes in blood flow.
- The penis starts to get smaller with age.
- Taking longer to reach orgasm (just what women have always wished for!).
- If there is orgasm, the force of ejaculation is reduced.
- There are fewer contractions.
- More time is needed between erections.
- Peyronie's disease is a condition that affects approximately 10 percent of older men, causing their penis to shorten and curve during erection.

Diabetes is the most common cause of male impotence, yet, interestingly, 80 percent of diabetic women do not lose their sexual desire or ability to orgasm. In *The Fountain of Age,* Betty Friedan conjectures that the explanation for this disparity might "simply be that male sexuality is equated with 'erectile capacity,' and not with total sexual responsiveness, which remains unimpaired in female diabetics." Friedan wonders, as do I, whether, if we moved the focus of male sexuality from a preoccupation with the erection to a more all-over sexuality, diabetic men wouldn't remain sexual the way their female counterparts do.[1]

Erections

We pay way too much attention to the importance of an erect, hard penis. More accurately, men pay too much attention to this,

and, all too often, if erectile dysfunction (ED) inhibits their erections, they will lose confidence and interest in sex. Some will
blame their older wife and seek out younger partners; however,
this doesn't always work out. A younger woman may be more
physically attractive, but she may be expecting the youthful, phal-
lic model of sexual intimacy, even though a sizable percentage of
women (if not most) are unable to experience orgasm from intercourse alone and require extended clitoral stimulation. A confident older woman can bring more to the bed: experience, empathy,
and understanding—especially an understanding of her own sexuality and the reality that her pleasure is not exclusively dependent
on penile penetration. The late Dr. Helen Kaplan was a
world-famous sex therapist and the director of Human Sexuality
Program at New York Hospital–Cornell Medical Center. When
interviewed by Betty Friedan for *The Fountain of Age,* she said, "The
older woman who is loving and sure enough accommodates herself to these age-related changes—they have oral sex. Do it in the
morning, whatever. . . . The paradox is the older woman is likely to
be much more accepting of his reality and his vulnerability. . . . A
man can have a million dollars but his penis is still sixty-eight
years old. An older man can be a wonderful partner, a wonderful
lover, if they both can get away from that obsession with the penis
and the performance."[2]

If men insist on trying to repeat the youthful model of sexuality in the Third Act, they will miss out on discovering the pleasure and intimacy that can occur later in life, when the slowing
down and showing up of two mature, trusting, fully realized people allow for a deeper intimacy and more holistic sensuality. Older
women have a greater potential for sexual agency, claiming their
pleasure without fear of being too forward, while, conversely,
older men are freed to experience a deeper connection and intimacy. At last, perhaps, the two genders can come together with
greater sexual compatibility than ever. For most of us, this doesn't
just happen. It takes working at it with courage, humor, and
intentionality.

Differentiation

In *Passionate Marriage,* Dr. David Schnarch writes, "Sex isn't a natural function—at least, not intimate sex. Intimate sex is a natural *potential* that requires development for its fulfillment.' "[3] Part of the development that Schnarch writes about is "differentiation"—that is to say, when an individual stands on their own two feet and becomes a whole, more confident, self-validated person, unafraid to claim their desire. "Differentiation" is another name for what Carl Jung called "individuation," which I discussed in the last chapter. Many older women, myself included, were raised feeling that "good girls" didn't show desire. We were recipients of the desire of others, pleasers who dared not ask for what we needed for sexual fulfillment. This harmful double standard is still all too prevalent today, and girls are harmed because of it. As I wrote in the last chapter, women in their Third Acts tend to gain confidence, self-understanding, and self-control, and become more able to stay in relationship to themselves while in a relationship with a partner. When we feel confident, we are more able to reveal all of ourselves to a partner. Intimacy requires a stable identity.

As Dr. Schnarch writes, "If sexual intimacy has to do with disclosing yourself through sex, people who can let themselves be known have more potential for profound sexual experiences."[4] It took me longer than some, perhaps, but I know that because I have finally become my own person now—with a lot of work, on my own and in therapy—I am also a better, more sensuous lover than when I was younger. I've kept my body in pretty good shape, but there is no way that a woman in her seventies can have as taut and toned a body as a younger woman. Gravity takes its toll; the skin loosens. Still, when I think back to the time when, physically, I was at my peak, neither my pleasure nor the pleasure I gave was as deep as now or as much fun. As Dr. Schnarch writes, "It's not about how your body looks or how you position it, it's about your frame of mind and emotional connection with your partner. It's not about frequency of sex; it's about eroticism. It's not about technique; it's about integrating your head with your genitals."[5] Language, self-confidence, and self-awareness permit us to bring meaning to sex beyond just the knee-jerk reaction of lubrication, erection, orgasm. We can talk to each other, gaze into each other's eyes. "The brain," says Dr. Schnarch, "is our biggest sex organ."[6] He also points out that "emotional stimulation is often a more powerful determinant of genital function and satisfaction than is touch."[7] Happily, this coincides with the age-related changes in sexuality that can be offset, to an amazing extent, by a shift from the biological drive to thoughts and feelings as determinants of our sexuality.

Freed of the need to "perform," men who have trouble getting erections may be able to experience a whole new type of sexual intimacy that has no boundaries. The entire body becomes sexualized, and the experience can last for hours. Just what women have longed for! Now, when both women and men need more tactile stimulation—touching, massaging, stimulation with hands and mouth—we need to get comfortable about asking for what we want instead of thinking that "if he really loved me, he would just know." Our partners aren't mind readers, and what may be good for them may not do the trick for us. He might love knowing how to please you more. Tell him. Show him. Teach him. Read the books. Read them together. Ask him to tell you what he likes, and then implement what he asks for. This will encourage him to do the same for you. Don't leave out his nipples. Many men's nipples are highly sensitive, and suckling on them may be just what he needs to get aroused.

We must not assume that lack of erection means the man is not attracted to us or is unable to provide exquisite pleasure. "Remove the belief that sex is intercourse," writes Dr. Marty Klein, "and all those non-erect penises become non-problematic. . . . That's what modern older people need—a new way to think about sex so that they can be sexual regardless of physical capacity." [8]

I like what Gail Sheehy writes in her book *New Passages*: "The mature man is ready to graduate from adolescent 'racing-car sex' to 'body-surfing sex.' Imagine riding the waves of love, moving up with the swells of pleasure when sexual energy is high and down with ebbs of intensity, when love and stroking can be enjoyed, then up on the next pleasure wave, and down in the rest cycle, when partners just lie there breathing and holding each other and whispering love, until they feel the next wave of sexual energy starting to rise again."[9] This requires trust and the investment of time. It means giving up the performance-oriented striving for orgasm. If orgasm does come, it will be much more profound, because the body is so ripe with sexual energy. Whether or not there is orgasm, whether or not the penis is erect, this approach to lovemaking demonstrates the matured power of the man to give and receive pleasure and love.

Erica Jong, the author of twenty-one books of poetry, fiction, and nonfiction, including the acclaimed novel about women's sexuality *Fear of Flying*, told me that when her husband takes medications to keep his blood pressure down, it makes sex difficult.

"So," Erica explained, "we've discovered tantric sex, which I always thought didn't exist. Boy, was I wrong. It took a long time to get there, but we have amazing sex when we can stop running around and arrange to be alone together."

In her original *Passages* book, Gail Sheehy postulates that the holding back of orgasm so as to extend pleasure, what is called tantric sex, was developed by the Chinese because, unlike Western culture, age is venerated in that culture, so they want us to keep having fun![10]

"How did you discover tantric sex?" I asked Erica.

"We started to do oral sex and touching and looking at each other, and he discovered he could have an incredibly intense orgasm when I came through oral sex."

I asked my friend Dr. Bill Stayton, the sex therapist I wrote about in the previous chapter, how he would define a really good lover. "The best lover," Stayton answered, "is the one who really enjoys the *process* of lovemaking without it having to have a certain goal—the old orgasm goal-oriented model. The process is what's very exciting. The process is making love. When you're orgasm-oriented, everything is the orgasm, the erection. Think of all the fun you have getting there." Lucky Erica Jong. Clearly her husband fits Stayton's description of the best lover.

"One of the things we know is that as a man gets older, he has less need to ejaculate," Dr. Stayton explained. "It is important that men know that erection, orgasm, and ejaculation are three separate events and are not dependent upon each other. You can have an orgasm without an erection or an ejaculation. You can have an ejaculation without an erection or an orgasm."

There's no doubt that the sexual landscape will continue to change as those in the huge cohort of baby boomers enter their Third Acts. Age simply isn't going to get in the way of their interest in and enjoyment of an active, robust sex life. After all, numerous studies have shown that, in addition to providing pleasure, an intimate, satisfying sexual relationship reduces the risk of heart disease, depression, migraine, arthritis, and stress, and boosts the immune system. My friend Reverend Debra Haffner (who is also a sexologist and a boomer) puts it this way: "Boomers will change

Reverend
Debra Haffner

how the culture thinks about sex and aging. We think we discovered sex, and we're not going to give it up easily. With new medications such as hormone replacement therapy, Viagra, Cialis, Levitra, et cetera, our knees and backs will give out before our genitals do!" Tell me about it!

Match.com, the world's leading online dating service, claims that people over fifty are the fastest-growing age group using its site. And X-rated films showing older women and men are reputed to make up the fastest-growing area of the video porn market!

Women's Bodies

Alongside men's age-related changes, there are plenty of changes happening to women's bodies, and we do well to anticipate and understand them.

- There will be less vaginal lubrication, and lubrication will take longer.
- The lining of the labia thins and becomes more apt to tear.
- The vagina loses some elasticity.
- We experience fewer uterine contractions with orgasm and, because of a drop in estrogen, the pressure sensors deep in the cervix will lose some of the sensation of thrusting. This may be remedied with estrogen replacement, which I will discuss further in the next chapter.
- According to a Kaiser Family Foundation report, the aging process itself seems to increase women's susceptibility to infection . . . possibly due to thinning of the vaginal walls and abrasion resulting from insufficient lubrication.

If you have been celibate for a long time and then begin a new love affair, be aware that your vagina is likely to need some attention. You would do well to have a gynecologist to turn to for answers to your questions and for prescriptions for such things as bladder, urinary tract, and yeast infections and tears in the vaginal walls.

Some women find that intercourse is painful because their vagina has shrunk. I interviewed gynecologist Dr. Michelle Warren, medical director at the Center for Menopause, Hormonal Disorders, and Women's Health at Columbia University Medical Center New York. She told me, "I had a patient the other day who has just remarried; she is in her seventies. She called me from Florida and said, 'Even with the vaginal estrogen you have given me, I just can't have intercourse, and I don't know what to do.' I sent her some vaginal dilators, a series of progressively larger plastic molds that you insert into the vagina for twenty minutes to an hour a day and gradually they expand the vagina, and she came back and said, 'Oh, you saved my life!' She used the dilators along with the estrogen and she was able to resume an active sex life." Conversely, the vagina may have stretched so that the man's penis doesn't experience enough friction to cause ejaculation. In this case, regularly performed Kegel exercises that strengthen vaginal and pubococcygeus muscles are helpful. I explain these exercises later in this chapter. If, because of childbearing, these pelvic muscles have been badly torn, an operation can be performed to repair and tighten them. Such an operation requires about six to eight weeks of recovery before intercourse can be resumed.

Just because our culture assumes that women want to be sexual only in the context of a monogamous love relationship shouldn't cause us to ignore the possibility of recreational sex with a partner of any age—or even without a partner.

The most important message in keeping sexually active is keeping sexually active. *Use it or lose it.* A broken arm atrophies. Penises that aren't being used have more problems with erectile dysfunction. Vaginas that aren't being used have more problems with elasticity. As a result, if you are experiencing any of these problems and want to prepare yourself for an active sex life, all the experts I have talked to recommend masturbation. This can be with your hand, your partner's hand, or a vibrator.

Masturbation

A 1995 study by the National Opinion Research Center showed that fewer than half of all women in the United States masturbate; even fewer do so regularly. Dr. Louann Brizendine, a pioneering neuropsychiatrist at the University of California, San Francisco, and the founder of the Women's and Teen Girls' Mood and Hormone Clinic, says, "Studies in nursing homes have shown that a quarter of women age seventy to ninety still masturbate."[11] Dr. Michael Perelman told me, "I think it would shock some of your younger readers the extent to which older individuals will use sex toys and enjoy them. Again, that is another wonderful adjunct and it can be done by people of all ages merely to help create variety, or it can be something that can help as an assistance, much in the same way someone would use a cane. A vibrator provides more stimulation, and especially as people age, the use of these toys could be quite helpful, and I think the next generation is probably more likely to do that than the current generation of very elderly people."

Obviously, a loving relationship of mutual pleasure-giving is preferable to solo masturbation, but that is not always an option. If we want to stay ready for love, it is good to keep our sensual selves tuned up—you never know what will happen a week, a month, a year or two from now. As I said earlier, I was celibate for seven years after my marriage to Ted Turner and thought that was the end of it. I was wrong!

If you are not used to masturbating and your own hand is not sufficient to excite you, I recommend that you buy a vibrator and some of the newest lubricants, make yourself comfortable, maybe even try reading a book while you masturbate so you are more relaxed and forget about what you're hoping will happen. This is no time for performance anxieties! Please try to get over any concerns you have about the appropriateness of pleasuring yourself. Think of masturbation as a medical necessity: You may find that it will not only improve the health of your vagina but your general disposition, as well.

There are so many different kinds of vibrators. Almost any good pharmacy sells the long, white, plug-in vibrator called the Magic Wand, made by Hitachi, with two intensities, high and low. It is sold as a body massager. The Eroscillator, which has been highly recommended by Dr. Ruth Westheimer, oscillates rather than vibrates, and does it at thirty-six hundred oscillations a minute. The sensation is gentler, faster, and feels like the wings of a flying hummingbird. It has five interchangeable attachments and comes with a book written by Dr. Ruth that explains how to use the attachments.

Then there is the Rabbit, a vibrator that became famous when it was featured in an episode of *Sex and the City*. It is so named because a little rabbit resides at the end of a rotating and vibrating shaft with about 5 inches of penetration. The ears of the Rabbit vibrate against the clitoris while the shaft is whirling around and stimulating the erogenous places in the vagina.

The most high-end, cutting-edge sex toys I've found on the market today are made by two companies, LELO and Jimmyjane. They are apparently made from medical-grade silicone, and must be used with water-based lubricants only. Using silicone lubricant with a silicone-based sex toy will eventually ruin it. If cared for properly, good sex toys can last for many years.

At the end of this chapter are the names of two sources of sex products for women; both companies will send you their catalogs. From either one, you can get two classic books about masturbation, *Sex for One,* by Betty Dodson, and *For Yourself,* by Dr. Lonnie Barbach. These have been in print for thirty-five years, proof that women continue to view masturbation as a loving ritual.

In the old days, K-Y Jelly was all you could get, but today a wide variety of lubricants are available. Some are more viscous than others. Lubricants come in two basic types: silicone-based and water-based. Silicone-based lubricants are known to last longer and provide greater stimulation and, as a result, are used primarily for intercourse. Water-based lubricants come in a variety of flavors and are used more for oral sex and when using sex toys. The lubricants that I have heard recommended most often are Pjur (pronounced *pure*), which is made in Germany, and Sliquid. These apparently do not contain glycerine and sugar, which can encourage yeast infections. Both companies make both silicone- and water-based lubricants. Sliquid comes in a variety of flavors such as green apple tart and blue raspberry.

Try things out until you find what works best for you. With or without a partner, lubricants are the friends of Third Acters, and you should take their use for granted.

During my interview with psychologist Dr. Michael Perelman, he said, "I think one of the tricky things, because of the politics of our time, is to understand how well being selfish in bed can work; that everybody needs to take care of themselves a little bit. You want to be a sensitive lover, but you also want to make sure that you are not worrying so much about pleasing your partner that you fail to please yourself. It is kind of a paradox; the more you can lose yourself in experiencing pleasure with the other person, actually the more pleasure they are going to get from realizing how desirable they are and how sexy they are, because look at how excited you are getting. If you worry too much about just pleasing the other person, and not getting excited yourself, you are actually depriving them of having that same reaction from you."

Practical Suggestions

Here are some practical suggestions for achieving a more satisfying sex life:

- It's critical to try to resolve any issues you have with your partner. Anger and resentment are surefire libido killers.

Talk things through, or find a good couples counselor or sex therapist and be brave enough to work through it.

• Besides anger, boredom can take a toll on sexuality, so try doing new things with your long-term partner, both in bed and out in the world. In bed, masturbating together can be a delicious new way of revving things up. Explore other parts of your bodies and discover new ways to give each other pleasure, especially a man's nipples. Many if not most men need this particular stimulation now more than ever.

• Learn about the G-spot. The G-spot, named in honor of Dr. Ernst Gräfenberg, a prominent figure in early-twentieth-century gynecology, is a small region of the female anatomy many regard as an erogenous zone responsible for intense orgasms. The G-spot, which is commonly considered an element of the female prostate, is located on the front vaginal wall, approximately two or three inches inside the vagina. When the area is stimulated, powerful sexual arousal and female ejaculation may occur. There is ongoing controversy over the physiological structure and exact location of the G-spot, but recent research utilizing ultrasound imaging does provide information with regard to the G-spot's location and how it relates to erogenous stimulation in women who have orgasms during intercourse.

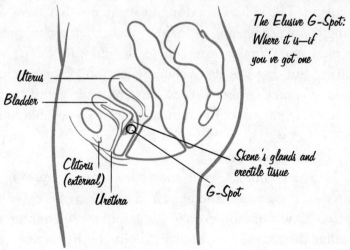

The Elusive G-Spot: Where it is—if you've got one

Uterus

Bladder

Clitoris (external)

Urethra

Skene's glands and erectile tissue

G-Spot

• Try reading sexy books together or watching sexy videos. Whereas the older erotic videos were made primarily to stimulate men, today there are videos made by and targeted for women (though men can enjoy them as well). The *Psychiatric Annals* mentions Candida Royalle (Femme Productions) and Jane Hamilton (also called Veronica Hart) as good examples of producers.[12] The couples in this new genre of erotica seem more loving and genuinely turned on, and it is the women who initiate sex. Videos showing tantric sex are more woman-friendly. And a growing number of videos feature older couples being erotic. By the way, if your partner likes to watch erotic pictures or videos during lovemaking, don't feel it means he finds you unsatisfying. Just keep in mind that men respond more to visual stimulation than women do and that older men in particular need more stimulation. Instead of letting it upset you, think of it as his way to be a better, more aroused lover for you. The very fact that you are the one to bring home a new video and propose watching it changes the dynamic, and puts you in charge, and you may find that you enjoy watching as much as he does. A sex therapy video series, Guides to Sexual Pleasure, was created by three of this country's top sex therapists: Reverend Dr. Bill Stayton, Dr. Herb Samuels, and Dr. Joy Davidson. The videos are done in segments that show real, loving couples engaging in loving touch, then techniques of foreplay, and, finally, intercourse. I find the videos very exciting, but they are also a therapeutic tool. Each one has a "therapy choice" where suggestions are made about how to view each segment, followed by suggestions on what a couple can do after watching the video. (See the end of this chapter for more information.)

• Learn to stimulate your and your partner's senses in the bedroom, suggests sex therapist and psychiatrist Dr. Barbara Bartlik. "One common exercise," she told me in an interview, "is called the Five Senses. I tell my client, 'Each time you make love, bring into the bedroom something that stimulates one of your senses.' So that might be that you bring a glass of wine into the bedroom and drink it from each other's mouths. Or you bring in chocolate sauce and lick it off each other. Drape a red scarf over your bedside lamp to create a dim, sexy aura. Learn to talk dirty to each other, read an erotic story out loud. Try the synthetic body scents or pheromones made by the Athena Institute, which can help with arousal. They mimic the body's own pheromones, which are secreted by the underarms and genitalia in the highest concentrations. As you get older they get less strong." You can find out more about pheromones from AthenaInstitute.com.

• Try having sex in the morning or afternoon, when you both are less apt to be tired.

• Start an exercise regimen so that you feel better and more confident about yourself. Your body will be more toned and—most important—flexible. Try dancing or yoga, something that involves the whole body.

• Start doing Kegel exercises. Named after Dr. Arnold Kegel, these are exercises to strengthen the pubococcygeus (pew-bo-cok-si-JEE-us) muscle, a hammock-like band of tissue that stretches from the pubic bone, in the front, to the

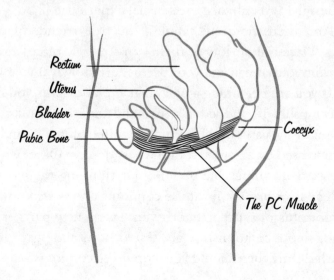

Rectum
Uterus
Bladder
Pubic Bone
Coccyx
The PC Muscle

tailbone, in the back, and to tighten the vaginal muscles. They also help prevent urinary incontinence. The PC muscle is sometimes called the "love muscle" because, along with supporting all the pelvic organs, such as the bladder, it helps the vaginal muscles work. Directions for doing Kegels are at the end of this chapter.

• Take an anti-inflammatory such as Aleve twenty minutes before sex so you won't feel the aches and pains.

• Take a romantic bath or shower together.

• Choose the sexiest turn-on music you can find. In fact, make a point of collecting sexy music you both like. Load the music onto an iPod so you'll have it all in one easy-to-transport place.

• Take a course in giving a massage or get a good video of erotic massaging and treat each other to one. It has been said that, along with the brain, the skin is the most erotic part of the body. The book *Erotic Massage,* by Charla Hathaway, is a classic about the art of this loving ritual. I can also recommend the DVD *The Joy of Erotic Massage,* produced by the Sinclair Institute and narrated by the notable sexologist Louise-Andree Saulnier. Try using scented massage oils (the Kama Sutra line is very desirable), organic lubricants, or other love oils designed to enhance the sensual experience.

• And then there are candles, the true friends of older lovers. Place them—lots of them—in strategic places around the room so that you and your partner are shown at your best.

• If you are beginning a new sexual relationship, you must protect yourself! Individuals fifty and older account for 11 percent of the cases of AIDS in the United States . . . and this has increased by 22 percent in the past decade. Older women are especially vulnerable because our thinning vaginal walls can tear so easily. We must use condoms unless we know the health status of our partner. If you have a new partner in a monogamous relationship, get tested now, and again in six months. Only then should you stop using condoms.

This chapter has been about the ways in which sex changes with age. The following chapter talks about some of the ways we can mitigate those changes.

Some Suggested Readings, Videos, and Sex Shops

The Good Vibrations Guide to Sex by Cathy Winks and Anne Semans (Cleis Press, 1994)—how to have safe, fun sex . . . tips and techniques from the folks who run one of America's favorite sex-toy stores

Good Vibrations—books and sexual products for women and couples
1210 Valencia Street
San Francisco, CA 94110
(415) 974-8990

Eve's Garden
119 West 57th Street
Suite 1406
New York, NY 10019
(212) 757-8651

Sex therapy video series (*Sexual Pleasure*, available in three editions: *Heterosexual Couples*, *Lesbian Couples*, and *Gay Couples*). For information visit www.HSAB.org.

KEGEL EXERCISES

The goal is to squeeze and release your PC muscle 200 times a day, using both slow movements and rapid ones. (See page 221 for diagram of muscle location.) You can start slow—three slow sets a day five days a week—and work your way up. This gets easier as you do more of them.

The Slow Squeeze

Squeeze for 10 seconds as though you're trying to stop the flow of urine, then relax for 10 seconds. Do this 10 times. (You may want to start with 3 seconds and work up to 10, but the squeeze and the release should always be of the same duration.)

The Quick Squeeze

Squeeze and release the PC muscle as rapidly as you can for 2 minutes; don't forget to breathe normally throughout.

Try to do the exercises in various positions—standing, lying down, sitting—including on the toilet while urinating. Think of trying to stop the flow of urine.

Your ob-gyn can provide you with a prescription for small weights of graduating heaviness that are inserted into the vagina while you perform the Kegels. This focuses your awareness and gives you something to resist . . . a vagina workout, if you will.

CHAPTER 14

CHAPTER 14

The Lowdown on Getting It Up in the Third Act

Those searching for the fountain of youth may be surprised to learn that perhaps the easiest and most natural way to achieve healthy aging isn't found in the doctor's office, drug laboratory or rain forest, but in the bedroom.

—ROGER LIBBY

In our relationships, how much can we allow them to become new, and how much do we cling to what they used to be yesterday?

—RAM DASS

IN THE OLD DAYS—BACK IN 1998, WHEN VIAGRA WAS FIRST APPROVED for commercial sale—the thinking was that as long as a man could get an erection, a good sex life was ensured. According to a 2007 report from the *New England Journal of Medicine,* one out of seven men use the sexual pharmaceuticals Viagra, Levitra, or Cialis. There's no question that these phosphodiestease inhibitors, or PDE5s as they're called, have done a lot to enhance sexual capacity. For some men they can turn back the clock, say, ten years. But a panacea they aren't. If a man and his partner expect these drugs to be the Fountain of Youth, they will be disappointed. On their own, the drugs don't produce an erection. What they do is make the blood flow into the penis possible. But without desire on the man's part and a great deal of direct stimulation of the penis (way more than when we were young), the erection won't happen.

Drugs and Other Methods to Address Erectile Dysfunction

Let's look at each of the drugs currently on the market. But first of all, remember that, erection-wise, the results of each drug will vary from man to man. And these drugs are not without possible side effects, some of which may be serious for certain people, so you really must consult your own doctor about all of this.

Generally, Viagra is effective for from one to four hours. However, because the pill works fastest if it is taken on an empty stomach, a guy who is planning to have sex in the evening needs to time things rather carefully. Gone are the days of having a long romantic dinner with good wine, going straight home while there's still a buzz, and getting right to it. Now he will probably want to wait for an hour or so after dinner and then ingest the pill, then wait thirty to sixty minutes for it to take effect. Alternatively, the pill can be taken prior to dinner, but some men may experience indigestion as a result. The effects of Levitra can be very similar, but Levitra may be taken with or without food. The effects of Cialis are supposed to last thirty-six hours, but you can't always count on that, either. Some men have told me that they take Cialis and then, after a while, as the time for sex approaches, they add a Viagra for a little bump. Combining erectile dysfunction medications can be quite dangerous, however, so never mix and match unless you are instructed to do so by a medical doctor who is experienced in prescribing these drugs (and then follow instructions carefully).

It can be important, at this stage of life, for both partners to know if sex is on the agenda on a given day or evening. The pills are not cheap. It can be a source of irritation if the man has taken a pill, expecting to have sex, only to discover that his partner isn't interested. Talk about crossed signals: One night I took a sleeping pill just as my partner came in telling me he'd taken a Levitra. We proceeded (lazily) down his chosen path and it was not uninteresting (hated to waste all that money), but we won't make that mistake again. Let's face it: Sexual spontaneity may be harder to come by or a thing of the past for many Third Acters. Then again, advance planning—anticipation and fantasy—can be sexy in itself.

Dr. Michael Perelman, a clinical associate professor of psychiatry, reproductive medicine, and urology at Weill Cornell Medical College, explained to me that "it's particularly important for some men to realize that just taking the pills will not give them an erection. Yes, sexual pharmaceuticals can restore function, but you still need the same kind of friction you always needed, only more of it for a longer time, and you need romantic or hot, sexy thoughts for the pill to result in the best experiences sexually." They should put this advice on the label: *Take pill. Add friction and fantasy.*

Besides the pills, there is a tool called a penis ring, a thick, flexible rubber ring that comes in varying widths and tightnesses. You slide it down the shaft to the base of the penis and it keeps the penis engorged with blood in the same way a tourniquet works. This is important because many older men experience venous leakage. There is one valve that allows blood to enter the penis and another one that keeps the blood in the penis and then lets it out. When that valve develops a leak, the man can get a hard-on but loses it right away. Pleasurable results can also be had by encircling the testicles within the ring as well as the shaft. Such a ring should be thicker and softer as well as larger. Then a second cock ring could be added, just around the penis, to give added strength to the erection. In fact, in general, softer and thicker is better than harder and thinner. Such skinnier rings can be painful. It may take a while before you or your partner finds a ring that is the right size and fit, but it is worth the investment! Some top-of-the-line rings come with vibrators on top for stimulating the clitoris as well as the penis during intercourse. Properly positioned, these rings can give tremendous pleasure to both partners. Along with lubricants, penis rings should be a permanent part of any senior's sexual tool kit. Rings should not be worn for more than thirty minutes without taking them off for a short break to avoid any potential damage to the delicate penile tissue. Never fall asleep with one on!

Penile injections before sex can be effective. They are done with a very fine needle, and if applied at the part of the shaft where there are no nerves, they are painless. Eighty percent of the men who try these respond very well. It gives a man a predictable, reliable erection about five minutes after the injection. But as Dr. J. Francois Eid said in an Internet videoconference about erectile dysfunction, "I have a lot of compassion for men who try injections. It takes courage and also it doesn't feel natural. Each time you want to make love, you have to excuse yourself and take an injection." Dr. Eid also noted, "I have to tell you that approximately 80 percent of patients will drop out of injection therapy the first year. Over 50 percent of the patients that start injections stop in the first two months of therapy. So yes, it is effective. It is a good treatment. But it takes a lot of motivation to do it."

Dr. Perelman said, "One thing to point out is by working with the man and his partner, we can actually improve that 80 percent dropout rate by helping the couple introduce their intimacy again in a way that takes into consideration the female partner's needs as well as just providing an erection."

Perhaps the partner could learn to give the injection and the couple could learn to see this joint effort (pardon the pun) as part of foreplay. I know it sounds so dramatic, sticking a needle into a penis, but with few nerve endings in the area where the needle is inserted, you really can't feel anything.

The **vacuum pump** is a plastic tube that is placed over the penis. A hand-powered or battery-powered pump will activate the vacuum, drawing blood into the penis in the same way a breast pump works. Like injections, the vacuum pump works for 70 to 80 percent of men. Personally, I always found that breast pumps were too painful, and many men have found these pumps to be the same. The hair at the base of the penis may need to be trimmed or shaved and then, after an erection has been obtained, a rubber penis ring is rolled off the end of the pump to encircle the base of the penis so as to keep the blood trapped inside. The pump is a simple, one-time purchase that requires a prescription. If the erection from use of one of the ED pills begins to wane, the pump can be used to get it up again. Doctors at the Mayo Clinic say that the pump can also be used apart from intercourse as a way to exercise the penis by bringing blood into it, irrespective of intercourse.

Self-administered intraurethral therapy (Muse). This treatment involves using a disposable applicator to insert a tiny suppository, about half the size of a grain of rice, into the tip of the penis. (A flashlight will help you see exactly what you are doing! Try holding a small one in your mouth during the insertion to light your way.) The suppository, placed about two inches into the urethra, is absorbed by erectile tissue in the penis, increasing the blood flow and causing an erection within approximately three minutes. Absorption is helped by rolling the penis between the palms of the hands for a minute or longer. The erection should last from forty-five minutes to an hour. Side effects may include pain, burning, minor bleeding in the urethra, dizziness, and formation of fibrous tissue in the urethra. In fact, 10 to 20 percent of men experience pain or burning with Muse or injections. If your urologist prescribes Muse, be sure that both you and your partner go on the website to get all the instructions. Doctors don't always explain everything, but you can ask. For instance, it was only on the website that I learned that you should hold the penis upright before and during insertion of the pill and then, after rolling the penis between your palms, as previously described, walk around for a few minutes, holding the penis upright, to increase the blood flow.

If the sexual pharmaceuticals, injections, vacuum pumps, and suppositories have not worked for a man, the next thing to consider is the penile pump.

The penile pump consists of two or three devices. The pump is inserted through a small incision in the scrotum and placed invisibly within a fatty deposit between the testicles. A reservoir cylinder is placed next to the bladder, in the lower abdomen, and another

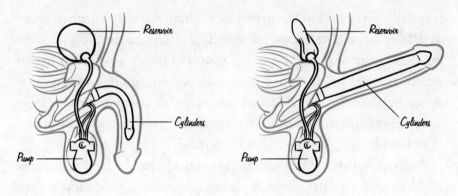

soft cylinder goes into the penile shaft. None of the penile nerves
are cut or damaged. When the pump is squeezed, a saline solution
is pumped from the reservoir into the cylinder in the penis to create an erection for as long as is desired. When sex is over, the solution is pumped back into the reservoir.

When flaccid, the penis looks entirely normal—locker room
safe. No one can tell that a device has been implanted. I am told
it looks and feels so natural that some men never let on, and their
partners don't know. I think that if a man is in a committed relationship, there should be full disclosure and the implant and
pump should become part of foreplay in the same way that putting on a condom can become a sexy act. The pump, after all, is
evidence that the man is truly committed to giving as well as
receiving pleasure.

Because the penis itself has not been damaged, the man has the
same feelings as he did during intercourse prior to the procedure,
and he can still have an orgasm and father children. For men suffering from Peyronie's disease, which causes pain or bending of the
penis during erection, the pump may be the best solution. For
healthy men, infection rates are low; men with diabetes are at
higher risk of infection. The insertion currently involves a
forty-minute procedure requiring a twenty-four-hour hospital
stay; as of this writing, costs run between $12,000 and $20,000,
depending on the hospital. Coverage of this procedure by medical
insurance depends on one's insurance policy. Medicare now covers

it completely, except for the co-pay. Other insurers will cover it if it is in the man's contract and depending on the cause of the ED.

The device needs to be replaced, on average, every ten years. I am told that, according to many doctors treating sexual dysfunction, the penile pump has a 99 percent satisfaction rate. Dr. Tom Lue, an internationally recognized expert in the treatment of male sexual dysfunction at the University of California, San Francisco, says, "The reason for the high satisfaction rate is that, first of all, you look like a normal person. No one sees any difference. But you can pump it up anytime you want and it will last as long as you want it to. Think about that. You can have sex twenty-four times a day if you want. It can last two hours, three hours, as long as you want!"

Can Sexual Pharmaceuticals Make for a Good Sex Life?

These advances in penile enhancements and drugs may be great for many men and their partners, but Dr. Perelman, who views sexuality from a psychological as well as a physical viewpoint, says, "Restoring a man's erectile capacity does not necessarily make for a good sex life for either the man or his partner because there is a whole range of psychosocial-behavioral-cultural issues that impact people's sexuality. Both the men and their partners need to understand where these medications will make a difference and where they won't."

They won't help mend marital conflicts. According to Dr. Perelman, the problem in about 10 percent of the cases he sees is that the woman is not receptive, and a pill won't help the man become a more sensitive lover so that she will become receptive. The man may come home having popped a Viagra, eagerly looking forward to the joy of putting his erect penis to good use. *"Hey, honey, I took this pill, let's go!"* But women are more contextual; they need foreplay (so do older men!), and this can create conflict.

So imagine, instead, this alternative positive scenario: The man calls ahead and says, "Sweetheart, I've been longing for you all day and I'm feeling like I should take the pill right now before I get home, *but I want you to want it, too.* What do you think about turning on some romantic music and lighting some candles so you'll be in the mood when I get there?"

Or the man comes home and his wife is preparing dinner at the sink. He comes up behind her and begins to kiss and nibble her neck. "How about we move to the couch and make out a little," he tells her. "I'm hungrier for you than for dinner right now." When he sees that she is getting turned on, he asks, "Should I go get a pill? Would you like that?"

In these kinds of scenarios, the erection occurs within a mutual context of desire. Then, once this happens, the partner needs to let the man know what she likes him to do now that he has his erection—what positions, what speed, more foreplay, and so on. Whatever happens or doesn't happen, why not celebrate and be grateful that your partner brought his erection home to you rather than to someone else! Perhaps thinking about that fact alone can be a turn-on.

The Mental Aspects of Arousal

Clearly there is a dynamic balance between mind and body, and it isn't static. Dr. Perelman says, "Being turned on is mental and physical, and so is being turned off. Positive mental and physical factors increase the likelihood of a response, while negative mental and physical factors inhibit the sexual response." Because women's sexual response is generally more context-sensitive than men's, a combination of medical and psychological treatments can be especially effective. And Jane Brody notes, "While a Viagra-like drug is not yet an option for women, use of the antidepressant bupropion (Wellbutrin at 300 milligrams a day) may improve sexual arousal and satisfaction in women who are not depressed."[1] However, numerous clinical trials are currently being conducted worldwide to identify compounds to assist women with their sexual response.

Dr. Bill Stayton, sex therapist and former executive director of the Center for Sexuality and Religion at Morehouse School of

Medicine, pointed out to me that one of the biggest culprits in sexual dysfunction is being an observer of yourself. A man may wonder, he said, " 'Am I going to get it up? Is it going to stay up? Is it going to come too quickly? Am I not going to come at all?' So, on his side, you've got two people in bed, you've got the guy thinking about it and you've got the guy trying to do it. And then you have another two people in bed on the other side when the partner begins to think, 'Is it me? I mean, why isn't it working? He took the pill, what happened? Maybe he's really not turned on by me?' So now you've got four people in bed. What's going on is between the two observers, and the two actual people in bed get shot out the window. So," Dr. Stayton noted, "pharmaceuticals can be great if they are in a proper perspective and the person is really turned on to making love and not observing. First thing we do is kick the observers out of the bedroom."

Creating a combination treatment by adding counseling and education to the mix, along with the pharmaceuticals, may be what is needed to create a positive sexual tipping point for the couple. Right now, however, too few doctors may take psychosocial, behavioral, or cultural factors into account when treating sexual dysfunction. In a 26,000-person study done in 2005, "only 14% of adults in the United States reported that a physician asked about their sexual concerns within the past three years."[2] Dr. Perelman feels that ignoring the nonphysiologic factors of sexual dysfunction—such as anxiety, anger, depression, early trauma, fear of failure, loss of confidence, and relationship issues—is what lies behind the 20 to 50 percent discontinuation rates reported for current erectile dysfunction treatments. A pill is not a magic bullet.

Erectile Function After a Prostate Operation

I asked Dr. Perelman what the current practice is to restore erectile function in men who have had various kinds of prostate operations or radiation. "What the medical profession is doing now to help restore erectile capacity is what we call penile rehabilitation right after surgery," he said. "The trick is to get these men getting erections as quickly as possible based on numerous theories, including one that brings blood flow and oxygen to the penis. The hope is that this will help the recovery process. So now urologists will give Viagra, Levitra, or Cialis to most men on a daily basis, or every other day, and begin to restore erections in that manner. But does restoring erections make for a good sex life? I think of it as something very helpful but not sufficient in and of itself. It depends on what else happens."

Male Orgasmic Capacity

Dr. Perelman told me that for some men, sexual-enhancement drugs and implants actually create a new problem. "In general, as men age, it becomes a little more difficult to reach orgasms for the same reasons that we don't hear as well, we don't see as well, our touch isn't as sensitive. The drugs are restoring their erectile capacity, but they are not helping them with their orgasmic capacity. Some guys can be kind of naive, and go, 'I must be turned on, I have an erection,' but they have an erection because they took a pill, or injected themselves, or they have a prosthesis"—a pump—"that is providing them with an erection. So they are presuming they are excited, and their partner might presume they are excited because, after all, he has got an erection, and maybe he hasn't even told her he has done this. So she is thinking everything is fine, and they make love, and he is unable to reach orgasm because he may not really be excited."

The problem is, Dr. Perelman explained, that "he is artificially induced into an erection, which would be much the same thing as a woman who is using too much lubricant and isn't really turned on, but she is able to have intercourse because she is so wet, the penis slides in. So men are starting to have this problem that we used to only hear about from women, about not being able to reach orgasms. Initially, the woman will feel, 'Oh, there must be something about me, it's my fault.' But then she will start getting angry and we begin to see the same sort of compulsive 'How come he's not coming?' that you see in some men who are dragging their wives and girlfriends in here saying, 'I want to see her have an orgasm, a real orgasm, none of this vibrator or clitoral stuff. I want to give her one!' The men, of course, are very distressed because it is a loss of something that was vital to both their sense of themselves as a man and their capacity. Right now I am describing probably 3 to 5 percent of men benefitting from medical assistance. I will predict for you, though, that this will be a greater percentage of individuals because it really hasn't been documented before."

The sexual pharmaceutical drugs are not meant to treat delayed ejaculation. There are, as of this writing, some off-label drugs designed for this purpose but nothing that is FDA-approved.

The Problem of Denial

Then there's the problem of denial. Dr. Perelman explained that the average man spends two to three years in denial about his erectile dysfunction before he seeks help. By then a new sexual equilibrium has taken place between the couple; they may have simply adjusted to not having much sex or to having a different kind of sex or to no sex at all. "What makes things worse for many partners of these men," said Dr. Perelman, "is that the men will begin to avoid any kind of intimacy, especially affection, because the presumption is that if they are affectionate, she may mistake this as an initiation of sex and he doesn't want to fail. Who wants to do what they won't do well, if you will?"

I find it so sad that couples will deprive themselves of the sensuality of touch, of playing, of the whole cornucopia of intimate and sexy things they could do without thinking about intercourse. Almost nothing brings home to me as forcefully as this the toxic nature of masculinity as it is currently defined by our culture and internalized by men and boys. They are so vulnerable to being shamed because they might not perform the way they think they should that they and their partners miss out on pleasure.

Communication Between Patients and Doctors

As I have said before, simply writing a prescription isn't enough. Erections, with no context, aren't enough. I think many doctors need to spend more time talking with their patients so as to get a holistic understanding of the landscape of the particular relationship. Along with others in his field, especially some of the women doctors, Dr. Perelman is a big advocate of getting the partner into the consultation session. "We should see both people," he said. "Not just the men. So, I did a little study of sexual medicine specialists who are urologists, across the country, and found out that less than one out of ten of them ever saw a partner at all, let alone every time that they saw the guy. For the most part, some of the men do not want the partner to come in, some of the men are not even telling their partners that they are going for help because they are so embarrassed about it, and in a very small percentage of cases they are not telling the partner because they plan on using it elsewhere."

Dr. Tom Lue told me that it isn't that doctors don't want to see the partners but that, very often, the partners don't want to come in. "Interestingly," Lue said, "if the men become impotent because of medical reasons like a prostate cancer operation, radiation, or whatever, 90 percent of the time the wife will come with the man. She will feel sympathy: 'My man has cancer, I should help him.' But if the man becomes impotent for other reasons—diabetes, high blood pressure, because those happen gradually—then quite often the woman thinks the man must be having an affair, or the man does not like her anymore. In those situations, the women don't come."

If the partner wants to come in and the man wants her to come in, then discussing their issues together with the help of a sex therapist can lead to big changes. Consider this scenario that Dr. Perelman described: "If the man has always been insensitive to her needs and she has satisfied herself with masturbation without him knowing about it for forty years, but she always secretly hoped or was too shy to ask him to touch her, then if you can actually get her into the office and have a consultation and discover that information, and find a sensitive way of communicating that to him that doesn't humiliate him or embarrass her, it is actually a win-win, and those are very happy people when they leave. Because now you have reestablished a new sexual script that is actually designed to satisfy her, not just to satisfy him. Then she is very happy about him getting help because she loves him, she cares for him, and a lot of things have been good in their lives, but sex was not one of them. Those situations are pretty easy to fix."

Medical Insurance Coverage

As beautiful as the outcome of a couple's sex therapy can be, a systemic problem stands in the way of this sort of therapy being broadly available. Sex therapists and urologists are concerned about managed health care and Medicare, which has meant that doctors rarely have more than six or seven minutes to talk to patients. As Dr. Perelman points out, how can the doctor, in a few minutes, "take a history, do a diagnosis, figure out what is going on with him, figure out what is going on with her? Does she need a referral to a gynecologist, does she need hormone supplementation, does she need to practice dilating herself so she might be a little more comfortable with intercourse?"

Medical-Psychological Combination Therapy

Understanding that just writing prescriptions and giving out pills isn't enough for many people, Dr. Perelman wants to work with the pharmaceutical companies to develop and disseminate an easy-to-replicate, affordable model of therapy that provides both the medical options and the counseling in combination to create a sexual tipping point. He sees it applying to women as well as men, and he feels that due to the drop-off of men who regularly refill their prescriptions, the pharmaceutical companies may be motivated to fund such work. In a field dominated by penis fixers, it would be a huge paradigm shift to move into the areas of relational intimacy, especially male intimacy, which heretofore has been all but ignored.

The Women's Part of the Equation

If it is the need to develop intimacy that is ignored in men, in women, especially older women, what's ignored is understanding their sexuality. "The problem is that there hasn't been nearly enough research done on women's sexuality," says Dr. Louann Brizendine, a neuropsychiatrist at the University of California, San Francisco. During our interview, Dr. Brizendine told me that several years ago she worked on a segment for CNN with one of her female patients who was around sixty-five. CNN wanted to explore the issue of women's brain and sexual function during menopause. The news editors cut it. "They were okay with the estrogen and the 'keeping the brain healthy' aspects," Dr. Brizendine told me, "but they didn't wander into the sexual area that we had done. My patient was a little bit miffed. She felt it was really important for women to know that you can keep yourself and your body and your mind and your sexual organs healthy and have a good sex life with your partner even when you're older and that it takes knowledge about what to do and what not to do."

Dr. Brizendine smiled as she related one of the best things about women she sees who have crossed the menopausal divide. "The kids are out of the house," she said, "and they are into the next phase of their lives, and that is about how they can maintain their brain function, their sexual function, their libido. They are still very much interested in sex, but so often they come to me with very out-of-balance hormones. There has to be a hormonal balance in your brain and in your sexual organs so that all the parts are working."

Men's sexual issues are visible, they are external, and they make up a large part of a man's sense of himself, and perhaps that is partly why the research funds favor men. Women's sexual parts are inside and may be neglected if—or as long as—doctors and researchers think that the erection is the be-all and end-all of sex. This is bad enough on a personal level, but it becomes a virtual nonstarter when it comes to studying older women's sexuality.

Women's Hormone Replacement

As you may recall, in 2000, the Women's Health Initiative issued findings that hormone therapy (HT)—that is to say, replacing the decreasing levels of estrogen in women approaching menopause— did not prevent heart disease and, in fact, increased cardiovascular risk factors. The report hit like a bombshell and frightened untold numbers of women away from HT. In the view of the study's critics, this has led to a generation of women suffering needlessly from menopausal symptoms, some of them acute, that could be safely treated.

The problem, as many experts have explained it to me, was that the study was misleading because the women participants were recruited from Medicare rolls, their average age was from sixty-three to seventy-nine, many were obese or smokers or both, and some two-thirds of them had never been on hormones before and thus had been estrogen-deprived for many years leading up to the study.

It is my understanding that the optimum time to begin HT is at menopause. Dr. Michelle Warren, medical director at the Center for Menopause, Hormonal Disorders, and Women's Health at Columbia University Medical Center, told me, "If you start HT at menopause and continue with it, there is protection against bone loss and vaginal atrophy and probably some protection against heart disease and other problems that can occur before, during, and after menopause. Some recent data also shows that the death rate is decreased in women taking hormones, and that the increase in heart attacks is not significant. Recently, they went back and saw that for the women who had been on estrogen alone, the hormones were really protecting the heart. Additionally, the study showed that in the women who were given estrogen alone as opposed to estrogen together with progesterone, there was no increase of breast cancer after almost seven years. This fact got little attention. The absolute relative risk is very small—.8 per thousand per year. I don't think the hormones are causing breast cancer. They may be fueling the growth of some atypical cells that are present in the breast, but the risk is very, very tiny. The estrogen-responsive cancers are very responsive to treatment, and after you stop the estrogen, the risk of cancer goes away."

In their book *Successful Aging,* Drs. John W. Rowe and Robert L. Kahn cite the Nurses' Health Study, which followed fifty-nine thousand women for sixteen years. They note, "The consensus of this research is that postmenopausal hormone replacement reduces the risk of heart disease an average of 44 percent, and increases life expectancy by 3 years—a dramatic effect."[3] The study goes on to say, "For women with one risk factor for heart disease (such as smoking, hypertension, diabetes, or a sedentary lifestyle), the benefits of hormone replacement outweigh the risks. This holds true even for women with a first-degree relative (mother or sister) with breast cancer. However, the equation shifts for women with no risk for heart disease and two first-degree relatives with breast cancer. For these women, HT carries more risk than benefits."[4]

According to its proponents, HT helps keep the brain healthy by preventing shrinkage, and it can lead to more brain-cell volume. HT can actually help the speed of brain functions, and studies have shown that when begun early in menopause, HT may be able to delay dementia symptoms. Additionally, say these advocates, estrogen helps preserve bone and works with other hormones to increase bone mass. The hormone also helps bones absorb calcium, but only as long as you use it: When you stop taking estrogen, the bone loss resumes. The Mayo Clinic does not recommend taking estrogen just to prevent bone loss, however, as the risks outweigh the benefits in many women.

Postmenopausal women who are not on HT and who are at heightened risk of developing osteoporosis are those who have suffered food addictions such as bulimia and anorexia, smokers, very slight women, those who have been particularly sedentary, those who have suffered from intestinal tract problems (which impede the absorption of calcium), and those who have experienced frequent fractures. These women should consider being screened for osteoporosis. The most up-to-date screening method is called a dual energy X-ray absorptiometry test (DEXA). It is rather expensive and is currently covered by Medicare.

Dr. Warren, like other gynecologists I spoke with, feels that it is almost inevitable that postmenopausal women who are not on estrogen will suffer vaginal dryness and atrophy. As she described it, "There are three layers to the vagina. The top layer completely disappears and the other two layers shrink, and you lose collagen as well, so the vagina starts to shrink." There are also urinary symptoms associated with age due to thinning of the urethral lining. Dr. Marianne Legato, in her book *Eve's Rib: The New Science of Gender-Specific Medicine and How It Can Save Your Life,* says that a reliable way for doctors to determine if a woman has enough estrogen is to "examine a sample of her vaginal lining under the microscope: A well-estrogenized lining is many layers thick."[5] If there is a lack of estrogen, the vagina will no longer be plump and juicy, but it can be treated with vaginal estrogen that lubricates the bladder as well. One medication that I use is Vagifem. It acts on the vaginal tissues only and is not absorbed into the bloodstream. Vaginal estrogen creams and a vaginal ring with estrogen are also available. Dr. Warren notes that the creams should be given in low doses and that both they and the ring are thought to be low-risk when appropriately used.

When women choose to take HT, those who have a uterus should take both estrogen and progesterone, to protect them from endometrial cancer; those who have had their uterus removed should take estrogen only. Besides strengthening bone and improving the skin, the hair, the brain, and the health of the vagina (which reduces pain during intercourse), HT may also increase sexual desire.

I strongly urge older women to have their blood tested for hormone levels, not just estrogen but free testosterone as well. Testing for free testosterone is not an automatic. You have to ask for it, as doctors are just learning to test older women for testosterone deficiency. In discussing the bottoming out of sexual desire in women, *The Psychiatric Annals: The Journal of Continuing Psychiatric Education* reported, "It has been postulated that, 'No matter how hard a woman might try to assemble the building blocks of healthy sexual functioning—the required amount of the hormones, a loving partner, adequate stimulation, possibly a good sexual fantasy—it cannot work if she does not have the basic foundation of enough testosterone.'"[6]

Dr. Brizendine has been prescribing testosterone replacement for her women patients since 1994. She says that sexual dysfunction in women is often an above-the-waist matter, residing in the brain. The upsides of testosterone replacement are increased libido and the sensitivity of the genitals, especially the clitoris; heightened energy; and better mood, mental acuity, and muscle and bone growth. The downsides may include lower voice, facial hair, body odor, acne, and thinning hair. The particular form of testosterone that can actually get into your brain and cause an upswing of libido is known as "free testosterone." The normal range of free testosterone for a woman—the amount thought necessary to maintain her sexual interest—is 20 to 70 of what are called picograms per milliliter. "Here's the thing," says Dr. Brizendine. "If you were to start taking estrogen in the form of an oral birth control pill or oral hormone replacement, it goes straight to your liver and makes more of this big, sticky globular protein called SHBG, or sex hormone binding globulin. I think of it as a big, sticky teddy bear that goes around in your bloodstream and gobbles up all of your testosterone, and then your testosterone isn't free anymore. So you may have a good total testosterone level as a woman, but if you don't have any that is free, you don't have any that can get into your brain. The normal range for your sex hormone binding globulin is 100 to 150. If you are getting a workup for low libido, you want to know the level of free testosterone, because that is what counts in terms of your sex drive in the brain." (Remember: The brain is the biggest sex organ.) Dr. Marianne Legato writes, "Before you take testosterone, make sure your doctor has measured your serum lipids and that your HDL (high-density lipoprotein or 'good cholesteral') is over 45 mg/dl."[7]

The hormones can be administered in several ways. Some women, like me, prefer the estrogen patch. The Vivelle-Dot seems to be a favorite. These patches provide transdermal creams, which may not go through the liver as much as oral doses. The Vivelle-Dot patch is small and transparent; the only way you see it is because it's shiny. It also comes in different concentrations. If you don't want to wear a patch, there are now very good gels, creams, and a spray that deliver estrogen through the skin. It's not true for all women, but I took oral estrogen for six years and it went right through me—didn't even register when they tested my blood levels—and it was probably creating those sticky teddy bear–like globulin proteins from the liver that killed off all my free testosterone. But who knew? Then, for many years, I used a low-dose Vivelle patch twice a week. But when a noninvasive cancer lump was discovered in my right breast (and removed), I had to stop all estrogen therapy.

Some women prefer and benefit from oral estrogen therapy because their good cholesterol (HDL) goes up. For some, the estrogen by itself is enough to raise their sex drive. For others, some testosterone, either in patch or gel form, will jump-start their libido and increase their energy and sense of overall well-being. For testosterone gel, you smooth a nickel-sized blob on your abdomen or inner thigh. It doesn't take long to experience the results. Talk to your doctor!

The type of doctor we need to turn to for HT should be an ob-gyn who practices postmenopausal hormone replacement therapy, as opposed to one who specializes in pregnancies and deliveries. Dr. Michelle Warren calls such doctors "menopause-friendly" and says they can be internists as well.

Human Growth Hormone

While we are on the subject of hormones, let me say a few things about human growth hormone (HGH), which has become a popular drug at many anti-aging clinics. HGH is naturally produced in the pituitary gland, at the base of the brain, and serves to fuel growth throughout childhood. Around the time a person hits thirty, the pituitary gradually reduces the amount it produces. Injections of synthetic HGH stimulate the pituitary gland to produce more of the hormone, and this can increase muscle mass and reduce body fat. But there are no free lunches. HGH can be harmful, causing aching joints, fluid retention and swelling, and carpal tunnel syndrome; most important, its long-term use may cause cancer by fueling the growth of small tumors. We won't even go into how expensive it is! As I said in Chapter 5, many doctors believe that the best way to stimulate growth hormones naturally is to get enough sleep, because that is when growth hormone and testosterone production peak.

In conclusion, hormone replacement therapy is a very individual matter—as are many of the current sexual-enhancement drugs—so please make sure you have a doctor who is knowledgeable, experienced, and up to date on the newest research when it comes to hormone therapy. And if you are still interested in making sexuality a part of your Third Act, why not consider paying a visit or two to a sex therapist with your partner—just for a little tune-up to your largest sex organ: your brain!

CHAPTER 15

Meeting New People When You're Looking for Love

**Love is everything it's cracked up to be. . . .
It really is worth fighting for, being brave for,
risking everything for.**

—ERICA JONG

IN THE NEW WORLD OF SERIOUS LONGEVITY, "TILL DEATH DO US part" has become profoundly challenging. Centuries ago, when that phrase was embedded in the marriage vows, we didn't live eighty, ninety, even one hundred years. Face it: It is hard to find a mate who is not only right for us in the early, family-building years but still pleasingly appropriate for our middle and autumn decades. As I said in a previous chapter, I am a believer in the value of long-term commitment, but—as is true for many others, too—it hasn't worked for me. This, then, is a chapter about ways to find new love.

Dr. Gloria Steiner is a friend of mine from Atlanta. When Gloria was fifty, her husband of thirty years told her that he was homosexual and wanted a divorce.

"I'm not at all judgmental—it wasn't that," Gloria told me. "I am still very fond of him, I respect him, and I'm glad he still lives close by. But I thought I would be with him forever. There was all that history—lost. That's what made me sad. The loss. My sense of self before that was entirely different from my sense of self afterward. I was knocked off-kilter and was trying to come back to center. That took a while."

"How did you do it?" I asked.

"About a year and a half after the divorce, I got into dancing and music. I adore music. Any kind of music. It became my salve and I lost myself in music, dancing."

"How? Did you go to, like, Arthur Murray's or—"

"No, no. I just went to a salsa place. I found people who loved to dance and I hung out with them and that made me feel alive."

"And did you have actual dates?"

"Yes, but not many fix-ups. Mainly, I would go to the symphony and somebody would sit down next to me and we would get to talking, and we would have a common interest and we would go out."

"So when you went dancing or to the symphony, you'd go alone?"

"A lot of times, yes. That is why I loved living in Atlanta. I never minded being alone. I have a lot of friends getting divorced who just can't stand being alone. Just the thought of being alone makes them feel as though the whole world is looking at them."

"I felt exactly that way for two years following the end of my second marriage, as though I were a leper," I confessed to Gloria. "So for thirteen years you were single and dating?"

"Yes, but the dating part was uncomfortable for me. It was so different after thirty years of being married. And you are searching for your identity. You go out in these situations and you say to yourself, 'Is this what my identity is now as a single woman? I don't want this to be my identity. How do I work on a new identity?' The thing I missed the most of anything about dating were the hugs. Hugs are so important, but once you encourage that, you encourage more than you want. They think you're asking for the whole kit and caboodle. You can't just ask for a good hug. So I got my hugs from my kids and got massages for the touching."

When I met Gloria she was with an attractive man named Scott who I assumed was her husband. I was wrong. She and Scott have been lovers for almost four years, although they've known each other for ten or fifteen years. Scott and his wife had moved into Gloria's building, and they would invite each other over for dinner.

When Scott's wife died of pancreatic cancer, Scott and Gloria got together.

"Do you live together?" I asked her.

"No, I live here on the twelfth floor, and he lives upstairs on the sixteenth."

"Would you ever want to live with anybody, with your ex-husband or Scott or anyone else, again?"

"You know, I say no . . . but who knows? I really don't. We spend a lot of time together, but it's when we want to be together. It is really nice having your own space."

"I guess he knows how to hug."

"Oh, yes. He is wonderful."

Clearly, getting out and about in situations where you are apt to meet like-minded people, the way Gloria did, is a good idea. So is telling everyone you know, including your children, that you're looking to date.

Younger women and men who want to meet someone go to bars or clubs. I wouldn't feel comfortable doing that, and I doubt most older women would either . . . or men, for that matter. That is a main reason why online dating has become such an important part of socializing in the Third Act. Frankly, I was stunned when a close friend of mine in Atlanta told me she'd been to a lunch with ten or so female corporate executives and that a number of them were dating or had married men they'd met online. With Internet services such as Match.com, PerfectMatch, and eHarmony, you can find out more about someone in a short amount of time because the process makes it so efficient. You can initiate, move things to the next step, or back out, all the while remaining invisible until you want to present yourself.

Mary Madden was sixty-two when I interviewed her in her attractive but not extravagant home in Atlanta. She had been divorced for fifteen years, and though she knew many people in Atlanta, she had never happened to meet anyone to date, nor been introduced to anyone. She had been a technology entrepreneur who started her own business and took it public; she now works with a turnaround firm, where she helps companies facing bank-ruptcy run more efficiently.

A few years before I met her, at age fifty-nine, Mary had gone on both eHarmony and Match.com, using them simultaneously. She explained, "A friend of mine who has her own business went on Match.com and met someone she then married. She told me, 'You are going to have to go through seventeen or eighteen guys. So prepare yourself. It's like making sales calls.' She's a salesperson and she was absolutely right. I corresponded briefly with seventeen men before I met the man I am with now."

I learned from Mary that to start, you sign up for an account with one or more of the companies. She said they are not expensive and that one, the Right Stuff, is free if you can prove you attended an Ivy League school. Once you have opened the account, you are asked to fill out a questionnaire describing yourself. You may also decide to write an optional essay that goes into more depth about you as a person. For example, what are your likes and dislikes? What do you want out of life? Are exercise and staying fit impor-tant? Do you enjoy travel? Do you like spending time with your children and grandchildren . . . or not? (If a man wants to be with his grandkids every weekend and you don't like kids, you may not want to waste your time developing a relationship with him.) Are you an avid reader?

Mary told me, "I put down that I read a lot and I listed all the things I read, and one guy sent me a response saying, 'Well, the last thing I read was my automotive manual. But I am in south Georgia and I am an auto mechanic and I would really like to meet you.' So, saying no to that one was easy."

Mary also mentioned that a Jewish friend of hers from Los Angeles who had used JDate, the Jewish dating site, told her that her personal essay was too serious. "So I rewrote it to make it less serious," Mary said. "I put in that I have been responsible for people all my life and right now I really do not want to be responsible. I just want to have a good time. This is actually what caught the eye of the man I ended up being with. He liked that. He is pretty independent. He doesn't really want somebody taking care of him. Although we do take care of each other. I get him bananas and little stuff."

Not all people post a picture. A friend of Mary's has a business in Atlanta and felt she couldn't let people know that she was looking to date online, so she never posted a picture of herself. "Yet she ended up meeting a highly placed corporate executive," Mary told me, "and they have been together the last couple of months." Since she didn't share her friend's concern, Mary did post a photo of herself along with the questionnaire; but after the JDate friend said the photo was also too serious, Mary got a professional portrait taken.

In her book *Prime: Adventures and Advice on Sex, Love, and the Sensual Years,* the sociologist Dr. Pepper Schwartz says that you can decide when to post your picture. You can do it right away, or you may want to wait until you feel there are a few men who seem compatible and then ask them if they want to see your photo. "A crisp, clear, recent picture showing your face and body type is the safest, most honest way to proceed. But make sure it shows off your best attributes," Pepper says. "If you are voluptuous, why waste your time (and the man's) if he prefers slender, small-breasted women?" Pepper adds, "Likewise, you need to see a clear picture of any guy you are considering meeting. Men in sunglasses, or with blurry pics, or pics that don't indicate their body type should be avoided."[1]

If there seems to be an interest on both your parts from the posting and emails, the next step is a phone call to see if the man's voice and attitude seem right for you. If there's no phone chemistry, you probably won't want to extend it into a meeting. Whatever you do, do not give out your phone number. The guy may turn out to be a real pain, and you'd have to change your number to get rid of him.

The man Mary has spent the last two and a half years with never even posted a profile, but he read Mary's and emailed her out of the blue. "It was interesting," Mary said, smiling as she remembered. "He said, 'Reading your profile is like sitting in a movie theater in Connecticut watching *Bull Durham* and being the only one laughing.' And I am going, 'This is the weirdest thing I've gotten.' And

I don't know why I answered, but I did. We emailed back and forth for a while, and then we met for a glass of wine and eventually started dating. But I did all these things—like, I called my friends and said, 'I am meeting this guy for a glass of wine.' I called when I came back home; I said, 'I am back home.' And I think I did the same thing on the second date."

I asked Mary what they had in common. "He is very cultured," she replied. "He belongs to the High Museum, he goes to the opera, to the ballet. And, like I said, he's very independent."

"And are you planning on getting married?" I asked. Mary explained that he's been married three times, so no. "But he wants me to live with him. He lives in a condo downtown that he has a mortgage on. I own this house. I love this house. He is not here half the time because he travels all over the world selling agricultural equipment. I keep saying to myself, 'Why would I want to live in a place I don't like when he's not even here?' I've grown to like having my own space."

I have spoken with a number of women and men who feel it can be good to extend the emailing and phone calling for weeks, even months, so that you really get to know the person before moving to the dating phase. However long you wait, be sure that you feel there is a real potential for compatibility before arranging a meeting. Like Mary, when you do meet, do it in a safe, public place and tell someone what you're doing and where you will be, and carry a cellphone with you. Don't commit to spending more than thirty minutes or so the first time. If he's a dud, you don't want to get stuck. And, under those circumstances in particular, offer to split the tab with him.

Out of the seventeen men she exchanged emails and phone calls with, Mary met only four of them face-to-face. I asked her if it was clear to her right away that they weren't right. "Oh yes," she said. "There was one guy I met twice. He told me he was going to join the Peace Corps, and I thought, 'Well, that's got nothing to do with me!' But he was the only one I met more than once. When I look back on it, I feel like it really wasn't going to work out with any of those guys."

"How long did you date the man you're with before you had sex?"

"Probably about three weeks."

"And was it hard? I mean, in terms of you having been single for—"

"No, it wasn't," Mary said with certainty. "We went to Friday night at the High, where the museum has martinis and a jazz band and you can look at art. Then we went to eat. It was just a very nice evening and . . . no, it was not hard."

If and when the time comes that you want to have sex with your new friend, be sure to be prepared with condoms and lubrication. If he resists using a condom, he's probably not for you.

It can be tough when you think the first date went well but he doesn't call again. Keep in mind that older men, far more than most older women, are looking for a serious, long-term commitment. "A perfectly nice date may not result in a follow-up if they don't sense that you are exactly what they are looking for," cautions Dr. Pepper Schwartz. "A quick rejection doesn't feel good—but it's the style of dating these days. People take their best guess right away. . . . If that's their decision, there's nothing to be done about it. . . . If he's not calling, he's not for you."[2]

When and if a relationship does develop, be sure that the two of you have a clear understanding of what each expects out of it: Do you want a completely monogamous commitment, or to continue seeing other people? Do you envision getting together once or twice a month or more regularly but without moving in together? And if he won't give you a home phone number or allow you to meet his children and friends, beware: He may be married.

Mary Madden wasn't alone in finding it hard to tell a man she wasn't interested. "You feel kind of sorry for them," she said. "A Vietnam veteran emailed me one day because he'd spent the whole day at the VA hospital because he could not hear and he could not walk. I was like, this is just not going to work for me. But it was hard. It pulls on a lot of heartstrings."

My heartstrings got pulled in the Third Act just when I felt certain I didn't care anymore and wasn't looking. Five days before I was going to have knee surgery, I was in Paris shooting (in French and English!) a commercial for L'Oréal skin-care products for older women. A pal of mine, the wonderfully funny writer Carrie Fisher, sent me an email to let me know that a longtime friend of hers, the music producer Richard Perry, upon discovering that I would be stuck in Los Angeles for at least a month because of the surgery, had asked her to organize a dinner where he could reconnect with me. I had first met him thirty-five years earlier, when he brought together a group of music industry heavyweights in his home to support my then husband, Tom Hayden, in his campaign for the U.S. Senate. I remembered the house, perched atop a hill overlooking all of Los Angeles, with a pool and a tennis court and tastefully decorated in an Art Deco style. (He still lives there . . . and now so do I, much of the time.)

Ten years later we ran into each other at a party in Aspen. Tom had chosen to stay home with the children, so I arrived alone, and when I saw Richard I asked him to be my date for the evening. We danced together all night; and I didn't see him again for twenty-five years. But there was that distant memory. And there were the songs he produced, hit after hit. Many of them I would use in the Workout classes I taught. I guess "Slow Hand," by the Pointer Sisters, was the one that always made me wonder what Richard was up to. I have to tell you, when I saw his name in Carrie's email, my heart did a little flip. I showed the email to Matthew Shields, my hairstylist. "See this name? Richard Perry? This could be fun." Barely ten days after the surgery, when I was still on crutches, we had our "reunion" dinner, and he's been my honey ever since. At seventy-one it felt good to feel good again and also to know that I can remain who I am, not trying to tailor my personhood to meet a man's fancy—well, maybe a little. When we've grown up (and that took a while for me), we are clearer about who we are, what we want and don't want, and this can mean that later in life the unexpected can always happen—if we remain open to it.

PART FOUR

PILGRIMS *of the* FUTURE

Left to right: Gloria Steinem, me, Eve Ensler, Charlotte Martin, and Isabella Rossellini at an event to mobilize young women to vote that was put together by Eve's organization, V-Day: Until the Violence Stops

CHAPTER 16

Generativity: Leaving Footprints

Old age is like a minefield: if you see footprints leading to the other side, step in them.[1]

— GEORGE VAILLANT

If the task of young adults is to create biological heirs, the task of old age is to create social heirs.[2]

— GEORGE VAILLANT

OTHER THAN DISEASE, THE PARAMOUNT DANGERS OF ACT III are loneliness, depression, and lack of purpose. These are, to a large degree, matters that have to do with the personal choices we make at this stage of our lives, what we choose to do or not do. When we feel we have purpose in our lives, the loneliness and depression seem to fade more into the background. *Okay, so my back aches, but I'm passionate about what I'm doing. Sure, I lost my network of friends at the office when I retired, but I'm going out and making new ones.*

Just as the Third Act is the time for journeying inward to allow the flowering of consciousness and growth, it is also the time to radiate that consciousness outward as a resource not only for our own self-fulfillment but for the world, as well.

Think of the bright blooms that burst forth from invisible, underground rhizomes to catch the sun. This new spring growth carries the sunshine—transmuted to sugar, thanks to chlorophyll— back to nourish the root. In us humans, the process is also circular:

The outward manifestation of our inner growth is what loops back and ensures that our inner self is nourished.

But it is the outer—what we *do*—that becomes our personal footprint, our ultimate identity. We are what we do.

Life can be taken away without death. We can let depression, self-pity, resentment, and grumpiness fossilize us so we're not of much use to anyone. But why shortchange ourselves, now of all times? Is that what we want our legacy to be? Why not deliberately start to live so that the breakdown of the youthful self can lead to the breakthrough of an emerging elder self?[3]

The Jungian analyst Helen Luke wrote, "To our wonder, we may find that now it is time to become aware of our oneness with everything and everyone other. Instead of 'I am not this, I am not that person or thing or image,' we begin to affirm, 'I am both this and that' and to glimpse the meaning of 'I am' as the name of God."

We can consciously cultivate these inner qualities in ourselves—trustworthiness, less ego, acceptance of differences. This is how we assume the role of sages, shamans, wise women who radiate a vision that beckons those who are younger more fearlessly into their own Third Acts. The very young may no longer need us to forage for food, an evolutionary imperative for grandmothers in hunter-gatherer times, but they need us to teach and inspire them. It is understandable for us, especially those of us at the far end of Act III, to feel a special affinity for children. Unlike those in midlife, the very young share with the old a proximity to what Joan Erikson called "the shadow of non-being," the thin membrane that separates life and nonexistence, which is forgotten in the glare of midlife.

There's a lofty word for this nurturing of the younger generations, or of individuals of any age: "Generativity." It's something the experts all agree is a central component of successful aging. The psychiatrist Erik Erikson coined the term to describe moving from a focus on oneself to a focus on a broader social radius, giving to the community and to the larger world. It involves the ability to care for and guide the next generation, to give of oneself to those

*With my
son, Troy,
in 2007*
KURT MARKUS

*Me as the
Easter bunny
in 2011, with my
granddaughter
Viva (second
from right)*

coming up, by mentoring, coaching, guiding, nurturing them. The young have inherited certain traits genetically; we can pass on other traits to them through teaching and example.

Generativity also means being concerned with the future of the planet. You can think of it as revolutionary. If Generativity were more widely embedded in our social fabric, with all the caring and compassion for young people that it signifies, everything would be different.

For me, the word conjures up the notions of generation, generating, and creativity: Our generation must generate (with creativity) caring and nurturance for things and people other than ourselves. We must become advocates for the future.

There's lots in it for us, too, including physiological benefits. It has been shown that endorphins that strengthen the immune system and increase our longevity are released when we are fully engaged in "broadening our social radius" by helping others, especially the younger generations—and this is what Generativity means.

Dr. George Vaillant, in his book *Aging Well,* based on the thirty-year-long Harvard Study of Adult Development, writes that in all the groups that were studied, "mastery of Generativity tripled the chances that the decade of the 70s would be for these men and women a time of joy and not of despair." Surprisingly and deliciously, the study also revealed—as I said in the Preface—that among the women, "mastering Generativity . . . was the best predictor of whether they reported attaining regular orgasm"![4]

In *Man's Search for Meaning* Viktor Frankl wrote, "Mental health is based on a certain degree of tension, the tension between what one has already achieved and what one still ought to accomplish, or the gap between what one is and what one should become." I like the metaphor Frankl uses to illustrate why the tension of striving, even in the elderly, is positive: "If architects want to strengthen a decrepit arch, they *increase* the load which is laid upon it, for thereby the parts are joined more firmly together."

I think one reason Katharine Hepburn remained strong into her advanced age was because, like an old arch, she assumed the load of the elder. When we worked together on *On Golden Pond,* she very deliberately took me under her wing, using every opportunity to pass on her wisdom. She let me know she'd been watching as I overcame my fear of doing a backflip for the film and said that mastering something you fear is what keeps you from getting "soggy" in life.

One day while we were having tea together, Hepburn told me how she would get up every morning at five to write about her life's experiences. One chapter, she said, was called "Failure." "You know, Jane," she remarked, "we learn far more from failure than we ever do from success."

Katharine Hepburn,
Dad, and me on the set
of On Golden Pond
AFP/GETTY IMAGES

KEYSTONE/HULTON
ARCHIVE/GETTY IMAGES

She made me understand the value of self-consciousness. We tend to think of self-consciousness as something bad—as being awkward or uncomfortable with oneself. But the way Hepburn made me see it was more as a *consciousness of self,* an awareness of how our presence affects people. "This is your package," she said to me once, pinching my cheek. "We all have our package, what presents us to the world. What do you want your package to say about you?"

My late friend the singer Michael Jackson spent several days visiting the set and watching Katharine and my father act. In between

RON GALELLA/
WIRE IMAGE

scenes, Hepburn would make a point of having Michael pull up a chair next to her so she could tell him stories. One of them was about Laurette Taylor, one of the great American theater actresses. Katharine had seen Taylor early in her career, when she had been "absolutely brilliant" in Tennessee Williams's *The Glass Menagerie*. A number of years later, when Taylor had become famous, Katharine saw her

again in that role. "The magic was gone," said Hepburn, watching
Michael to see if he was paying attention. "She'd become too successful. Lost the hunger. Sad, sad, sad." It was an important lesson for a
rising star, which Michael was at the time. Hepburn never hammered
me over the head with her wisdom. She simply layered it into our
daily contacts in ways that made me think and feel challenged.

I work with teenagers, through my nonprofit organization in
Georgia, the Georgia Campaign for Adolescent Pregnancy Prevention. When I am with them, I try always to remember what my
friend and mentor in the field of youth development, Dr. Michael
Carrera, says: "Young people may forget what you say or what you
do. But they will never forget how you made them feel." Helping
the young feel worthy, loved, challenged, and hopeful is what will
make them strong and resilient. And more often than not, what
they need is for us to listen, really listen—with our hearts, counte-
nancing them with our eyes, not tuning out while we figure out
what to say back to them.

These are the footprints we want to leave behind, ones they can step into confidently as they move through midlife and into their own Third Acts.

In Santa Monica, California, I discovered a real hub of Generativity at WISE & Healthy Aging. The center has been around since 1976 and has gained a national reputation for its innovative programs for seniors, especially its Peer Counseling Program, where volunteers become trained paraprofessionals, supervised by a licensed therapist. I talked to a seventy-one-year-old woman who was a retired lawyer. She told me, "I found that after law, I needed to utilize a different part of my brain, and volunteering here provides that opportunity. I meet people that I probably would never meet in day-to-day life, and the problems that they face are sometimes extremely difficult—insurmountable health problems, financial problems, problems with their children. I feel very gratified in thinking that in some way I can improve the quality of their lives, and I feel the quality of my life has been improved substantially as a result of the training here and my involvement with the group."

An elderly widower told me he had been suffering from depression when a friend urged him to come to the center and volunteer. "Depression isn't contagious, you know," the friend had told him. "It works the other way." "He was right," the man said cheerily. "When I started volunteering I got over the depression. It's a whole new life."

The men and women volunteers, all seniors themselves, have been able to replace the lost social networks they had at work or through marriage with a new network that includes their clients and their fellow counselors.

A retired school psychologist loves her work as a volunteer. "I had all that background and thought I should use it for something," she told me, adding that the greatest part for her are the new relationships she's formed with the people she works with. "It's just so wonderful. We're not just chatting; we have such meaningful exchanges."

Lois has been a counselor at the center for twenty-two years and believes that this is what she always wanted to do. "I was very busy my whole life helping my husband with his real estate business," she said. "I had no choice. I felt obligated to my husband. So this was like getting a second chance at a new life."

I met Jake, who volunteers with the center's Friendly Visitor Program and brought with him his ninety-five-year-old client Karl, who lives in a nursing home and can't get around on his own anymore. Karl has bonded with Jake. Karl is the man I quoted earlier who, when I asked how old he was, replied with the playful humor that seems so characteristic of the very old: "I don't know how old I am, but I was around when the Dead Sea was only sick." I hated to think what life would be like for Karl if he didn't have Jake to talk to. "We see eye to eye on so many subjects—politics, humor," says Karl of Jake.

Evelyn Freeman, the beautiful ninety-one-year-old founder of the Peer Counseling Program, says, "If I were going to look for one word that describes what goes on here with the counselors and the clients, the word would be 'joy.' The joy of being productive. The joy of doing something meaningful. The joy of knowing that you can enlarge your life at a time when many people think it gets smaller. The joy of knowing that each of us has the potential for change for as long as we live."

Another wise woman practitioner of Generativity is my friend Dr. Johnnetta Cole, about whom I wrote in Chapter 13. A vibrant woman, Johnnetta said her Third Act well-being has to do with her sense of purpose and her active engagement with living. "Let me tell you about my fiftieth reunion at Oberlin College. I'm very close to one of my former roommates, Chitie Edgett, and her husband, Dick. Well, Sister Jane," she said in her characteristic style, "there were a few folk at our reunion who, whether in wheelchairs or not, seemed to have lost eye contact with living. But I'm happy to say that the majority of my classmates were clearly moving through life in a very different way. What was the difference? Despite the health challenges that Chitie, Dick, and I, along with many of our classmates have, we are not only looking at life straight on, we are busily trying to find enough hours in each day to do what we must do and what we want to do. I am really convinced that this Third Act can be at its best when we are truly engaged in something we are passionate about. I know that the more engaged I am intellectually and involved in causes that I care about, the better this Third Act is going to be. Of course, we have to acknowledge our infirmities and the physical expressions of growing older. I chuckle when I recall hearing Maya Angelou say that at a certain point in her life a woman can watch a race between her two breasts to see which one is going to drop the quickest. Having a sense of humor about how the natural process of aging is expressed on one's body helps to keep fun and joy in the process of becoming a seasoned citizen."

Her whole life, Johnnetta has been fighting against the isms: racism, sexism, classism. "And," she added with fervor, "I also signed up in strong opposition to heterosexism, ageism, ableism"—discrimination against people who are physically challenged—"and any other ism. My way of looking at and moving through the world has been shaped by experiences growing up in the South in the days of legal segregation, participating in the civil rights and anti–Vietnam War and women's movements, and, yes, by academic training in anthropology, women's studies, and African American studies. Now I can bring all of the knowledge and experiences from Acts I and II together with what this Third Act has to offer and, hopefully, I can make a few more contributions in our ongoing struggles against all systems of inequality."

For a number of years, Johnnetta was closely involved with the Johnnetta B. Cole Global Diversity and Inclusion Institute, founded at Bennett College for Women in Greensboro, North Carolina. When the institute was at its height of success, it annually convened the Chief Diversity Officers Forum. I had never heard of a chief diversity officer (CDO), but Johnnetta explained that more and more corporations are appointing CDOs to provide leadership for the necessary tasks of increasing workforce diversity and creating an inclusive culture that is welcoming to all employees. Such actions, Johnnetta pointed out, are necessary if a company wants to successfully compete in the increasingly diverse global marketplace. Attracting and keeping a diverse workforce and creating an inclusive culture is not only the right thing to do, Johnnetta said, it is the smart thing to do. In short, there is a business case to be made for diversity.

Actually, Johnnetta's Generativity is not only about encouraging diversity in the corporate world; she is passing on her wisdom and experience so as to build a younger generation of leaders. Power Girls, another program of the institute, brought fourteen- to seventeen-year-old girls from the United States and several other countries to Bennett College for a two-week leadership training program. "One way to have a vigorous and exciting Third Act," Johnnetta said, "is to hang out with young'uns!"

A year and a half ago, Johnnetta explained, "I received my third F minus in retirement as I assumed the position of director of the Smithsonian National Museum of African Art. And," she added, "I could not be happier because in this Third Act of my life, I have the joy of bringing together my passion for African art, my knowledge of anthropology and African studies, my belief in education as a powerful instrument for change, and my responsibility to be of service."

For some, having a purpose can mean getting better and better at what you're already good at. I once saw an inspiring photograph of the bedridden Henri Matisse still painting from his bed, with a brush attached to the end of a pole. Winston Churchill's last tenure as England's prime minister began at age seventy-seven. Michelangelo was sculpting up until a week before he died, at eighty-nine. At age ninety, Albert Schweitzer was working with lepers.

Sure, it's easier to keep doing what you love doing to the end if you're your own boss, a stand-alone artist (which actors aren't, at least not movie actors), or a constantly reelected politician. It's a lot harder when your work depends on other people's decisions, as it does in the corporate world. But you might think of ways to go back and develop old interests you never had time for, such as writing, ceramic sculpting, working with young people, coaching, or teaching adults to read. Explore new interests or find a way to use your special skills and knowledge in new guises.

My friend Scott Seydel, a biochemist, built an international textile-dyeing business. In his Third Act he is using his scientific expertise to help New York City, Walmart, and other companies use recyclable products and packaging. His wife, my close friend Pat Mitchell, told me, "I find him at three A.M. sitting at his computer at the dining room table writing a PowerPoint script for a

The Honorable Robin Biddle Duke (left) with friends

speech on recycling." Scott views his new life as "atonement for having been part of the industrial complex." Atonement or not, he's making a difference.

The gorgeous Robin Biddle Duke was eighty-three years old when I interviewed her. Her whole adult life has been devoted to expanding life choices for women and girls through her work with the United Nations Population Fund (UNFPA). She has an activist spirit coupled with an abundant talent for diplomacy that was honed by her long marriage to Angier Biddle Duke, President Kennedy's chief of protocol. No on-the-arm-of wife she, Robin used her contacts and positions to promote international cooperation on behalf of women's human rights. Angier was killed in a Rollerblading accident when Robin was seventy-three, but she kept right on going.

"Sitting around waiting for something to happen is certainly not the name of my game," she told me. "I mean, come on. You pull your weight in a boat. If you've been as lucky as I have in life, you put your oar in the water and you keep rowing. So what if I don't row as fast as I once did? It's more fun to be involved." At eighty she decided to learn French, partly to be useful to the International Rescue Committee in the French-speaking African countries and partly because, as she said, "I wanted to see if I could still learn. You know how your machine gets rusty." She told me that she enjoyed being the oldest person among the young students. "I try to stay on top of my game, but I am a bit slower," she admitted. She doesn't go to all the receptions, she said, and she's begun to cut back her to trips to Africa (to only twice a year!). Assuming the role of sage, Robin had just brought her granddaughter along on a trip to Africa when I interviewed her. "I wanted her to see the on-the-ground realities of the developing world and how much work there is to do," she explained.

Another wonderful example of having a purpose in late life comes from my friends Eva and Yoel Haller, both seventy-seven years old when I interviewed them. They met when they were fifty-seven and she was a widow running a major international marketing company that she and her fourth husband had created together. Three years later, Eva sold her marketing company to the employees, Yoel retired from a long practice as an ob-gyn in San Francisco, and they have worked together ever since on numerous philanthropic efforts. "I don't play golf, don't play tennis, don't play bridge," Eva told me. "I don't do luncheons and I don't pour tea. I've always been a social activist. I can't think of another way of living. What other reason is there to get up in the morning? What are you going to do with your day? You need to have a reason to live."

Eva describes their activities as "incubating" new youth organizations. One major nonprofit she chairs is Free the Children, which has built more than five hundred schools in Africa, Asia, and South America. "It is organized, run, and financed through fund-raising by young people," she told me with pride. She also sits on a variety of mostly international boards of nonprofits that are dedicated to education, the environment, and improving the lives of women and children in developing countries. The Hallers speak of the young people they work with as their extended family. "We take them under our wing," said Yoel. "They stay with us and share our lives." Eva added, "It's very nourishing. We get more than they get out of it, but of course I never tell them that."

Over and over again, I have found this true in my own relationships with youngsters. As Carolyn Heilbrun wrote, "The secret . . . of successful—and therefore continuing—association with the young lies in knowing that they are more valuable as suppliers of intelligence than receivers of it."

Eva and Yoel Haller NORMAN-MARQUEE PHOTOGRAPHY NEW YORK

Janet Wolfe was ninety-three when we met at a party in South-hampton. She radiated such good humor and vitality that I asked to interview her. She took me to a restaurant close by her small New York apartment, where she eats lunch every day: spaghetti alle vongole (she brings the leftovers home for dinner) and a glass of pinot grigio.

What surprised me, given her ebullience, was that Janet has had a very difficult life, one that could well have made her bitter. She told me, "I had a mother who hated me. She'd say, 'You ugly thing, you'll never amount to anything.' In her will, she left everything to my two brothers and a dollar to me, so I wouldn't break the will. My father didn't know how to cope with her." Janet's father was a Wall Street broker. They were wealthy but lost everything in the Depression. "I'm the most successful failure," Janet said. "I could have been a good actress, or a director in the theater, but I didn't stick to anything. I never had a sense of worth. I worked a little in Hollywood as an extra. Danced in some pictures till they found out I couldn't dance." She headed the officers' club for the Red Cross in Rome during World War II. Despite her ability to make friends and make people laugh, at sixty and supporting two daughters, Janet was running out of money. She asked the chairman of the New York City Housing Authority if he could give her a job.

He said, "What can you do for the housing authority?"

"Nothing," she answered.

"Tell you what," he said. "I grew up in the projects and was never exposed to classical music. Could you start a symphony orchestra for us?"

That's just what she did, and she was still running the orchestra when I interviewed her.

The orchestra Janet founded has produced fifty public concerts every year for residents of housing developments in New York City—at public schools, in prisons, and in city parks—and has performed annual concerts at some of the city's most prestigious halls. This is the work of Janet's Third Act. She used to sneak in black musicians from Juilliard who were being pushed into jazz because there was a perception that blacks couldn't or shouldn't play classical music. The late Max Roach, a famed composer and percussionist, who performed with the orchestra, said of Janet that she "has provided more work for black, Hispanic, and Asian players than anyone in New York. It's probably the only orchestra in the country that gives minority musicians, including black composers and conductors, an opportunity to perform classical music with a symphony orchestra."

Janet has a wonderful, self-depricating sense of humor about herself. She told me over lunch that she's always trying to raise money for the orchestra. "I said to this wealthy man recently, 'If you give me enough money, you won't have to sleep with me.' And he replied, 'How much is enough?' " Despite health problems and a painful past, Janet is doing well by doing good.

We know that just about everything that is part of the world around us right now will continue on after we are gone. Therein lies the sadness. I take comfort in the thought, expressed by Zalman Schachter-Shalomi, that by using our later years for Generativity—for guiding and nurturing others, especially the next generations—we ensure that our lives are "saved" in the same way we save something we've written on our computer to ensure that it lasts and isn't wiped away by a power outage. The accumulated experience of our lifetimes, synthesized through failures and successes, are "saved" as legacies to others, long after our bodies have shut down.[5]

I looked for organizations that enable seniors to give back, and I found the following listed in the International Longevity Center's book *The Longevity Prescription: How to Maximize the Three-Decade Dividend.*

THE EXPERIENCE CORPS: The mission of this organization is to "partner with schools and local community organizations to create meaningful opportunities for adults over 55 to meet society's greatest challenges." The Experience Corps has programs in place in twenty cities across the nation. The website is www.experiencecorps.org.

RESERVE, INC.: Its mission is to connect experienced retired professionals with compensated service opportunities that challenge them to use their lifetime skills for the public good: www .reserveinc.org.

CIVIC VENTURES: This group seeks to encourage experienced workers approaching retirement to redeploy their expertise to address serious social problems in areas such as the environment, education, health care, and homelessness: www.civicventures.org and www.encore.org.

It has been my experience that the most powerful and rewarding forms of Generativity are those that have personal relevance. For instance, I enjoy and am good at working with (and creating organizations that work with) adolescents because I so vividly recall how difficult my own adolescence was and what it was that I lacked: someone to listen to me and make me feel safe with self-revelation. Similarly, I am drawn to work within organizations such as Eve Ensler's V-Day: Until the Violence Stops because so many women I know—including my mother—have been victims of violence and abuse and I'm sure that, if we can stop the violence, just about every single thing in the world will change! In doing this work, I am moving from the core of my being and with my heart. I do not view it as charity! Charity, as I see it, means creating safety nets. But people can get caught in safety nets. True Generativity is creating trampolines, not safety nets.

CHAPTER 17

Ripening the Time: A Challenge for Women

Another world is not only possible, she is on her way.
On a quiet day, I can hear her breathing.

—ARUNDHATI ROY

What is required today is after all what the great
religions have asked of human beings, to treat others as
we ourselves want to be treated, to accept social
responsibilities and to exercise stewardship over all
creation. We don't know if or when the time will be ripe
for such a transformation, but we do believe that all of
us should be striving to ripen the time.

—PAUL ERLICH

WE'VE LIVED FOR FIVE, SIX, SEVEN, EIGHT DECADES OR MORE, long enough to know that the world is in major trouble. Call me an alarmist but, to paraphrase my friend Robin Morgan, being an alarmist is a principled choice when there is cause for alarm.

This is way beyond equal wages and glass ceilings. I have come to the conclusion that nothing less than the long-term survival of our species—of our planet, actually—will depend on women moving into leadership positions in every arena: electoral, judicial, spiritual, financial, psychological, community-based, artistic.

Far be it from me to be holier-than-thou in the denial department; I've done plenty of denial in my time. I understand that to face what's happening means being called to act, and that's tough. Some of us have a need to cling to what we want to believe despite evidence to the contrary. One's identity can be bound up in a certain belief system, and to examine it is to throw one's very being into question—*If this isn't true, then who am I?*

We need to answer the question "Then who am I?" with a resounding "We are wise enough women, ready to speak our truths to power even if it means dredging up the truths we've been trying to bury." Some anthropologists believe that with age, women reclaim their assertive, aggressive traits, which they may have repressed during the parental years. In studying twenty-six different societies, the anthropologist David Gutmann found that this was true in fourteen of them, and that in none of them did men's dominance increase.[1]

We are also members of the trailblazing sixties generation. We have experienced what it means to confront outmoded, discriminatory status symbols; to throw ourselves behind efforts to achieve equal rights for people of color, for ourselves; and to create new role models of citizenship in the process.

We can't wait for the young, though we must lead and inspire them. But they are absorbed in becoming and getting—getting a degree, getting a job, getting a partner, getting a house, getting a family, getting a promotion, getting a grip. The middle-aged are in the midst of the fertile void, anxious about youth and about power slipping through their fingers. They're still scared of elderhood. We're past that, and, for the most part, we're through with the "getting," too.

You may wonder why I speak of elder women (together with girls and men of conscience) as being the ones more likely to lead society toward a new paradigm that is less violent, less unequal, less ageist, racist, sexist, and homophobic. For one thing, many men have been trained to think that the ideas of diplomacy, peace, and equality are effete, too humanistic—sissy stuff that challenges their manhood. In *The New Earth,* Eckhart Tolle writes that while the ego has gained "absolute supremacy in the collective human psyche," it is harder for the ego to take root in women than in men because women "are more in touch with the inner body and the intelligence of the organism where the intuitive faculties originate [and have] greater openness and sensitivity toward other life-forms and [are] more attuned to the natural world." As Gloria Steinem has said, "It's not that women are morally superior to men, it's just that we don't have our masculinity to prove."

For another thing, there are more elder women than ever before: forty million—51 percent of the aging boomers. Women are the single largest demographic in U.S. history.

Then there's the fact that women navigate changes and adjustments more easily than men and so have an easier time with aging. While men's lives have tended to be focused mainly on job or career, women's have been marked by discontinuity: having babies, balancing careers while keeping house, moving as our husband's jobs dictate, raising children, then sending them off (often to have them return till they become economically independent, which is happening later and later!). The women's movement inspired many of us to examine and reappraise our roles in life and work. Then there are the major changes brought on by hormonal shifts. We've learned to adjust to discontinuities. The cultural anthropologist Mary Catherine Bateson points out that although for much of our lives these discontinuities were seen as vulnerabilities— *women's ways*—as we age, our adaptability becomes an asset, a core of our resilience. Besides, we have less to lose from change than men do. Too few of us have ever really been in control within our nation—perhaps even within our families; we've suffered the most from the status quo, and in Act III we're no longer in the marketplace, trying to please. What have we got to lose?

Ready or not, here we are, with more time and experience on our hands and less fear about upsetting anyone. It's time to scrounge around in our house of memories and pull up the things we once knew and then forgot we knew because knowing meant

authenticity—being who we are fully, in the truest sense—and authenticity was dangerous. Let's bring back the girls we once were
before we became the women our husbands or bosses thought we
ought to be. The girl with hands on hips, jaw jutting, saying, "Oh
yeah, says who?" Bring her back, nourish her with our hard-earned
wisdom, and let her guide our footsteps as we face our challenges.

One of our challenges is to help one another understand the
new global reality and redefine our nation's place in it. We face a
shrinking, congested planet with diminishing resources. Globaliza-
tion may be creating one sort of unified world, but for it to be a
peaceful, just, sustainable form of unity, our global consciousness
needs to catch up to it.

The new reality demands internationalism, multilateralism,
diplomacy (with humility), and compassion. But these approaches
are considered "effeminate" or "effete" by too many men we've
elected to office. If you study the gender gap—which exposes the
differences between how women vote and poll on issues and how
men vote and poll—you can see that these are, in fact, overwhelmingly women's values. But men are wrong to view them pejoratively.
These are the values that will save us. And, on a hopeful note, when
the gender gap does narrow—as it appears to be doing on war and
peace issues, for example—men are moving in women's direction,
rather than the other way around.

I've said in many different ways why *elder* women are best suited
to take the lead in saving the world. Let me say it again: We have
the time, the wisdom, the breadth of vision, *and the numbers.* We have
less to lose, and now we're not afraid to be angry. At least according
to some anthropologists, we've become the more assertive gender.
And there's the future of the young—in some cases our own grandchildren and step-grandchildren, nieces and nephews—to motivate us further.

It seems overwhelming, doesn't it? The idea that we can actually
change how the world's institutions conduct themselves? But think
of a trim tab! A trim tab is a miniature rudder, a tiny thing that is

attached to the edge of the big rudder at the back of an ocean liner. If you move the trim tab just a little bit, it can, with hardly any effort, build up a low pressure that pulls the rudder around. Women constitute a critical mass, and older women are the critical mass *within* the mass. Women over eighty-five are the fastest-growing age group in the world! Let's become the trim tab on the rudder of the ship of state.

In the time of the founding of our nation, the trim tab was a council of elder wise women who chose the chief for the Six Nations of the Iroquois Confederacy. The women weren't chiefs themselves, but it was recognized that they were the ones who would know which man had the appropriate qualities of leadership (which meant the ability not to go out after things but to hold things together). It was the elder women who decided when to go to war and how to maintain the peace. So successful was the government of the Seven Nations that our founders used it as a template for our Constitution. Except that—surprise!—they left out the elder wise women part.

If we really wrap our minds around what's at stake and bring all our experience and wisdom to the task, we can not only choose our chiefs; we can *be* the chiefs.

The cultural anthropologist Mary Catherine Bateson has written a book about aging, *Composing a Further Life: The Age of Active Wisdom,* and, like me, she feels that the growing number of older people has the potential to play a major role in bringing about change. "You and I are living at a turning point," she told me. "The rise of feminism was a turning point, and the awareness of climate change as an environmental danger is a turning point. And this extension of longevity is a turning point. The question is, Can we contribute to the process of change in a way that really enriches and deepens lives for people of all ages; will we claim the right and mobilize the energy and find our voices again and do it?"

In his *Letters to a Young Poet,* Rilke said, "Life and Death are the greatest gifts—and usually go unopened." Shouldn't our ultimate task be to tear open our gift of life and use our wisdom and deep-ened consciousness to ripen the time? We ourselves are ripe—"going to seed," as they say. So let's sow those seeds far and wide and see what grows! Might this not be our ultimate evolutionary purpose?

CHAPTER 18

Don't Put Off Preparing for the Inevitable: One of These Days Is Right Now

One of the things I have come to feel ... is that if you think you know what you're going to be doing in five or ten years, you're wrong. But if you don't have an opinion on it, you're in trouble. In other words, go toward the future with a plan that you're willing to let go of.

—MARY CATHERINE BATESON

NOW, IN THE FIRST HALF OF MY SEVENTIES, I REALIZE THAT MY future is right now, today, this very minute. Never has the expression "If not now, when?" been more relevant. Let's not blind ourselves to the realities that lie just around the corner, realities that, with proper forethought, can be manageable—or, with denial, can make our last decades miserable. *One of these days I'll make a will, start saving money, figure out what will happen if Bill dies first . . .* This Second Act thinking is a recipe for trouble in the Third Act. Backing out of the bedroom to avoid displaying a dimpled rump is one thing; backing into our futures is quite another! I hope younger women reading this book will begin to prepare for the future right now, when it can be easier and less costly.

"People generally overvalue the present and undervalue the future . . . and it's very clearly a phenomenon that applies to decision-making about money," writes Dr. Laura Carstensen in her book *A Long Bright Future: An Action Plan for a Lifetime of Happiness, Health, and Financial Security.*[1] "We'll let our future selves deal with living on less so we can live on more now," says Dr. Carstensen, the founding director of the Stanford Center on Longevity.

In an effort to see if virtual reality might be used to help people better relate to their older selves, researchers at the Center on Longevity work with young volunteers who don virtual-reality helmets, look into computer-generated "mirrors," and see their own older self, their own avatar, looking back at them. Half the volunteers see themselves at their present age; the other half see themselves forty-five years in the future, bags, jowls, wrinkles, and all. The researchers then have the "aged" volunteers perform different interactive tasks with their avatar, and this appears to enable them to connect emotionally with their older selves. "At the study's conclusion," writes Dr. Carstensen, "participants are asked to decide how to allocate a $1,000 windfall. Interestingly, participants who see their older selves in the mirror allocate significantly more money to retirement."

Not all of us can avail ourselves of this morphing technology, so we have to try hard to envision ourselves at, say, sixty, seventy, and eighty. Have we saved money? Possibly not. Only half of the older baby boomers are saving enough for a comfortable retirement. This is a serious dilemma for women, in particular, since older women are twice as likely to be poor as men. During our lifetimes, the one-paycheck family became less common. Women in ever-increasing numbers entered the workforce; many of those women have been widows and divorcees, and they weren't working for "pin money." These women needed to increase their Social Security benefits and maintain their health care coverage. But women start off earning only up to 81 percent of what men earn (often doing the exact same work), and, because we live longer, the effects of reduced benefits in an economic downturn are especially onerous for us. It's a burden, particularly for the more than two million divorced women, who far outnumber the widows. In their book *Project Renewment,* Bernice Brattner and Helen Dennis write, "The annual median income for women 65 and older is about $3,000 above the Census definition of poverty, or $11,816. Ninety percent of all women, at some time in their lives, will be totally responsible for their own financial welfare."[2]

Financial Planning

Ask yourself these questions: Do you have investments, and how much are they likely to earn for you? What benefits—your own or your husband's—will support you? If you are married and your husband has a private pension, has he elected to provide survivorship coverage for you? If he has a 401(k) retirement plan at work, are you sure you are named as the beneficiary? Similarly, are you the beneficiary of any life insurance policies on your spouse? Has he told you that you will inherit "everything" in his will—but created a trust that keeps you from making withdrawals without permission from his estate-planning attorney, who will act as trustee?

Believe me, all of these things happen to smart women who think they will be provided for upon a spouse's death!

Have you discussed these matters with your husband or has he told you, "I've got everything under control"? Maybe yes, maybe no, but you have a right to know. Our income in our seventies and eighties may determine our outcome.

Women may be single by choice or by circumstances. But since women live longer, the odds are that we will live our later years on our own. It's worth thinking about and planning for right now.

Draw up a baseline budget that you will need to live on when you stop working. Include in it the cost of long-term care should you need it, and start right now figuring out how you're going to fund it.

One of the best books about financial planning for your retirement that I've read is *The New Savage Number: How Much Money Do You Really Need to Retire?* by Terry Savage.[3] I often urge friends to buy and read it. When Terry says that within every woman there is a secret fear of being a "bag lady," you know she is talking to you. (Terry's website is www.terrysavage.com.)

Savage says that there is easily accessible and inexpensive help for planning your retirement. Let me summarize a few of her points about the key issues: You need to start saving, and investing to increase your savings. Then you should carefully plan your withdrawals from your savings after retirement *so you don't run out of money before you run out of time.*

THREE QUESTIONS

Terry Savage asks us to start our planning by answering three questions. They are basic but require you to put some starch in your spine and remove any blinders of denial.

1. How old do I expect to be when I die?
2. How do I rank the following three retirement solutions?

    -   Working longer before retiring
    -   Lowered standard of living in retirement
    -   Saving more now

3. If I knew I could get trustworthy advice about how to save, invest, budget, and withdraw, would I be willing to confront the financial issues of retirement?

Terry's first step is to help you get a realistic perspective on how long you're likely to live. (You may be surprised, since women over age eighty-five are the fastest-growing demographic!) For some insight into the question of longevity, Savage sends you to a website: www.Livingto100.com. You enter information about your age, health, and eating and exercise habits, along with some information about your parents' longevity, and you'll get a personalized estimate of how long you might live. Once you're armed with that information, Savage suggests going to www.choosetosave.org, a website created by the nonprofit Employee Benefit Research Institute. Click on the "Ballpark Estimate" tool for help in determining how much you should be saving, given your earnings and your life-style and when you hope to retire, so your standard of living doesn't drop sharply when you stop bringing home a regular income. Using this online calculator, it's easy to see the impact of working longer, contributing more, changing your investment style, or a combination of those variables.

You may discover that you are unable to save more or that your investments aren't bringing in big enough returns to give you a secure retirement. In that case, you may have to consider working longer hours now or continuing work for more years to allow your nest egg to grow. Or perhaps you can convince your company to keep you on part-time. Older workers have enormous things to teach incoming, younger workers. Research shows that companies that make it possible for older workers to stay by rearranging hours, creating new job descriptions, and so forth, wind up earning more profit. Or you might investigate the possibility of using your skills—computer, sales, management, leadership skills—for salaried work in a nonprofit organization. Or go into teaching your skills to other people.

Monte Carlo Modeling

When you're approaching retirement, you'll need some advice about how to invest with less risk (since you will no longer be making big contributions to your retirement plan) and how much money you can safely withdraw every month so you can make your money last as long as you do. For that kind of planning, simple averages or casual guesswork just won't do.

Savage explains the strangely named Monte Carlo modeling process, a sophisticated computer program that takes in all your answers to a detailed questionnaire and models multiple alternatives to come up with investment and withdrawal strategies for your retirement years that have a high probability of meeting your goals. The Monte Carlo process can also be used if you're younger;

it will show you, among other things, how much you should be saving, whether you are investing appropriately, how much money you can afford to take out every month, how inflation will affect your savings, and what your income goals should be.

"Monte Carlo modeling goes far beyond the law of averages," says Savage. "It illustrates the range of probabilities so that you can observe the trade-off between risk and return."⁴ Monte Carlo modeling is available at a number of leading financial services firms. Which firm may be appropriate for you depends partly on whether you are in what Savage calls the "accumulation phase" or the "withdrawal phase."

THE ACCUMULATION PHASE

You are in the accumulation phase if you are still working, still trying to save, or still contributing to a retirement plan at work. If this is the case, Savage says, "Your company 401(k) retirement plan (or 403(b) savings plan for non-profits) isn't the only place you could be saving. If you're self-employed or own your own small business, you can set up a Keogh plan, an IRA, a SEP-IRA, or an individual 401(k) plan. These plans differ in their contribution limits and in whether those contributions are made by the employee or employer." You can find definitions and instructions for opening these accounts at any major mutual fund or brokerage website because they also offer the mutual funds and stocks to make your retirement plan grow.

"It can be difficult to force yourself to save, so the trick is to do it automatically—to have the money taken out of your paycheck before you see it and spend it," notes Savage. But the really tough part is deciding how to invest that money, how much risk to take, which investments to use, and how to maintain a disciplined approach to your investments even when the stock market is plummeting. For that you need professional help—and it doesn't have to be expensive. Many of the nation's largest employers offer 401(k) investment advice to their employees through independent services.

FINANCIAL ENGINES (www.financialengines.com). Savage likes this firm's modeling services for those who are still in the accumulation phase. It includes modeling for your tax-deferred accounts, your non-tax-deferred accounts, employee stock options, and multiple goals. You are asked to fill out an extensive questionnaire that asks about your financial matters as well as your goals. Financial Engines is an independent firm that receives no fees for its buy-and-sell recommendations. You simply follow the suggestions to switch investments among the funds in your company plan.

But you need different advice—and investment choices—as you enter retirement. Savage advises that you not leave your money in your company 401(k) plan after retirement because your firm's type of investments are more suitable for the accumulation phase than for the withdrawal phase; also you have no choice over the investment decisions. In addition, many company IRA or 401(k) accounts require immediate distribution of the funds when you die, which prevents your heirs from spreading out distributions and delaying taxes on withdrawals. She suggests instead that when you retire you roll your company 401(k) plan into an individual retirement account (IRA). And then be sure to name a beneficiary for the account.

THE WITHDRAWAL PHASE

The withdrawal phase is just what it sounds like: the time when you have fewer if any earnings beyond your investments and you have to carefully prioritize what you spend: Do you get a new car or a new dress, or downsize your home?

SOME SOURCES FOR MONTE CARLO MODELING

T. ROWE PRICE (www.troweprice.com). T. Rowe Price Advisory Services was one of the first to use Monte Carlo modeling. It sees the accumulation and withdrawal phases as integrated parts of the advice process. It advertises itself as offering a top-performing and diverse group of mutual funds and providing individualized investment advice. The service is available to company retirement plans and to individuals who pay a fee ($250 as of this writing) for the initial analysis and annual updates. You do not need to have an investment with T. Rowe Price to use this service.

FIDELITY (www.fidelity.com). Fidelity offers a more all-encompassing financial service that may be attractive to baby boomers. The Fidelity Retirement Income Advantage program starts with Monte Carlo modeling and goes further, notes Savage, "providing the framework for planning, investing, withdrawing, and reassessing all your retirement assets, from Social Security and pension checks to IRA rollover assets and other savings, whether invested with Fidelity or elsewhere."[5]

VANGUARD (www.vanguard.com). The Vanguard Group manages some of the largest funds, specializes in index funds, and has provided a type of Monte Carlo modeling to its clients for years. As of this writing, fees for its services range from free to $1,500, depending on the size of the account. The standard fee covers a one-time consultation with a certified financial planner, who is supposed to help you examine your choices and develop a plan, using both Vanguard and non-Vanguard investments. A complete and ongoing money-management service is also available, at a higher cost.

Professional Advice

Terry Savage points out that even with all these amazing tools and services available online for people who, like me, are challenged in technological and financial domains, there is nothing like a trusted, certified, experienced professional to help make sense of it all. To find such a person, Savage suggests going to the website for certified financial planners (CFP), www.cfp.net. There you will find a search engine that gives you a list of CFPs in your area and lets you check a planner's credentials and find out if they have anything questionable in their history. Some CFPs charge an hourly fee for creating and updating a plan; plus, they receive commissions on products they sell, such as life insurance or mutual funds. Fee-only planners receive no commissions on sold products. Fee-only planners are credentialed through the National Association of Personal Financial Advisors (NAPFA). NAPFA members can be reached at www.napfa.org.

Never give any financial adviser the power to make independent decisions without your knowledge. If you don't understand what is being offered, ask questions—and keep asking—until you do, and be sure you understand all the risks. You can check out any financial professional's disciplinary history at www.FINRA.org, the website of the Financial Industry Regulatory Authority.

One last word of advice from Terry Savage: "If it sounds too good to be true, it usually is! There's nothing wrong with keeping a significant portion of your money in what I call 'chicken money' investments, such as short-term, insured bank CDs or money market accounts. You won't get rich with these low-yielding investments—but you won't get poor either! They give you peace of mind so you can invest the balance of your money for growth and income."

Long-Term Care

It may surprise you to learn that 80 percent of older people are fully independent. The 2005 National Health Interview Survey revealed that only 7 percent of people between the ages of seventy-five and eighty-four and only 25 percent of those over eighty-four depend on someone for their personal care. Still, elderly women over sixty-five are three times as likely as elderly men to be widowed, sickly, indigent, and in need of assistance from their children—usually this means their female children since, like all forms of care, caring for elderly parents falls predominantly to women. One English study found that women spent nineteen

minutes in the most arduous care of elderly relatives for every minute their husbands spent.[6]

It is possible that you will not be able to afford long-term-care
insurance. Many Americans cannot buy this type of insurance
because it is expensive and their savings may be gone by the time
they need such care. I saw, up close and personal, what lack of
long-term care can do to a family. I had an uncle who developed
Parkinson's disease. His was a very protracted illness that ended up
draining all the family's savings. This is why you should try, if at all
possible, to have your estate planning include insurance coverage
for long-term incapacity, including assisted living, nursing homes,
and in-home care, which Medicare does not cover long-term. If
you're old and impoverished, the state will put you in a Medicaid-
funded nursing home. If at all possible, it is wise to identify an
attorney, accountant, or estate planner who can work with you to
develop a plan to cover long-term care when rising insurance premiums may be more than you can afford. For information on
long-term-care insurance policies, go to www.MagaLTC.com—
independent agents, specializing in this type of insurance. Different strategies can include reverse mortgages or living trusts. The
younger you are when you take out long-term-care insurance, the
less expensive the premiums will be.

Mary Madden is a sixty-two-year-old Atlanta businesswoman
who is dating a man she met online. She told me, "I just recently
got long-term care, and I asked when I got it if I got married what
it would take to put someone else on it. Turns out the other person
can be included pretty easily. Because that's what worries me—the
long-term care if we ended up together and one of us got sick. If
you are getting married at this point in your life, you need to make
sure everyone has long-term-care insurance because otherwise it
could jeopardize what you leave your children. So I talked to my
life insurance agent and we moved things around so I would have
long-term care."

You can go to AoA.gov for information on many elder care services, including housing and seniors' rights, and Medicare.gov/

nhcompare for information on the quality and performance of every nursing home in the country that is certified by Medicare or Medicaid.

Making Your Will

Many people put off making a will. It does, after all, require facing the time when you'll no longer be around. My estate planner, with whom I started working thirty years ago, when my children were very young, tells me that many of her clients have to be dragged kicking and screaming into the process, whereas I see it as a fascinating, ever-evolving exercise that forces me to imagine what my children and grandchildren will become and which of my organizational efforts I want to endow if I am able and in what form. So, if you haven't already, get to work on a will or a revocable living trust and make sure that all legal documents, deeds to your house, insurance policies, and so forth are with a lawyer or in a safe-deposit box that has a signer you trust.

Durable Power of Attorney

Another document you need is a durable power of attorney. This gives the authority to make legal decisions to a child or other trusted individual should you be incapacitated. In this way, you make it possible for them to avoid legal hassles with banks, doctors, and so on. This document should be created in conjunction with your will, or the person to make these decisions can be the "successor trustee" of your revocable trust. Think carefully about the person you choose for this responsibility; it should be someone who loves and understands you, and who will be available in an emergency situation.

Palliative Care

Knowing from my own family experience the agony an ill person and their loved ones can go through as disease wends its way through all facets of their lives, I was eager to find out about a relatively new field of care known as palliative care, which has grown up in the last decade or so. Palliative care provides emotional, spiritual, and practical care for patients who are ill but not necessarily terminal; a serious illness can take a toll not only on the patient herself but on her family as well. By the year 2009, more than 1,530 U.S. hospitals (62 percent) were providing palliative care.

I assumed palliative care was the same as hospice care, the value of which I had witnessed when a beloved aunt was dying. The hospice worker enabled my aunt to actually look forward to the experience. My aunt called me the night she died to say goodbye and tell me she'd put on her favorite lipstick and nightgown and "was ready to die." But when I interviewed Dr. Diane Meier, who heads the Center to Advance Palliative Care (CAPC) at Mount Sinai School of Medicine in New York, she made clear that hospice and palliative care are different.

"Hospice is one version of palliative care specifically for the terminally ill," Dr. Meier explained. "And, in fact, to get hospice in this country, your doctor has to sign a piece of paper saying you are dying within six months, and you—the patient—also have to sign a piece of paper saying you are willing to give up life-prolonging treatment in return for hospice care. It's not human nature to accept the reality of death, nor to give up the hope that more treatment will prolong your life. As a result, the majority of people don't start getting hospice until the last few weeks of their lives, and more than 60 to 70 percent of Americans who die never get hospice at all because of those barriers, those eligibility barriers. Late referral means that people and their families miss out on the care and support they desperately need during the typically many-year duration of a serious illness. This is why palliative care outside of hospice is not limited to the dying."

Palliative care, Dr. Meier went on, is "for anyone living with a serious illness who may have years to live but have consequences of their illness: distress due to psychological, physical, practical, or spiritual issues, as well as family burdens." As with hospice care, palliative care can be provided at home, in a nursing home, or in a hospital. I learned from Dr. Meier that palliative care teams look at the patient's entire situation, including their ability to access transportation, manage their pain, understand what is happening to them, and arrange for massage therapy; workers will also help members of the family handle their own stress. "Thanks to modern medicine, we can keep you going for a very long time with some pretty debilitating illnesses," continued Dr. Meier. "So palliative care developed as a field in an attempt to focus on the quality of all this extra time. It gives the patient this sense that no matter what happens, you're going to walk with them and be with them and listen to what matters to them—the patient is at the center. This kind of support and attention is profoundly reassuring and, unfortunately, in the absence of palliative care, is not something that characterizes modern medical care in this country. Most people with advanced illness have six specialists and no quarterback, no one really in charge. And even if they once had a quarterback, a primary care physician, once the serious illness develops, that person often recedes into the background, is out of the loop, is no longer controlling the care, and the patient is sort of left to the hospitalist, the oncologist, the cardiologist, or the neurologist, who does not see him- or herself as a primary care physician or as the person who is going to keep walking with that patient and family no matter what happens. They're the specialist. They treat the heart failure, they treat the cancer, they treat the Parkinson's disease, but the needs of the patient go far beyond the disease-specific issues."

Even though palliative care is currently offered in 70 percent of our large hospitals, not enough patients are accessing it, because doctors have not been trained to understand its value and patients and their families have not yet learned to ask for it. This is more important than ever now: A recent study showed that cancer patients who get palliative care along with standard cancer treatment actually lived quite a bit longer than patients who received only standard care. If palliative care can help patients feel better, perhaps it's not surprising that it also prolongs life!

Where and How Will You Live?

Then there's the issue of where you live. Maybe it's time to make changes to your home that will make it easier and safer for you as you age. Having had a hip and a knee replacement, I know that in a few years' time I will want a home without stairs. I'm aware of the hazards of falling at my age, so I've gotten rid of all throw rugs that might slip. I also make sure there's nothing lying about at night that I could trip over. Ted Turner has installed grab rails in the showers and baths of his homes and was generous enough to offer to do the same for me. I've known too many people who've fallen in the shower, and I don't intend to be one of them.

There are a variety of housing arrangements for people who cannot or no longer want to live alone and be responsible for all that it entails—cleaning, cooking, gardening, and so forth. There are independent senior communities with private apartments and twenty-four-hour emergency-call services, as well as social activities. Continuing-care retirement communities agree under contract to provide residents with housing and services for life; these usually require a one-time entrance fee and monthly payments. Assisted living facilities can be nursing homes or part of a retirement community; they cost on average $32,000 a year. A semi-private room in a nursing home costs $65,000 a year. As I said, Medicare covers the expenses for only a limited time, while someone recovers from an accident or surgery. Start saving and budgeting!

Only 5 percent of people over sixty-five are in special-care institutions, and that number has been dropping since 1982. Dr. Marion Perlmutter told me, "I think we are moving away from institutionalization, which is good. People do much better at home if they can stay at home. What we know now about the memory system is that it is so context-dependent. If I can't remember something I was going to do when I was in the next room, all I have to do is go back into the other room and that context reminds me. Well, if you move to a nursing home, you have lost the entire context of your life. It's so disorientating. and they get into this vegetative state. But this isn't a necessity of old age. We know that now."

Elderly people who are confined to nursing homes do remarkably better, physiologically and psychologically, when they have some control over their day-to-day lives. Homes should, perhaps, allow patients to keep a pet, have some say over their schedules, and decorate their room. "It's not responsibility that kills, it's the lack of control," says Dr. Estelle Ramey, a professor of physiology and biophysics at Georgetown University Medical School. "The driver isn't under as much pressure as the passenger."

End-of-Life Care

You should also prepare a health care power of attorney document, which will appoint someone to make decisions about your end-of-life care or cessation of treatment. This would go into effect when your doctor determines that you are no longer able to make such decisions yourself.

A Living Will

Another important document is a living will, in which you state what life-support procedures you want or don't want. This is extremely important if you want to avoid putting your loved ones in a situation where they may have to fight with the doctors about what to do. When developing a living will or power of attorney document, you will need to know what your state's laws say about such end-of-life advance directives.

If you prefer not be resuscitated should your heart or breathing stop, you will need a Do Not Resuscitate order (DNR). This should be signed by a doctor and put into your medical records. These orders are accepted in all states.

I know that these are all difficult issues to come to terms with, but I strongly encourage you to accept the challenge—not one of these days, but right now.

CHAPTER 19

Let's Hear It for Revolution!

The meaning or the lack of meaning that old age takes on in any given society puts that whole society to the test, since it is this that reveals the meaning or lack of meaning of the entirety of the life leading to that old age.

—SIMONE DE BEAUVOIR, *The Coming of Age*

AS I HAVE SAID BEFORE IN THIS BOOK, THE PRESENT GENERATION of boomers and seniors is redefining what it means to age. In record numbers, we are surviving, thriving, and defying stereotypes. I believe we are collectively moving into a more productive and creative vision of retirement. New research has shed light on the aging process, and the span of healthy living is increasing. Government programs instituted in the twentieth century have begun to reduce poverty and isolation among older citizens. With years of vitality both behind us and ahead of us, we are the face of what the late Dr. Robert Butler called the "longevity revolution."

We know that we matter. At least we should know. Having confidence about our place in the world is not only good for us psychologically, it is also critical for advancing the social and political issues that matter to us. If we are going to advocate for ourselves and others—if we are going to step up and offer solutions to pressing global problems—we need to believe we have the *right* to do so. We need to take stock of how much we contribute, become aware of the wisdom we have to offer. We should be proud of our deeds—even as we express our needs.

As a social group, we must remain aware of the negative stereotypes that can damage our sense of ourselves. One of the most destructive myths about older people is that of the "greedy geezer," the selfish, narrow-minded, stingy hoarder who shows little concern for others. I believe these portrayals are inaccurate. Considering all of the contributions older people make through spending, working, volunteering, donating, and caretaking, it is clear that we provide more to society than we drain from it.

The Ways Seniors Contribute

Older individuals participate in the marketplace by paying for specialized goods and services; they constitute what is called a "silver market." Economists argue that there is an important dividend that comes from the increasing number of older people who are relatively well-off and who now make up a greater proportion of the market share.[1] Many retirees have accumulated wealth and offer significant spending power, which stimulates jobs and financial growth. Older individuals make invaluable investments in real estate, continuing education, technologies for independent living, travel, tourism, health services, and the like. Our spending in the health care industry is not trivial, either. Economists have recently asserted that the health care industry is helping to prop up our nation's economy; it continues to add new jobs and serves as one-seventh of the economy.

WE SPEND MONEY

Some older people have been nicknamed Woofs (Well-Off Older Folks).[2] Identified as having golden spending power, this demographic is being closely watched by marketing companies, insurance companies, and wealth managers. A study by the MetLife Mature Market Institute reported that the estimated spending power of baby boomers will soon exceed $2 trillion dollars annually. Boomer households are believed to spend up to $45,000 per year. It is forecast that a shift in entertainment, advertising, and perhaps voting patterns will occur as boomers retire.[3]

However, the degree to which the silver market thrives is highly policy-dependent. In the countries where sound retirement plans are provided, older individuals feel secure enough to spend their wealth rather than save it. This underscores the critical importance of keeping Social Security solvent while also upholding incentives for private pensions. At present, no federal laws mandate that our companies—even our largest international corporations—provide pensions to their employees.[4] Worse yet, when workers save for retirement solely through private accounts, many find themselves woefully under budget. Currently, only 60 percent of American workers are saving for retirement, and about half of them have put away only $25,000. Yet IRAs and 401(k)s remain the common alternative for the company pension.[5] No matter how retirement savings are to be structured in the future, it must be understood that programs that support retirement security also support economic growth.

LATE-LIFE TECHNOLOGICAL INNOVATIONS

Beyond our spending power, our lifestyle changes have spurred significant technological innovation. According to the Stanford Center on Longevity, a host of mobile text-messaging systems and assistive technologies are being developed to improve personal and public health. High-tech inventions, including multisystem household sensors, motion detectors, and robotics, have been developed to help older people live safely and independently in their homes.

People have long been familiar with household accommodations for the elderly, including bathroom railings, motorized stairlifts, and lever-style door handles. But the most up-to-date technologies use sensitive monitoring systems to provide minute-by-minute information to outside caretakers. Environmental sensors can monitor stove and appliance use and household temperature and can indicate hazards such as high carbon monoxide levels, flooding, or gas leaks. Motion and pressure sensors can track when an older person gets in and out of bed and monitor in the event of a fall. Messages from passive sensors can be relayed to caregivers, who can then decide whether to call on the older person. Door sensors can be used to signal when an older person leaves the home, and location trackers can help pinpoint the location of an older person who is prone to wandering. These advances allow older people to live in their homes longer, even if they have a health condition, mobility problem, or complex medication regimen.[6]

SENIORS ARE READY AND WILLING TO EMBRACE NEW TECHNOLOGIES

Still, it is important to avoid stereotypes when considering how older people use technology. The majority of individuals entering retirement today are generally comfortable using cellphones, computers, and the Internet. Most are not technophobic. In fact, many aging baby boomers eagerly follow along with new advances in telecommunications and computer science. As a generation that identified with rock and roll and counterculture trends, they likely do not (and will not) identify with overly simplistic products designed for "the elderly." Technology designers appreciate that the over-fifty generation grew up in entirely different circumstances than their parents did; today's retirees enjoy experimenting with, learning about, and purchasing technology. Experts predict that baby boomers will embrace available technologies, especially social-networking sites, to reduce their social isolation—for example, sites such as eNeighbors and Microsoft's Virtual Senior Center, now used in New York City.

WE ARE GENEROUS

Not only do we contribute as consumers, we are by far the biggest charitable donors. Older individuals donate more money to universities, charities, and civic organizations than any other age group. According to the National Philanthropic Trust, by 2055 an estimated $41 trillion will change hands as Americans pass on their accumulated assets to the next generation.[7] The *Chronicle of Philanthropy* has reported that "mature donors" (those born prior to 1946) give the highest amount to charity (an average of $1,066 per year), give to the highest number of different charities, and demonstrate the highest rate of giving (77 percent of these individuals give). Close behind are the baby boomers. Among those born between 1946 and 1964, 66 percent give to charity, and they give an average of $900 each year.[8]

WE VOLUNTEER

Volunteering is another important way older people give. Many deeds by older citizens go unpaid, and we must not underestimate the social and monetary value of volunteerism. Older citizens are active citizens; their efforts as volunteers help uphold communities. They organize and participate in civic organizations, run election polls, mentor young people, support their peers in long-term care and hospice, lead recreation groups, and assist visitors at hospitals, libraries, schools, and museums. They are active in local, state, and federal governing bodies. Older Americans participate in the Peace Corps (with people fifty and over serving as 10 percent of the corps),[9] not to mention the many volunteers in the Senior Corps programs. Economists estimate that the tasks performed by volunteers, given the level of education and training that would be required, are valued at $20 per hour.[10]

WE WORK

Among AARP members, almost half (47 percent) work full- or part-time. The word "retired" does not necessarily mean one has wholly abandoned the workplace. It is estimated that about one-third of men and almost one-fourth of women between sixty-five and sixty-nine are in the labor force today. Furthermore, the rates of employment among older individuals have been rising. AARP projects that roughly one in three workers will be fifty or older within a matter of years.[11]

Employers frequently fail to recognize the valuable attributes of older workers. The abilities of older people are often underestimated, but they should not be. The depth of our expertise and the breadth of our knowledge base make us critical resources for our communities, families, and places of business. For instance, one's fund of knowledge and depth of expertise can serve as a cognitive strength well into old age. Similarly, our judgments and decision making in real-world contexts are often sound, having been tempered by experience. After all I have read and heard, I am convinced that whatever small declines come with age, they do not outweigh the strengths tied to our reasoned approach to problem solving and our depth of expertise.

Older people help others maintain their work-life balance. Family caretaking is often provided by older people in the form of care for grandparents, siblings, and peers. Caretaking duties have a direct impact on the well-being of families as well as on the economy. By providing child care and elder care, older people allow other family members to reduce their absenteeism and maintain their productivity in the workplace. Our collective efforts as caretakers represent the equivalent of millions of full-time workers serving the young, old, and infirm.

Problems Persist

POVERTY

Older people remain at high risk for poverty. For 30 percent of retirees, Social Security is 90 percent of their income, and 7.1 million individuals over sixty-five live in poverty. The current unemployment rate for "mature" workers is at an all-time high of 6.7 percent. In 2007, the average income among individuals sixty-five and over was $28,449; but the median income was only $17,382.[12] Without Social Security, almost half of all older Americans would be in poverty. Social Security is the most important source of retirement income for the majority of Americans.

SOCIAL SECURITY

The 2008 Social Security Trustees report projected that without any change in current law, the assets of the Social Security trust fund will remain solvent, but not for very long. The disability trust fund, one part of the Social Security umbrella, is projected to remain solvent over the next ten years. The combined fund for retirees and survivors insurance (OASDI trust fund) is expected to remain solvent until 2041. Similarly, the Congressional Budget Office has estimated that Social Security will have sufficient funds to continue paying full benefits on time through 2048.[13]

Many different solutions have been proposed to keep Social Security solvent for future generations. Experts have considered means testing (reducing benefits for individuals with higher incomes) and/or raising the age of eligibility for payout (the age is currently sixty-six, after being raised from sixty-five). The most popular proposal, however, is to broaden the taxable wage base that funds Social Security.[14] As of 2008, Social Security has been funded by a 6 percent tax on wages up to $102,000. Wages above that level were not taxed for Social Security purposes. Historically, the intent of the taxable wage cap was to draw from 90 percent of payroll earnings without overburdening those who earn higher wages. However, today's wage base for Social Security no longer includes 90 percent of payroll earnings because wages above the taxable maximum have increased more rapidly than wages in general. If the wage base were changed to match the historically intended levels, the maximum taxable wage would be $203,000.[15] This adjustment would significantly increase projections for Social Security solvency.

- *We deserve financial security throughout our retirement.*

- *Social Security should remain a public, government-run program.*

- *We deserve to see our political leaders resolve the solvency issues that will burden future generations.*

ABUSE, DISCRIMINATION, AND EXPLOITATION

Older people are vulnerable to victimization. Sadly, hundreds of thousands of reports of elder abuse—including physical, emotional, and sexual abuse—are made to social services agencies every year. Financial exploitation of vulnerable adults is common as well. It frequently occurs among family members and is difficult to enforce. Living trusts, which give outside parties decision-making power over funds, sometimes allow conservators and guardians to mismanage property. Older people deserve opportunities to seek redress in court in cases of exploitation and abuse, regardless of their ability to pay an attorney's fees. Elder abuse and exploitation must be categorized as criminal offenses and properly enforced.

- *We deserve support in our court system even if we cannot pay for attorneys.*

- *We deserve to be safe from abuse and exploitation.*

Age discrimination at work is another form of exploitation. Significant progress was made with the passage of the Age Discrimination in Employment Act (ADEA), which prohibited mandatory retirement in most professions. However, the ADEA does not permit victims of age discrimination to recover compensatory or punitive damages. Unlike other forms of discrimination legislation, the ADEA lacks stipulations that would serve as a deterrent to age discrimination. Futhermore, greater awareness needs to be given to subtle forms of age discrimination that persist in the workplace. Many older workers are disadvantaged at their jobs because they are denied opportunities for training, promotions, or access to benefits. Ultimately, the effectiveness of the ADEA is dependent on the responsiveness of the Equal Employment Opportunity Commission. The EEOC is responsible for monitoring and enforcing federal employment discrimination law.

- *We deserve greater protection from discrimination in the workplace.*

Ways for Seniors to Keep Working

Employers should support opportunities for older individuals to work by offering flex-time and part-time arrangements. Telecommuting and job sharing can make employment feasible for older individuals who want to maintain a work-life balance. For many, working more years is a preferred plan. Workers generally do not benefit from early retirement, because it can reduce their Social Security and/or pension payments for the rest of their lives. Additionally, staying employed after sixty-five provides social interaction, a sense of purpose, and mental stimulation. Do not forget, companies that retain older workers fare better. Older employees have proven to be more careful, with lower rates of on-the-job injuries. They report a high level of morale and loyalty to their employers. Although teenagers are often given frontline jobs as cashiers or service representatives, older workers are often better equipped to think independently and to properly analyze the features of a complex situation.[16]

Older workers are proven to have good attendance rates and low turnover. This leads to significant overhead savings for the companies that employ them. Labor economists estimate that the cost to a company when an employee leaves and a new employee has to be hired and trained is significant—somewhere between $2,000 and $3,000 per worker. For large companies, holding down turnover rates can result in millions of dollars in savings. As of 2005, companies that sought to hire and/or retain older workers included Home Depot, Walgreens, MetLife, and Pitney Bowes.[17]

Younger workers need not fear the retention of older workers. According to Kenneth A. Knapp, with the International Longevity Center, in New York City, there is an erroneous assumption that if older workers stay in the workforce, this will prevent younger people from getting jobs. However, Knapp has asserted that higher employment is a positive all the way around. Higher employment leads to greater economic growth, which ultimately leads to job growth.

- *We deserve flexible work arrangements in discrimination-free work environments.*

Special Concerns for Women

Nearly 72 percent of women in their fifties are in the labor force; thus, pay inequity is a salient issue for older women. As of 2008, women in full-time jobs had a median weekly wage 20 percent below that of their male counterparts. Working women are often the sole providers for their families, yet they tend to be concentrated in low-paying occupations. More than two-thirds of the part-time labor force is made up of women, leaving them with less job security and with far fewer employer-provided benefits. Furthermore, many low-wage workers are hired as part-time, contingent, or temporary workers. In these roles, low-paid employees lack job security, paid leave, and sick leave, and have limited legal protections.[18]

Retired women have different needs than retired men. For one, women live longer than men. Women outnumber men in nursing homes, and roughly three out of every four individuals over eighty-five are female. Women need long-lasting retirement funds, but, compared to men, most of them have earned less and spent fewer years in the workforce.

Our current Social Security program includes adjustments for disparities in pay, but privatized Social Security programs would not. Private savings accounts and investments would likely not provide women, low-paid workers, or the unemployed with adequate retirement savings.

- *Women deserve equal pay for equal work.*

- *Women deserve a government-run Social Security program that will not penalize them disproportionately, as a privatized system would.*

Social and Psychological Difficulties

Many of the difficulties associated with getting older are psychological. While the majority of older people become happier as they age, rates of suicide, depression, and substance abuse among a portion of the elderly are far higher than the public appreciates. The suicide rate for individuals over eighty is higher than the teen suicide rate. However, according to the National Council on Aging, state spending for community programs has been undermined by the current recession, resulting in a 10 percent cut, on average, to services to seniors. While the Older Americans Act includes provisions for lifeline outreach programs such as Meals on Wheels, many states have exceptionally long waiting lists and cannot properly execute the programs, and this leaves many seniors isolated.

The Older Americans Act was enacted in 1965 by Congress and was reauthorized and modified in 2006. The legislation supports older citizens' health and independence through community programs, including Meals on Wheels, civic engagement programs, senior centers, transportation services, support for family caregivers, health promotion, disease prevention, and service training for employment for mature workers. These well-conceived programs can be highly effective, but citizens need to make sure that they are properly funded and executed. Nearly 80 percent of states report waiting lists for home-delivered meals, and more than 50 percent have waiting lists for personal care, homemaker services, and respite care. This is important: Dollars spent on OAA programs save taxpayers money in the long run because the programs stave off premature nursing home placements and reduce Medicare spending by preventing malnutrition and controlling chronic health conditions.[19]

Meaningful community connections promote good health. A prime example of an effective community-focused program is the AARP's Blue Zones Vitality Project. Inspired by Dan Buettner's *The Blue Zone: Lessons for Living Longer from the People Who've Lived the Longest,* an initiative was carried out by the United Health Foundation in the city of Albert Lea, Minnesota. Older citizens participating in the program joined walking groups, volunteered with youths, attended neighborhood picnics, ate nutritious foods, increased their social networking, and attended "purpose workshops." The initiative included before and after measurements of respondents' overall wellness. As measured by the "Vitality Compass," an online tool that offers an estimate of life expectancy based on eating habits, sleeping habits, stress levels, and daily activity, participants in the project raised their life expectancy by three years.[20]

- *We deserve social outreach programs that decrease social isolation and increase public health in every community.*

- *We deserve a decrease in waiting time for social service programs.*

Medicare Doesn't Cover Everything

Everyone needs to understand what Medicare covers and what it doesn't. Medicare benefits are broken up into four categories. Part A includes hospital coverage, encompassing inpatient care, inpatient drugs, and limited home health care stays and stays in a skilled nursing facility. Inpatient stays longer than 150 days are not covered, and stays in a skilled nursing facility longer than 100 days are not covered. Part B includes physician services, some home health services that are not linked to a prior hospitalization, and outpatient services. Part C covers private health plans that contract with

Medicare. Part D covers outpatient prescription drugs. Medicare does not pay for long-term nursing home care after 100 days, and sets a 190-day lifetime limit on care in psychiatric hospitals. Surveys indicate that Medicare generally covers 50 percent of health care costs, with 25 percent covered by supplemental plans and 25 percent left uncovered.[21]

- *We deserve coverage for long-term nursing home care.*

- *We deserve extensions in coverage for stays at hospitals, including psychiatric hospitals.*

Isolation

Isolation is highly detrimental to older citizens with chronic health conditions. Older people frequently have problems communicating with physicians and navigating fragmented health care systems. This is made worse if an individual has difficulty driving to appointments, getting out to pharmacies, or keeping track of medications. Many seniors simply cannot execute their health care directives on their own—they are in need of palliative care.

I wrote about palliative care and its benefits in Chapter 18. Unfortunately, palliative care is not uniformly integrated in states' Medicare budgets. According to the National Hospice and Palliative Care Organization, A-grade palliative care was available in Vermont, Montana, and New Hampshire. However, F-grade care was observed in Oklahoma, Alabama, and Mississippi.[22] It is unsettling that one's locality can make such a difference in the ability to access appropriate care.

Advocates of palliative care support one-stop-shopping service delivery. Medical "homes" would include offices with multidisciplinary teams serving older patients. Ideally, these teams would allow for collaboration among doctors, nurses, psychiatrists, social workers, physical and occupational therapists, and other professionals. To allow individuals to stay at home, and to reduce the costs associated with long-term care, we need policies mandating that palliative care be covered by Medicare and made available in every community.

- *We deserve comprehensive coverage for palliative care.*

- *Access to quality palliative care should be universal.*

A Nursing-Care Crisis

According to Dr. Robert Butler, the author of *The Longevity Revolution: The Benefits and Challenges of Living a Long Life,* our country is facing a nursing-care crisis. Workers in long-term-care facilities are poorly trained and poorly paid, and often leave due to lack of appreciation and/or lack of opportunity for advancement. Care workers are not uniformly required to hold certification, and many are paid merely $8 an hour, with no health benefits. Only one in ten nursing homes meets basic federal standards in the United States. This problem cannot and should not be minimized. It is nothing less than a sign of ageism that we have 1.5 million people in nursing homes, but only 10 percent of those homes meet federal standards.

Nursing homes need properly trained, properly paid caretakers who are rewarded for their hard work. Caretakers need opportunities for raises, continuing education, and career advancement. To address this issue, an ongoing grant initiated by the International Longevity Center allows care workers to take classes at twenty-four community colleges in multiple geographical locations as an opportunity to move ahead in the field of nursing. The purpose of the program is to allow care workers, who are often big-hearted but disenfranchised, to move toward a career that provides them with greater security and dignity. Many are not paid even minimum wage.

- *We deserve properly paid, properly trained care workers.*

- *We deserve long-term-care facilities that uniformly meet federal guidelines.*

Lost Opportunities in Research

We are losing ground in scientific research and medical training. Dr. Robert Butler has stated that although the United States is usually at the forefront of medical and scientific research, we now fall behind other countries in terms of the percentage of gross domestic product allocated for science. Over recent years there has been a 13 percent cut in science funding. This limits scientists' ability to get grants, and many fine young PhDs who were trained in the United States are returning to their home countries.

- *We deserve to see the world's most advanced research programs on aging take place in the United States.*

Furthermore, medical training in geriatrics is inadequate in our country. Only a fraction of our 150 medical schools have specific training programs in geriatrics. Medical students are sometimes offered elective courses on the needs of older patients, but these classes are pursued by only a small percentage of students. Worse yet, clinical medication trials rarely include older patients (the FDA does not require that the elderly be included in medication trials), even though older people use 40 percent of all the medications available.

- *We deserve strong geriatric medicine programs in all of our nation's medical schools.*

- *We deserve inclusion in medication trials.*

Research on aging goes beyond the disciplines of biology and medicine. Dr. Laura Carstensen, founding director of the Stanford Center on Longevity, believes that quality-of-life advancements require cross-disciplinary efforts. Social scientists need to continue to examine which factors contribute to health in old age, and psychologists should design campaigns for social change. City planners should assess what is necessary to help older people maintain active daily lives, with less time spent being sedentary. These are broad goals—but they are not impossible. A wider view of life-span wellness is required across all sectors of society. To make a true breakthrough in "longevity science," a multitude of academics and professionals will need to dismiss the disease focus that currently defines old age.

- *We deserve more research on healthy living across the life span.*

A Revolution!

Some people think we are asking for a lot. Well, people at the forefront of revolutions do that. As we move toward unprecedented productivity and vitality through the life span, it is no time to lowball our demands. The longevity revolution requires us to raise public awareness so our contributions will be recognized and the reasonable supports we deserve will be put in place. Ultimately, aging is a universal experience that should unite our interests and efforts.

Let's act—individually and together—to defeat ageism and apathy.

CHAPTER 20

Facing Mortality

Without an ever-present sense of death life is insipid.
You might as well live on the whites of eggs.

—MURIEL SPARK

We do not know where death awaits us: so let us wait
for it everywhere. To practice death is to practice
freedom. A man who has learned how to die has
unlearned how to be a slave.

—MICHEL DE MONTAIGNE

OKAY, SO YOU THINK THIS IS MORBID AND YOU'D JUST AS SOON
not read this chapter. Try for a minute to imagine what it would be
like to live forever. There'd be no shape to life anymore, no meaning. What gives a thing meaning is the tension of its opposite:
Silence means nothing without sound; light means nothing without
darkness; even kindness without meanness or happiness without
sadness turns mundane. After a while, after we'd done everything
we wanted and needed to do, then what? Keep doing the same
things forever? Same old, same old. There'd be no urgency, no
incentive. When time is endless, moments lose their preciousness.

It's not just old age that we rehearse for—that I've been rehearsing for over the last twenty-some years. I've been rehearsing for my
death, as well. This may strike some people as gruesome, at least at
first. In the 1970s, the singer Michael Jackson came to visit me in
Santa Barbara. I pointed out to him a spot at the edge of a cliff

With my son, daughter, and stepmother, Shirlee Fonda, at the unveiling of the Henry Fonda postage stamp COURTESY OF THE UNITED STATES POSTAL SERVICE

overlooking the Pacific Ocean where I thought I might like to be buried, and I was stunned when he freaked out, screaming, "No! No!" It was incomprehensible and frightening to him that I could so easily accept my own death. Perhaps it was a blessing that he went out the way he did. I cannot imagine him living peacefully into old age.

From time to time I make an effort to imagine myself as very old. I see myself lying on a bed, frail and wrinkled. I can feel my soft little dog (alas, it probably won't be my current dog!) curled under my arm. My children and grandchildren surround me. Most of my closest friends are younger than I am, and I see them there as well—coming and going as their lives permit. I know that what I want most is to see love in their faces. I know that I will have to live my life between now and then so as to deserve that love. I know that in order to be able to recognize their love and respond to it, I need to keep my mind alert. I know that in my dying I want to try to communicate my love for them, along with a sense of the appropriateness of death as a normal part of life. My friend Joan Halifax, a Zen priest who works with dying people, wrote that "we have an intuition that a fragment of eternity within us is liberated at the time of death."[1]

Joan also told me about her father. Two days before he died, a nurse approached him and asked, "How are you feeling, Mr. Halifax?" and he replied, "Everything!" I'd like to be able to say this right before my death: *I feel everything, the pure interconnectedness and interdependence of us all.* I know that to do so I will need to learn to have an open, accepting, love-filled heart, and that doesn't just happen. It takes work.

I recognize my tendency to plan everything out according to my own vision, and I know that I mustn't cling too possessively to this death narrative, because such things usually don't work out as we've imagined. Still, the awareness of it helps me to live every day more fully.

During the writing of this book, I made a movie in France—in French—the first one after forty years in French! (Talk about a perfect brain workout and the activation of my higher-order cognitive functions!) One of the things that drew me to the movie was the way my character approaches her imminent death from colon cancer. She creates a lovely, vine-covered arbor, under which she intends to be buried; plants flowers; and plans on installing a bench next to her grave. ("I want to continue to receive guests," she tells a friend, "and, besides, rows of headstones just aren't my thing.") There's a scene I love where she tells the man who sells coffins that she doesn't like the classical brown and black coffins and wants her casket to be pink. "You only die once," she tells the salesman, "and I quite like the idea of surprising my guests the day of my burial."

The truth is that none of us can know what kind of death we will have or when it will occur. All we know is that we are all terminal. It could come instantly or be long and painfully drawn out. I may not be able to communicate at all when the end comes. But I am learning about the growing practice of palliative care and the amazing people, like Joan Halifax, who are trained to be with the dying and bring them and their families comfort. I will want to know someone like this who can be present with me and my loved ones when my time comes.

I've had a talk with my children about how I want them to deal with my body when I die. I hope my passing won't occur in a hospital, although for 80 percent of us in the United States that's how it happens. If that's where I end up, I want them to stand up to the nurses, take my body, clean it up, wrap it in a shroud, and put me into a hole at my ranch in New Mexico and cover me with earth. Simple as that. I want to be recycled, especially since I read somewhere that burials in America deposit 827,060 gallons of embalming fluid—formaldehyde, methanol, and ethanol—into the soil each year, and cremation pumps dioxins, hydrochloric acid, sulfur dioxide, and carbon dioxide into the air.[2] I've tried to live light on the planet. Why die heavy on it? I've told my children that I want a simple gravestone, though—something that my children and grandchildren can lay their heads beside. I like graves and headstones—always have. They give a tangible presence to the spiritual realm. I'm sad that Dad was cremated but never buried. Having a gravestone to sit by and touch would make it easier to feel as if I am with him.

I'm glad that I am thinking about all this even though, if I'm lucky, it may not happen for another twenty or thirty years! I'm grateful for this time when I can drive the four-wheeler around my ranch in New Mexico with Malcolm, my grandson, who, at this writing, is eleven years old. I explain the things I'm doing on the ranch so as to be a responsible steward of the land. I tell him why I'm cutting down so many of the trees on my property: how trees have become too plentiful ever since we stopped allowing forest fires to burn, so that now there isn't enough water for the expanded forests, the meadows have shrunk, leaving less grass and shrubs for wildlife, and bark beetles are turning landscapes into brown wastelands. I explain that we leave the chipped wood on the ground to mulch and hold water, and how, in nature, things have to die so new things can grow. I tell him that one day that land may be his and his siblings' responsibility, so he needs to pay attention. I hope I am instilling early the sense of the finiteness of things and the preciousness of time.

Letty Pogrebin, in her book *Getting Over Getting Older,* wrote "We teach our children to tell time, but not what to tell it."[3] I want to teach Malcolm and Viva what to tell time—that everything will someday end and that every day, every hour, every moment of time matters.

In 1982, my father died three minutes before I arrived at Cedars-Sinai Hospital in Los Angeles. When I came into his room, I could see that he was gone but I desperately wanted to sit with him, touch him, experience closure, and try to grasp what was left when the spirit has gone. The nurses would have none of it. They insisted that we leave so they could "clean him up."

Western societies do not psychologically equip us to confront death. It's viewed as an indignity that needs to be "cleaned up." But if you really think about it, life exists only in relation to death, just as light exists only in relation to dark and sound exists only in relation to silence. Death gives shape and meaning to our lives. Very old people know this. None of the centenarians I have interviewed were afraid of dying. On the contrary, their very proximity to it seems to give their lives exquisite meaning.

Rachel Lehman, who was 104 years old when I talked with her, told me she thinks of death quite often. "I am willing to accept it and I just don't care what happens," she said. Ben Burke, age 101, told me, "Well, we can't help thinking about death on occasion. But it seems I am so busy, so involved with my different activities that it is kind of on the back burner. But on the other hand I say, *Well, when it happens if I can only be plunking my banjo and pass off into the sunset, that would be the best of all*—while doing what I enjoy doing."

Not all societies are as death-denying as ours. All indigenous, preindustrial, precapitalist cultures not only venerate the aged, they consciously cultivate a life-affirming death awareness. In Vietnam, the bones of the deceased are buried in the fields so that they will fertilize the rice that feeds the deceased's families and, thus, it is believed, there is physical and spiritual continuity, and the children inherit the strength of their ancestors.

In Mexico you can see death all around you as part of everyday life: Souvenir shops display miniature skeletons dancing and playing instruments, and chocolate candies shaped like skeletons. On All Saints' Day, November 1, families load up on wine, bread, and cheese and camp out on their loved ones' graves, singing, reminiscing, and celebrating. All these customs demonstrate that part of life is rehearsing for old age and death, welcoming it with open arms, humor, and respect.

We can choose to sink into age, denying, resisting, and protesting, and thus miss the fruits of wholeness. Or we can be liberated to live a full and vibrant life by choosing to *grow* into age, accepting, letting go, embracing the emptiness to come with humility.

Death is a democratic inevitability for every one of us. In my opinion, there's something worse than death, and that is never having fully lived.

PART FIVE

THE SPIRAL *of* BECOMING

CHAPTER 21

The Work In

I practiced meditation to give my life a spine on which to hang my heart, and a view from which I could see beyond what I thought I knew.

—ZEN PRIEST JOAN HALIFAX

The real voyage of discovery consists not in seeking new landscapes, but in having new eyes.

—MARCEL PROUST

THE JANE FONDA WORKOUT BECAME A VIDEO PHENOMENON IN the 1970s, launching the video industry as well as the acceptability of women's muscles. But these days, while I continue to maintain my strength, flexibility, and aerobic fitness as best I can, I find myself turning more and more to the work *in*. This chapter is about how I got there. But there are many paths to the realms that lie within.

On several occasions when I was young and lost, I took off to somewhere entirely foreign in the hope that I would "find myself." The instinct was well-founded. As we learn from mythology, the passage to a new and important phase in life always required the hero (heroes were the only ones written about back then, although plenty of *she*roes had preceded them) to pass into the unknown, cut off from all that was safe and familiar. Joseph Campbell called it the "hero's journey."

The problem was, I didn't understand that the answers I was looking for could come only if I gave myself up to the foreignness, allowing myself to be a blank slate. Instead, although the environs were new, I remained the same old me, desperately seeking the safety of activity and companionship—usually male companionship.

Life in my sixties taught me that I didn't need to go somewhere "else" to get answers. I do need time alone, time for the introspection I talked about in the previous chapter, and over these last years I have spent weeks and sometimes months at a time by myself. When I am "public," I'm busily public and pack a lot into each day. Because of this, acquaintances think I have no downtime. They are wrong. I have many responsibilities, not the least of which is earning money to help support loved ones and fund my non-profit organizations. Because of this, I am disciplined in scheduling my downtime.

I have a ranch on a river in New Mexico to which I retreat. There's a routine that comes with it when I'm alone with my dog Tulea: Get up with the sun; make breakfast; hike or swim for an hour or so, depending on the season; go to my gym for weight work (and aerobics if the weather has precluded the hike or swim); then come back to the house to write or read or sit or, most commonly, a combination of the above. Several times a week I will go fly-fishing for the Zen of it. Two weeks before my seventieth birthday, I added something new: meditation. I had tried—oh, how I'd tried—over the years to meditate, but I could never still my mind, and although I knew it was something I needed (people were always telling me this), I wasn't motivated to stick with it. But as I was approaching seventy, every fiber in me told me the time had come.

I knew I was in transition, not sure what I was meant to do, uncomfortable with a relationship that had ceased to be meaningful to me. Rather than voyaging to a foreign clime, I decided that the new territory that awaited me was within my own mind—if I could learn to quiet it, that is.

Several months earlier, Jodie Evans, an activist friend who also happens to be deeply spiritual, had invited me to a June seminar at the Upaya Zen Center in Santa Fe. She'd told me that Joan Halifax, known for her work with death and dying, would be a speaker, along with Mary Catherine Bateson, daughter of Margaret Mead and Gregory Bateson. Mary's book *Composing a Life* had had a profound effect on me a decade earlier, and because I had begun work on this book, I wanted to hear what Joan Halifax had to say about the end of life.

It turned out that Joan is a Zen master and the abbot of Upaya. With her close-shaved head, shining eyes, and dimpled smile, she radiates such presence that it makes you want some of what she's having. During a break in the seminar, she took me on a tour of the center, which includes a large temple, magnificent and simple, with a glistening, black wood floor like ones I'd seen in Japan. Woven tatami mats raised about four inches off the floor, each with a flat black cushion on it, lined the bare, hand-troweled plaster walls. Joan explained that various *sesshin* retreats are held in the hall throughout the year, including an eight-day silent *Rohatsu sesshin,* at the beginning of December, focused on the enlightenment of the Buddha. "Hmm," thought I. "Pretty intimidating language, but— just so happens I will be all by myself at my ranch then, preparing to turn seventy." I started to get excited.

"What's a *Rohatsu sesshin?*" I asked, trying to say it right, the way she had, with the accent on the *shin.*

"*Sesshin* is an intense silent meditation retreat that unifies the heart and mind," she replied. "You become clear and open so that you can experience your true nature. *Rohatsu* means the eighth of December, when, in the Japanese Buddhist world, we celebrate the enlightenment of the Buddha but we also mourn our own stupidity." I got goose bumps. Finding my true nature was just what I needed before I hit seventy. Throwing in a little mourning of my stupidity would make it perfect.

"But I'm a Christian," I said, hoping this wouldn't render me ineligible.

"Many Christians come here," she assured me. "For us, Buddhism isn't a religion, it's a practice, a philosophy. One of my Christian friends told me her time here had made her a better Christian." Always a believer in trial by fire, I signed up then and there.

Five and a half months later, I was in that hall, sitting in silence with sixty women and men ranging in age from nineteen to eighty. My friends couldn't believe I was really doing it. "Aren't you scared?" they asked me. Several were positive they could never go eight days without speaking. Scared was the last thing I could imagine being. Excited was more like it. This was a wonderful chance to jump-start a regular meditation practice—and maybe even a deepening of consciousness. As for not speaking, I knew I would relish it. I'm not my father's daughter for nothing.

During the eight days, we weren't silent just during meditation. Even in our adobe guesthouses or as we walked to and from the hall in the early mornings and late evenings, the center was bathed in utter silence. We were asked to avoid eye contact and to fold our hands at our waists as we walked. I cheated, of course, sneaking furtive glimpses as I passed other guests and hating myself for being occasionally judgmental. "That one's a sure loser," I'd think.

Except for the first meditation period, at 5:45 A.M., and the last one, at 8:40 P.M., when we faced out into the hall, the rest of the time we sat on black cushions facing the wall, backs straight, hands folded in our laps in a ritual position—left hand resting in the cupped right hand, thumbs touching. That is when, in my case, all hell would break loose between my ears. Who knew there was so much chatter in there? If this was my true nature, I needed to be locked up. I tried to "follow my breath," as we'd been instructed. I tried shutting my eyes but would fall asleep. (I discovered that I can sleep in a perfect meditation pose without anyone knowing.) I tried opening my eyes a crack, so that just a faint bit of light would come through my lashes. I'd count—four breaths in, four breaths out—and less than five seconds would go by before some thought would come galumphing in and get stuck. Later Joan described it as having a "sticky" mind, like flypaper—all your poor little thoughts buzz around and get stuck and drive you crazy. I would remember to "let it go" and return to the breath, but in another few seconds a new thought would move in and get stuck. "Am I the only person here who is waging a war with my mind?" I'd think. Everyone else appeared to have it all together. Then again, I must have appeared that way, too.

Every forty minutes a lovely gong would sound and we would rise, bow to the center of the hall, turn to our left, and begin a walking meditation, single file, ever so slowly, our hands held in ritual position at waist height, back straight. We reminded me of the black-robed magicians marching up the dungeon stairs in Dr. Seuss's *The 500 Hats of Bartholomew Cubbins.* The first time we did this, I continually risked bumping into the woman in front of me. "What a loser," I remember thinking. "Why's she creeping along like that? She doesn't even know how to walk." After a while, trying to get from judgment to meditation, I began to focus all my attention on how each foot slowly touched the ground, heel first, then bit by bit rolling through the arch, the ball, the toes, until the full foot was flat on the ebony-dark hardwood floor. Only then would I lift the other foot. Before I knew it, I was walking just like the "loser." It was a humbling experience. Mourning my stupidity was becoming a full-time job.

Except for the chants that preceded and followed the meals, the food was served in silence, in a simple, highly ritualized ceremony in which servers would enter carrying large steaming pots, turn, bow to each of us as it was our turn, and kneel. We would return the bow with our heads and offer our bowl to be filled. As there were three bowls, this process would be repeated three times, each server bringing a different food. We'd been taught at the start exactly how to place our wooden spoon and chopsticks, fold our three cloths (place mat, napkin, and cleaning towel), clean our three bowls, and fold everything back up again. The simplicity and exactitude of the ritualized meals forced me to acknowledge the extent to which I was not, as I had thought, really "in the moment," paying careful attention to each gesture, each detail. I was spending too much time noticing what others were doing, judging if their napkin was folded into a better lotus-blossom knot than mine. It took several days for me to realize that when I really was in the moment, really showing up, for example, for the small head bows to the servers, I would experience gratitude. "So there is a deeper purpose for each step of the ritual," I thought.

By day two my back and knees were screaming in pain, and I moved from sitting in a partial lotus on the mat to a folding chair. I told myself that, after all, I was older than most of the others, and that the few who were older than I were also sitting in chairs. Although it never occurred to me to leave—I'm too proud—by day three I was asking myself why I'd come, why I was purposefully putting myself through this torture. What made it all possible—no, not possible; endlessly worth it—were the daily one-hour dharma talks given by Joan or one of the three other priests. "Dharma" refers to the teachings of the Buddha, and because this was a *sesshin* focusing on the enlightenment of the Buddha, the talks centered on enlightenment. We would carry our mats into a semicircle around the priests. They would sit on mats facing us as they talked, and it wasn't just the breaking of the endless silence that made their words so precious. Sometimes Joan would choose a koan, a brief Zen story that can be understood only when you let go of the mind and allow the *feeling* of it to penetrate you. I was reminded of the twenty-one sayings or puzzles attributed to Jesus in the Gospel of Thomas. He said that grasping their meaning would allow you entrance to the "Kingdom of Heaven"—which I take to mean achieving higher consciousness or wholeness.

Joan would help us understand the koan's meaning by weaving a personal, often hysterically funny story around it. She told us about the time when she was to give a talk at a big temple in Japan and walked out of the Japanese bathroom, forgetting to take off the bright red toilet shoes (with the word "toilet" written in kanji on the tops of them), and strolled "mindfully" down the public hallway to the lecture hall; her soon-to-be Japanese audience subtly brought her attention to her egregious cultural faux pas. She related this story to illustrate a verse by an ancient Japanese Zen master: "A splendid branch issues from the old plum tree; in time, obstructing thorns flourish everywhere."

This was a good talk for me, as my lessons in humility were advancing. It seemed like every insight I was having was accompanied by more stupidity and more "thorns." I was being taught that these obstructing thorns were all part of the package of life.

Every talk Joan and the other priests gave, every story, felt as though it had been chosen especially to help me see why I was there, and what I should reach for within myself. It was comforting when she told us that even the Buddha had had a hard time quieting his "devilish thoughts." "Whenever an unpleasant state of mind would arrive to the Buddha," she said, "instead of rejecting it, or judging himself, he would say, 'Hello, old friend. I know you,' and that would dispel the state of mind itself. It's an important strategy, the strategy of nondenial."

On the sixth day, I noticed that I didn't have to count my breaths anymore; I was *being breathed,* just as Joan had predicted. The nondenial strategy made my mind less "sticky" and helped me get to a new mind stillness and stay there for minutes at a time. I felt, then, suspended in what seemed like an intersection behind my forehead. Just floating. I was aware that my awareness of not thinking was different than thinking.

Joan describes this as the "nonadhesive mind"; like a mirror, it reflects what is, without judgment or attachment. It's not something you can make happen. It arises spontaneously. Joan used the metaphor of the mirror and the red balloon: As the red balloon passes the mirror, the mirror reflects the red. It doesn't judge the red or comment on the red. It just reflects it. But the mirror is not red. It is a clear, still medium (like our minds can be), and thus it can reflect things just as they are, without distorting them with projections or agitation. In other words, I got that it was possible to have an "unfiltered" experience of reality.

During the talks, Joan spoke of what she referred to as nonduality, but I didn't understand what that meant. Then, on the seventh day, as I was floating in that still void behind my forehead, the sixty people sitting as I was seemed to merge into a single energetic force that filled the hall. It wasn't that I *thought* of this; it just was.

For a fleeting moment I knew that everything—*every thing*—is part of an unbroken wholeness, constantly flowing and coherent. Tears poured down my cheeks. They tickled me. Joan had talked about this—not scratching when we itched, instead becoming the itch. I became my tears. I was beyond happy.

On the final day, we held council. All sixty of us, together with Joan and the other priests, sat in a circle, and each person spoke for a few minutes about what the eight days had meant for us. I learned that every one of us had been challenged in the mind-stilling department. As I heard the others describe their experiences and what had brought them there, all the "loser" labels melted away and all that was left was our shared, beautiful, fragile humanity. The poet Mary Lou Kownacki has written, "Is there anyone we wouldn't love, if we only knew their story?" I'd been broken open.

It is hard to put words to what the experience at Upaya did to me and for me. But upon my return, I remembered a letter that my grandaunt Millicent Rogers had written to her son Paul prior to her death in 1953—it was he who'd given it to me. Millicent was my mother's cousin, the daughter of Henry Huttleston Rogers, a cofounder of Standard Oil, and a woman of legendary style. Despite the fact that the Millicent Rogers Museum is in Taos, New Mexico, I had always avoided knowing about her because I wanted to disassociate myself from anything related to my mother and because I assumed Millicent was simply a fancy socialite. How wrong that assumption was! The opening paragraph of her letter showed me that she had attained, before her early death at age fifty-one, what it had taken me seventy years to begin to understand.

> *Darling Paulie,*
>   *Did I ever tell you about the feeling I had a little while ago? Suddenly passing Taos Mountain I felt that I was part of the earth, so that I felt the Sun on my Surface and the rain.*
>   *I felt the Stars and the growth of the Moon, under me rivers ran. And against me were the tides. The waters of rain sank into me. And I thought if I stretched out my hands they would be Earth*

and green would grow from me. And I knew that there was no
reason to be lonely, that one was everything, and Death was as easy
as the rising sun and as calm and natural—that to be enfolded in
Earth was not an end but part of oneself, part of every day and
night that we lived, so that being part of the Earth one was never
alone. And all fear went out of me—with a great, good stillness
and strength.

I set the letter down and marveled that I hadn't read it until my
return from Upaya, when I was totally open to her words. I won-

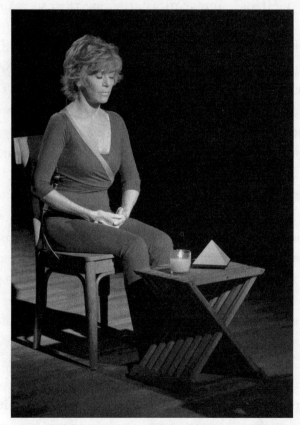

PHOTO BY JUSTIN
MARCEL LUBIN

dered if my ancestor Millicent hadn't been holding my hand as I'd
made my inner journey. Maybe she's why I have ended up spending
so much time in New Mexico. Seekers and sages say that we all have
councils of elders guiding us from the other side.

I can't pretend to carry the non-sticky, non-dual mind with me day to day, but I have begun a regular practice of meditation, and sometimes, when I reach that still intersection, it comes back to me. I can tell from my interactions with people and when I speak publicly that I manifest a different energy, one that encourages an easy give-and-take, often on a soul level—even with strangers. Dr. Laura Carstensen, founding director of the Stanford Center on Longevity, told me that the center is training young students in a Buddhist meditation on death and that the data the staff is collecting seems to indicate that meditation allows the students to experience the "Positivity effect," similar to what happens to so many people in Act III.

In the days that followed Upaya I was aware of being kinder and more careful of others. Colors appeared more vivid, sounds more acute, and my thinking felt different. Changing your thinking is so hard. Joan had said, "Don't believe your thoughts." How to get out from under our thoughts? I learned from Upaya that slowing down the thinking process lets you *feel* beyond or deeper than the thinking process, and thus to avoid being a toy to conceptions. I was to see that this changes the experience of thinking itself.

But the change I noticed most was what happened to time. It seemed to have doubled in volume, and I know why. It is because during the eight days, I had learned to pay deep attention to the Now. This allowed me to see that on a subjective level, time is what we make of it. We've all read or been told umpteen times that time expands if we fill it with newness. Remember when you were a child and summer vacation seemed to last a year because things were new? My experience at Upaya showed me that even within the familiar, time expands when we are paying close attention to life, detail by detail, moment by moment. Perhaps this is another purpose of the Third Act. Assuming we are able and want to reduce the to-ing and fro-ing of youth, we have more time to make time for time.

Since my experience at Upaya, I have read books about quantum physics, met scientists, and attended their lectures. I have come to feel that there is a beautiful intersection between the place where meditation leads us, the general falling away of differences that tends to happen with age, and the new physics. It is as if, even before we die (and if we encourage it), we are pulled toward the undefinable totality of flowing energy from which we all emerged and of which we remain a part. It is a place where poetry and science meet. The Vietnamese Buddhist master Thich Nhat Hanh said, "The four elements of space live within my body. When I die, my elements will separate one from the other and return to the mother elements. We are not separate from any being or thing." The physicist David Bohm wrote, "In a way, techniques of meditation can be looked on as measures which are taken by man to try to reach the immeasurable, i.e., a state of mind in which he ceases to sense a separation between himself and the whole of reality." Like the teachings of Buddha and Jesus, quantum physics cannot be understood through books alone; it must be experienced—in our body, viscerally. How do you viscerally experience an abstraction like space, infinity, or dark matter? Apparently by transcending the mind. Albert Einstein, for instance, didn't arrive at his theory of relativity through logic or deduction alone. Many have written about the fact that his theory came to him when he was in a deep, meditative alpha state.

To me, a layperson, it seems to go like this: For a long time, many in science took a mechanistic approach to what constituted the material world, believing that its "ultimate substance" would be found in the building blocks of atoms and even more basic particles, such as electrons, protons, and neutrons. These were thought to be distinct, unchangeable, independent entities. Einstein, with his theory of relativity, challenged the mechanistic understanding of the world. He said that instead of discrete particles, reality was made up of nonlinear, overlapping, ever-changing energy fields. Then scientists discovered that atoms, electrons, protons, and neutrons were not the "ultimate substances" at all, that they were continually transforming into a multitude of increasingly smaller, unstable particles called quarks and partons. Building on this, quantum science has revealed that everything we can see or touch or describe, including space and time, is simply an abstraction of some "unknown and undefinable totality of flowing movement"[1]— including us! How, then, to explain the apparently tangible, solid, visible world of the senses? Physicists see this "manifest" world as projections or abstractions of a higher, multidimensional reality.

To make it easier for us to grasp the concept, David Bohm used the image of a flowing stream: "On this stream, one may see an ever-changing pattern of vortices, ripples, waves, splashes, etc., which evidently have no independent existence as such. Rather they are abstracted from the flowing movement, arising and vanishing in the total process of the flow."

Okay, so my "true nature" turns out to be a ripple in the cosmic flow. In my midlife this would have been a downright uncomfortable proposition to accept—*Don't tell me that my Workout and all those new muscles we're creating are just energy waves, or that my Oscars are only abstractions!* But now, why not? I'm in my seventies. The wind isn't at my back anymore; it's right in my face. Going with the flow is actually a rather comforting notion. The more I can wrap my "mind" around this cosmic view, the more comfortable I'll be, when the "end" comes, stepping away from being an abstraction and becoming what I actually am—part of the cosmic energy flow. As Buddhists often say, "No thing–ness, or nothingness, is more real than thingness."

Still, why does this laptop I'm writing on seem so solid and my dog lying against my thigh so warm?

Bohm suggests that we couldn't get much accomplished in the practical reality of our day-to-day lives if we lived in the constant awareness of the multidimensional reality of ever-changing, interacting fields. So we've turned the illusion of a stable, fragmented, atom-based-building-block manifest world into the way things are, the ultimate truth. We've made the abstraction into our reality. And mirroring the old scientific view of that reality, a mechanistic culture of individualism, of us and them, of us versus nature, has come into being. What would happen if we were able to accept the manifest abstraction that we call reality as a practical way to get things done (do the laundry, board a plane, fall in love and have sex with a kindred abstraction) while simultaneously holding the awareness that on a deeper, indefinable level, we are all one—not just figuratively but literally?

Who knows if nuns and monks who spend their lives in prayer or yogis who spend theirs in meditation are intuitively tuned in to the cosmic reality. More and more of them are working with scientists to reveal the impact their mindfulness has on the "real" world.

We don't all have to go to a sanctuary to spend eight days in silent meditation. But we can seek times of solitude as well as activities that allow us to go inward: yoga, tai chi, life review, gardening, walking in nature, painting, meditating, poetry, prayer. These and other contemplative activities let us become permeable to the wisdom we all possess, to the reality of *inter*dependence instead of individualism, to the inevitability of our own death alongside the infinite flow of energy that is also us.

I want to close this chapter by quoting the final portion of "Monet Refuses the Operation," by Lisel Mueller, the poem I cited in Chapter 1:

> *I will not return to a universe*
> *of objects that don't know each other,*
> *as if islands were not the lost children*
> *of one great continent. The world*
> *is flux, and light becomes what it touches,*
> *becomes water, lilies on water,*
> *above and below water,*
> *becomes lilac and mauve and yellow*
> *and white and cerulean lamps,*
> *small fists passing sunlight*
> *so quickly to one another*
> *that it would take long, streaming hair*
> *inside my brush to catch it,*
> *to paint the speed of light!*
> *Our weighed shapes, these verticals,*

burn to mix with air
and change our bones, skin, clothes
to gases. Doctor,
if only you could see
how heaven pulls earth into its arms
and how infinitely the heart expands
to claim this world, blue vapor without end.

CHAPTER 22

Full Tilt to the End

**He allowed himself to be swayed by his conviction that
human beings are not born once and for all on the day
their mothers give birth to them, but that life obliges
them over and over again to give birth to themselves.**
—Gabriel García Márquez, *Love in the Time of Cholera*

THE PHILOSOPHER AND PSYCHOLOGIST DR. JEAN HOUSTON TELLS
this story about a series of life-altering encounters she had as a
young girl:

> When I was fourteen years old my parents got divorced, and
> I was just grief-stricken about it. I took to running down
> Park Avenue, late for school—I would run from my grief.
> And one day I ran into an old man and knocked the wind
> out of him. I picked him up and he said to me in a French
> accent, "Are you planning to run like that for the rest of your
> life?"
> I said, "Yes sir, looks that way."
> He said, "Well, bon voyage!"
> I said, "Bon voyage." And I ran to school. The following
> week I was walking my fox terrier, Champ, and I saw the old
> man coming out of a building. I lived at 86th, just off of Park
> Avenue, and the old man lived somewhere around 84th and
> Park.
> He said to me, "Ah, my friend the runner, you have a fox
> terrier. Where are you going?"

"Well sir, I take Champ to Central Park after school. I just think about things."

"I will go with you sometime, okay?"

I said, "Well, sure."

"I will take my constitutional."

Now he was something. He had no self-consciousness at all. He had leaky margins with the world. He had a long French name but he asked me to call him by the first part of it, which to my American ears sounded like "Mr. Tayer." So I called him Mr. Tayer. We walked for about a year and a half, off and on, mostly Tuesdays and Thursdays. He would suddenly fall to the ground and look at a caterpillar: "Oh, Jean, look at the caterpillar! Ah, moving, changing, transforming, metamorphosing. Jean, feel yourself to be a caterpillar. Can you do that?"

"Very easily, Mr. Tayer." I mean, here I was, a fourteen-year-old girl nearly six feet tall with red dots on my face—I felt like a caterpillar!

He said, "What are you when you finally become a *papillon*, a butterfly? What is the butterfly of Jean?"

"I don't know, Mr. Tayer!"

"Yes, you know, you know. I know you know. Now, what are you transforming into?"

"Well, I think when I grow up I'll fly all over the world, and maybe I'll help people."

"Ah! Bon, bon, bon." And he'd say, "Oh, Jean, lean into the wind!" There are these strong winds off of Central Park. "Ah, Jean, smell the wind! Same wind once went through Jesus Christ."

"Jesus Christ felt this?"

"Yes. Oh, Marie Antoinette, here she comes! Genghis Khan, not so good. Joan of Arc, Jeanne d'Arc! Be filled with Jeanne d'Arc! Be filled with the tides of history!" We had all these wonderful games about life: "Jean, look at the clouds, God's calligraphy in the sky!"

He would suddenly stop and look at you, and he would giggle and you would giggle, and he'd giggle and you'd giggle, and then he would look at you laughing and laughing as if you were the cluttered house that hid the Holy One. I would go home and tell my mother, "Mother, I met my old man again and when I'm with him I leave my littleness behind."

Toward the end of our walk together one day, he stopped suddenly and he turned to me and said, "Jean, what to you is the most fascinating question?"

And I said, "It's about history, Mr. Tayer, and destiny, too. How can we take the right path in history so that we even have a destiny? My friends at school all talk about the H-bomb, and I wonder if I'll ever get to be twenty-one years old. Mr. Tayer, you always talk about the future of man as if we had a future; I want to know what we have to do to keep that future coming."

He said, "We need to have more specialists in spirit who will lead people into self-discovery."

"What do you mean, Mr. Tayer?"

He said—and this is exactly what he said; I was taking notes because I knew I was in the presence of greatness— "We are being called into metamorphosis, into a far higher order, and yet we often act only from a tiny portion of ourselves. It is necessary that we increase that portion. But do not think for one minute, Jean, that we are alone in making that possible. We are part of a cosmic evolutionary movement that inspires us to unite with God. This is the lightning flash for all our potentialities. This is the great originating cause of all our shifts and changes. Without it there is nothing but struggle and decline."

And I said to him, "What do you call it? I've never heard of it. Can something as great as that even have a name?"

"You are right," he said. "It is impossible to name."

"Well, try to name it, Mr. Tayer. I've heard that once a thing is named, you can begin to work with it."

He seemed amused and he said, "I'll try." And then he said, "It is the demand of the universe for the birth of the ultra-human. It is the rising of a new form of psychic energy in which the very depths of loving within you are combined with what is most essential in the flowing of the cosmic stream."

I didn't really understand what he was saying, but I nodded sagely, and I said I would ponder these things, and he said he would also. One day toward the end of our time together—this was actually the last day that I ever saw him—Mr. Tayer began talking to me about the lure of becoming, a phrase that then became a part of my language. And also about how we humans are part of an evolutionary process in which we are being drawn toward something—which he called the "Omega point"—full of evolution. He told me that he believed that physical and spiritual energy was always flowing out from the Omega point and empowering us as well as leading us forward through love and illumination. And it was then that I asked him my ultimate question, the one that I must say has continued to haunt me all the days of my life: "What do you believe it's all about, Mr. Tayer?" His answer is enshrined in my heart. He started by saying, *"Je crois"*—I believe. "I believe that the universe is in evolution. I believe that the evolution is toward spirit. I believe that spirit fulfills itself in a personal God."

"And what do you believe about yourself, Mr. Tayer?"

He said, "I believe that I am a pilgrim of the future."

It was the Thursday before Easter Sunday, 1955. I had brought him the shell of a snail. "Ah! Escargot!" he said, and then he began to wax ecstatic for the better part of an hour about spirals and nature and art, snail shells and galaxies, the labyrinth on the floor of Chartres Cathedral—which later became a symbol of my work—and the Rose Window and the convolutions of the brain, the whirl of flowers and the circulation of the heart's blood. It was all taken up in a great hymn to the spiraling evolution of spirit and matter, "It's all a spiral of becoming, Jean!" Then he looked away, and he seemed to be seeing into the future and he said, "Jean, the people of your time, toward the end of this century, will be taking the tiller of the world. But they cannot go directly." He used the French word, *directement.* "You have to go in spirals, touching upon every people, every culture, every kind of consciousness. It is then that the newest in the field of mind will awaken and we will rebuild the earth." And then he said to me, "Jean, remain always true to yourself, but move ever upward toward greater consciousness and greater love." Those were the words that he said to me. Then he said, "*Au revoir,* Jean."

"*Au revoir,* Mr. Tayer! I'll see you on Tuesday!"

And Tuesday came and I brought Champ, and Champ whimpered; he seemed to know something. And my old man never came. Thursday, Tuesday, Thursday. Eight weeks I waited and he never came again, because it turned out he had died on that Sunday in 1955.

Years later, somebody gave me a book without a cover called *The Phenomenon of Man.* And when I began to read it, I said, "My God! That's my pal, that's . . . oh my goodness . . ." And I went to my friend and asked, "Have you got the cover to the book?" And she gave it to me and I flipped it over and, of course, there was my old man. No forgetting that face! Mr. Tayer had been Teilhard de Chardin.

Teilhard de Chardin was a great French philosopher, Jesuit priest, and prolific author. This lovely story about him is, for me, a perfect example of someone living full tilt right to the end: playful, generous, curious, overflowing with Generativity (what Dr. Houston calls his "leaky margins with the world")—inspiring the young girl to become a "pilgrim of the future," to act from more than "a tiny portion of herself."

I have—rather late in life—begun to feel the exhilaration of no longer acting from a "tiny portion" of myself. My wish is that all of us experience this and, thereby, become "pilgrims of the future," using our lives to complete ourselves—to develop our bodies, our minds, our hearts, and our souls to become all we can be and then use all of it for something beyond ourselves.

Ours is the first generation to be well prepared for a vital Third Act. As women, we've got the numbers, the consciousness, the health, and the knowledge to make us better able to meet whatever challenges this last act may bring. I believe that our actions, like stones tossed into a pond, will ripple to every inlet of society. As we shape our own last third of life, so do we help to transform the experience of age for ourselves, our men, and our children . . . modeling what it means to live an examined life of reflection, compassion, and balance.

Summary of Main Areas of Anti-aging Research

Calorie-Restriction Diet

Working with mice almost thirty years ago at UCLA, the behavioral geneticist Dr. Richard Sprott and his colleague and mentor, Dr. Roy Walford, discovered that you could start calorie restriction in middle-aged mice and still have the possibility of increasing their life span by 15 or 20 percent. Now the executive director of the Ellison Medical Foundation, Dr. Sprott discussed the effects of calorie restriction on life span at an Age Boom Academy seminar I attended in 2007 at the International Longevity Center.

"Here is the only experiment that actually changes life span," Dr. Sprott said. "It can extend life span from two to six times longer in mice, small worms, fruit flies, and dogs. There are ongoing experiments with a large number of self-volunteer humans, and with nonhuman primates, that appear to be working but are not completed yet. What it demonstrates is that if you reduce your calorie intake by 45 percent, or roughly down to a diet of 1,250 calories a day (but in the face of otherwise excellent nutrition so you create a state of undernutrition without malnutrition), this can, in these experimental models, produce about a 40 percent increase in life span." Dr. Sprott said that they do not know yet if a similar kind of change in diet would produce comparable increases in human life spans. "There are good genetic reasons why it might and good genetic reasons why it might not," he noted. "There are certain behavioral reasons why it is hopeless. Bob [Butler] and I both know the foremost human practitioner of this therapy, who bet his life on the fact that it would work, and it didn't." An experiment was started in 1989 with the rhesus monkey, a species closely related to humans. These monkeys can live up to forty years, so it's not a short experiment. Dr. Sprott said, "We are starting to see statistically significant improvement in survival and resistance to disease and favorable effects on brain aging."

SIRT1 and Resveratrol

In their research, Dr. Sprott and his colleagues discovered a universal gene. Found in plants, in bacteria, and in humans, it seems to control the aging process and appears to underlie many of the benefits of the calorie-restriction diet. The gene is called SIRT1, and it is activated by a molecule called resveratrol, which is found in the skin of red grapes (and is a constituent of red wine . . . but don't get your hopes up; you'd have to drink a thousand bottles a day to see any effect). Resveratrol is also found in mulberries, peanuts, and other plants, including an Asian plant called giant knotweed.[1] Dr. Sprott said, "When you feed this molecule into mice in a pure form, they live longer, they are almost immune to the effects of obesity, they don't get diabetes, cancer, or other age-related diseases. Most of these results have yet to be replicated in humans. In the only positive human trial, extremely high doses (three to five grams) of resveratrol in a proprietary formulation have been necessary to significantly lower blood sugar."

"But," he added, "the reason for doing the research is not because we think that it would actually produce these big increases in human life span. We believe that if we understood why it produces these increases in life span in other organisms we might discover promising therapies in the treatment of metabolic diseases, including obesity, diabetes, cancer, Alzheimer's, and other diseases of aging."

The Telomere Hypothesis

Perhaps you have read about the telomere hypothesis of cellular aging. I have already discussed how many of our cells are continually dividing. Every time they divide, the very tail ends of the chromosomes—called the telomeres—become shorter, until the time comes when they are too short to divide anymore. The cells don't die; they just quit replicating, for reasons nobody understands, and this is called senescence. Some cells that do not go through this dividing and gradual shortening into senescence are the reproductive cells known as the germ line. In these cells, a special enzyme called telomerase shuts off the process of telomere shortening. If you put the telomerase enzyme back into the cell, it puts the DNA back on the end of the chromosome, so that it doesn't get short. The result is immortality at the cellular level. Sounds like the Fountain of Youth, right? Trouble is, this is also what we call cancer. Tumor cells are immortal cells because they have been released from the telomere-shortening process.

Biomarkers of Aging

The anti-aging medical interests and the nutraceuticals industry issue a lot of promises about tremendous increases in life span and health if you'll just take the right supplements, human growth hormones, resveratrol, or all sorts of new elixirs. Look at all the longevity spas springing up all over the place. Dr. Sprott explained, "They run a series of tests on you, looking for what they call biomarkers of aging, and at the end of the tests they will tell you that according to those biomarkers you are in pretty good shape except that you have this system and that system that need a little tuning up—for the average cost of $25,000 a year for the rest of your life. What they don't tell you is that the only thing that is going to change very much is the thickness of your wallet. We just don't know enough yet. One problem is that National Institute on Aging grants are for a maximum of four years, but right now it takes one hundred and fifty years for scientists to know if an experiment to extend the human life span has worked. Biomarkers of aging could shorten up the whole process because they would show us the rate at which an organism is aging in less than the life span of that organism. Well, I spent a big chunk of my career and a big chunk of NIA's money searching for the biomarkers of aging, and I can tell you there aren't any."

Dr. Sprott feels that a danger of the current promises of longevity is that they are simply not true, and "it encourages the public belief that you can get health out of a bottle; that all you need to do is to swallow a pill rather than increasing your life span and health span by a combination of having chosen long-lived parents and living an appropriate, healthy lifestyle."

Stem Cells

Many problems that develop with age are not caused by disease or trauma and are difficult to distinguish from the process of aging itself. One example is what is called sarcopenia, or the age-related loss of muscle mass and muscle strength; this can make it harder for an older person to perform the activities of daily living that require muscle, such as lifting objects and climbing stairs. Muscle mass also diminishes in people who have low levels of growth hormone, testosterone, or estrogen, or high levels of cortisols, the stress hormones.

The Stanford Center on Longevity's deputy director is Thomas Rando, a stem-cell biologist. He and his team are applying targeted science and technology to understand ways to maintain muscle tissue so that people can remain strong and independent even into old age.

Stem cells are like building blocks that are able to become whatever tissue is needed—they can become skin cells when in the skin or muscle cells when put into muscle. But in order for stem cells to do their job of repairing injured tissue, they have to receive the right signals from the surrounding damaged tissue. Signals can come from uninjured cells in the tissue, from hormones and other factors in the blood, and also from cells of the immune system that migrate into the damaged area to clear away dying cells. Stem cells respond to those signals by dividing many times in order to generate enough cells to replace the cells that were lost. Because stem-cell repair is so much less robust in older animals, scientists believed that age causes stem cells to lose their efficiency. Dr. Rando's team at Stanford discovered, however, that when the old stem cells were exposed to factors in the blood of younger animals, the stem-cell activity in the old tissue was just as robust as that in young tissue. Turns out there are substances in old blood that suppress stem-cell function, and if scientists can develop a drug to block these suppressors, they may be able to modify old blood and allow for faster, more effective healing of old or damaged tissues.

The science of aging is growing fast, and there are real prospects: new theories, new ideas, and new technologies that can improve function in older people if we can just fund the needed research. Dr. Rando explained to me in detail how the new understanding of the human genome tells us about the genes that are affected in the ongoing biological processes of age and provides the possibility of doing genetic repair in a variety of ways. "If we know what genes are turned on or turned off as you age, maybe we can give you the proper gene product that you no longer have," he said. "Or maybe we can perform 'genetic adjustments' to give you the proper gene product that you need to repair a damaged tissue. Or maybe we can find ways—this is reasonably possible rather soon—to replace aberrant or damaged genes that increase the risk of developing some age-related diseases. I would submit, however, that none of these developments are going to produce dramatic changes in the life span of human beings. What it is going to change, we hope, is the health span of those same human beings."

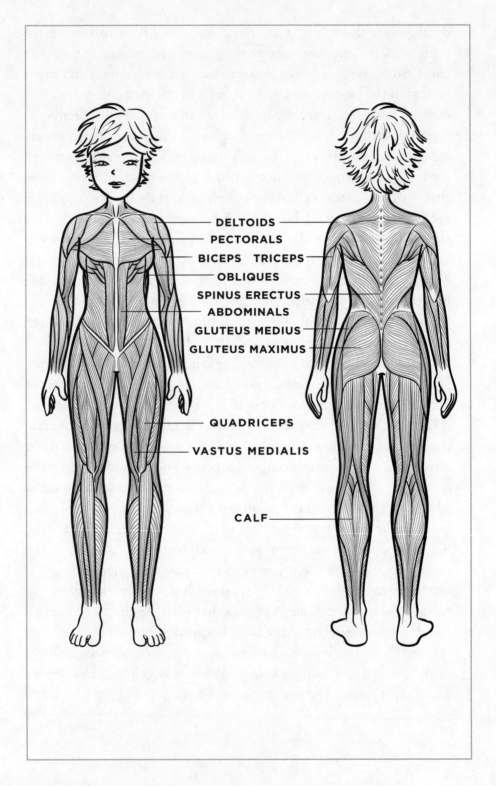

DELTOIDS

PECTORALS

BICEPS   TRICEPS

OBLIQUES

SPINUS ERECTUS

ABDOMINALS

GLUTEUS MEDIUS

GLUTEUS MAXIMUS

QUADRICEPS

VASTUS MEDIALIS

CALF

Prime Time Exercises

You will need a sturdy armless chair and hand weights. These can be dumbbells, cans of food, or bottles of water. Start with light weights and, as you get stronger, increase the weight until you can do the prescribed number of repetitions and no more. Be sure to read the instructions completely before beginning each exercise.

Warm-Up

We begin by warming up the major muscle groups with three exercises.

- While standing, reach up tall first with one arm, then the other. Really feel a stretch up your sides. Keep your abdominals pulled up and your spine extended upward.

- Standing with your arms on your hips and your feet a little more than hip width apart, bend and straighten your knees as far as is comfortable 5 times, putting your weight on your heels. Next, add a lift with your arms coming overhead as you bend your knees; bring them back down as you straighten. Exhale as you squat; inhale as you straighten. Do this 5 times.

- Stand tall and bring your arms out in front of you and then pinch your shoulder blades together by bringing your elbows back as far as you can, keeping your arms horizontal and at shoulder height as you do. Breathe as you do this and repeat 5 times.

Exercise 1 / SEATED PELVIC TILTS

These work the gluteal muscles, in your buttocks.

- Sitting up tall, pull in your abdominal muscles as though you were protecting yourself against someone about to punch you in the stomach.

- Keep your shoulders back and your chest lifted, but without letting your rib cage stick out.

- Now rock your pelvis forward and squeeze those gluteal muscles hard, tightening your abdominals as you squeeze. Hold the squeeze for 3 seconds and then release.

- Exhale as you squeeze, and inhale as you release. Repeat 15 times.

Exercise 2 / SEATED ABDOMINAL CRUNCHES

Strong abs pull in your gut and protect your back.

- Continue to sit up tall, as in the previous exercise.

- Contract your abdominals by tightening those muscles. Hold for 5 seconds and release.

- Exhale on the squeeze and inhale on the release. Repeat 15 times.

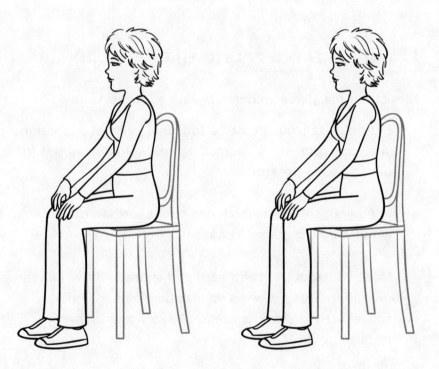

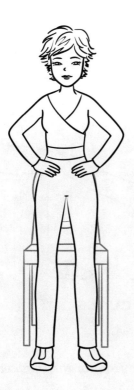
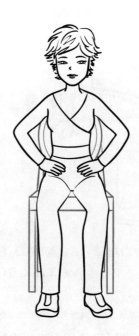

Exercise 3 / **CHAIR SQUATS**

These work your quadriceps muscles, in the front of your thighs.

- Stand up tall in front of your chair and, with your hands on your thighs, sit down and stand up. Do this 15 times, exhaling as you stand, inhaling as you sit. As you get stronger, put your hands on your waist.

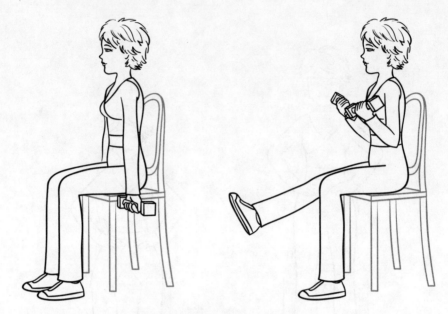

Exercise 4 / SEATED BICEPS CURLS WITH LEG LIFTS

These strengthen the muscles in the front of the thigh and the front of the upper arm.

- Sit up tall with your arms hanging down at your sides and a weight in each hand.

- Raise your right leg straight out to knee height, keeping that thigh level with the other thigh and squeezing those thigh muscles and the muscles around your knee. Hold in this lifted position for 2 seconds before lowering.

- As you do this, curl both weights up to your chest; lower them as you lower your leg. Control the weights—don't just let them drop. Exhale on the lift, and inhale as you lower the weights.

- Repeat with the other leg. Do this 16 times. Each leg lift counts as one repetition.

Exercise 5 / STANDING SIDE ARM LIFTS

These work your shoulder muscles—the deltoids.

- This exercise can be done standing or seated.

- Hold the weights in front of your body, with your palms facing down and your elbows very slightly bent. Your knees should also be softly bent.

- Exhale and lift your arms out to the sides, only to shoulder height—no higher!

- Inhale and slowly lower your arms to your sides. Repeat 15 times.

Exercise 6 / SEATED TRICEPS LIFTS

These work the triceps muscles, in the back of the arms.

- Sitting up tall in your chair, without letting your back touch the back of the chair, hold the weights with your palms facing inward.

- Lift your arms so they are straight up alongside your ears. Do not hunch your shoulders while doing this.

- Keep your back pulled up tall, stomach in, shoulders back.

- Now bend your elbows so that your forearms slowly move back and down.

- Do *not* let your back arch as you do this, and do *not* let the weights drop. Keep the movement controlled, so that you don't hit yourself with the weights.

- Then lift the weights back up so that your arms are straight overhead again. Repeat 15 times.

Exercise 7 / **BALANCE ON ONE LEG**

Maintaining or improving balance is critical as we age. Every thirty-five minutes an older person dies from a fall!

• Stand behind your chair. Don't hold on to it unless you have to. It's okay if you need to, but the goal is to do these without having to hold on.

• Stand tall on your right leg. Lift your left foot slightly off the floor and try to balance. Keep your hands on your hips.

• Don't forget to breathe, and keep your shoulders pulled back, your stomach pulled in, your head lifted, and your spine long.

• Hold for 15 seconds and repeat with the other leg.

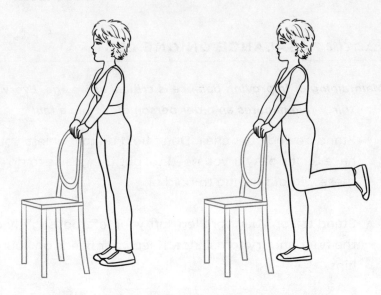

Exercise 8 / STANDING HAMSTRING CURLS

These work the hamstring muscles, in the back of the thighs.

• Standing behind your chair, balance on your right leg as you bend your left leg. Try to get your heel up to your buttocks. That's hard, but that's what to aim for . . . it's almost like you're kicking yourself in the butt!

• Make sure the thigh of the leg you are bending remains parallel to the thigh of the standing leg—only the lower part of the leg should move.

• Do this 15 times with one leg and then repeat with the other leg.

• As you get stronger, try doing this exercise without holding on.

• Make sure your abdominal muscles are engaged the entire time and that you keep breathing.

Exercise 9 / STANDING ELBOW TO KNEE

This exercise works the muscles in the pelvis and the back, the obliques (the sides of the abdomen), and the thighs.

- Holding on to your chair with your right hand, reach your left arm straight up.

- Bend your left elbow and bring it down to meet your right knee as it lifts, squeezing the muscles in your side as you do.

- Do this 15 times with your left arm and right leg, and then repeat with your right arm and left leg.

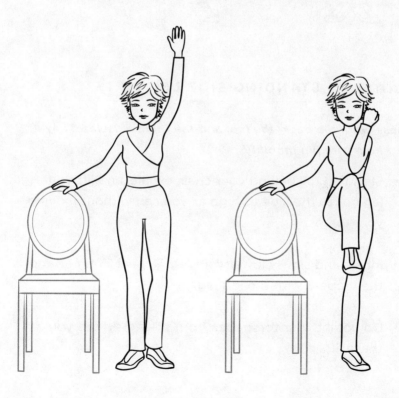

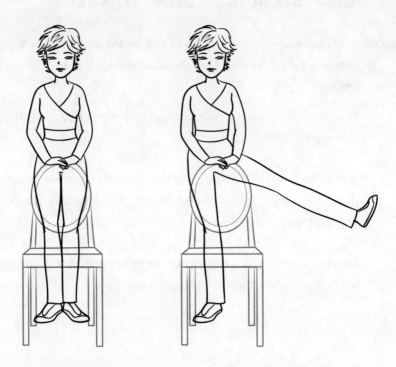

Exercise 10 / **STANDING SIDE LEG LIFTS**

These work the back, the hip, and the thigh muscles. They help with hip mobility.

- Stand up tall behind your chair, exhale, and lift your right leg out to the side as high as you can without moving your torso.

- Inhale and slowly lower your leg. Repeat 15 times and then repeat with the left leg.

- Do *not* let your torso rock from side to side as you do these lifts.

Exercise 11 / ISOMETRIC SQUATS

These will strengthen your thighs.

- Stand behind your chair. Place your feet wider than hip width and turn your toes slightly out.

- Bend your knees and come down into a squat.

- Your knees *must not* stick out beyond your toes. If they do, move your feet farther apart.

- Do not lean forward—keep your back straight.

- The goal is to lower your hips so that they are level with your knees. Getting there and holding the position may take a while. In the meantime, lower as far as you are comfortably able to and then hold the pose for one minute.

- Your thighs will begin to burn. This means you are really challenging these muscles . . . not to worry. The burn is a good sign. But if you must come back up for a moment, do so and then return to the squatting position.

- I like to keep my hands on my hips, but if you need to (until you are stronger), you can softly hold the back of your chair. Do *not* hold your breath!

Exercise 12 / FLAT BACK BEND-OVERS

**These stretch and strengthen your hamstrings and
strengthen your gluteals.**

- Stand up tall, inhale, and slowly walk your fingers down
  your thighs as far as you can go until your flat back is
  parallel with the floor.

- Keep your head and neck aligned with your back. Do *not*
  let them either drop down or crane up, as that will strain
  your neck.

- Keep a slight bend in your knees.

- Exhale as you come back up to standing, squeezing your
  gluteal (buttock) muscles as you reach the full standing
  position.

- Repeat this move—up and down—10 times.

Exercise 13 / **SEATED ANKLE CIRCLES**

Ankle mobility is important for balance.

- Lift your right thigh and circle the ankle clockwise 5 times.

- Repeat counterclockwise 5 times.

- If it is too hard for you to keep your thigh lifted, you may hold your thigh under your knee.

- Repeat with the other leg: 5 times clockwise, 5 times counterclockwise.

- Throughout this exercise, keep your abdominals pulled in and sit up tall.

STRETCHES. After working out, when our muscles are warmed up, is the optimum time to stretch. Stretching helps us stay flexible and helps prevent injuries. Each stretch must be held for a minimum of 20 seconds to get the full benefit.

Exercise 14 / **SEATED HIP STRETCH**

This stretches the muscles in the hip and buttock.

- Place your right ankle across your left knee. If your hip is tight, you can move your left foot away from the chair a little and put your right ankle on the leg just below your left knee.

- For more intensity, you may gently press your right knee down.

- Sit up tall while you do this, and keep breathing.

- Hold the position for 20 seconds.

- Repeat with the other leg.

Exercise 15 / **SEATED NECK STRETCH**

This stretches your neck and side.

- Place your right hand under the seat of your chair.

- Place your left hand on the right side of your head and tuck your chin toward your left armpit, near your collarbone—*not* straight forward!

- Gently press your head down with your left hand, feeling a stretch in your neck and up your right side.

- Continue to sit up tall as you do this. And breathe! Hold for 20 seconds and repeat on the other side.

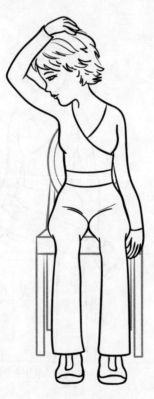

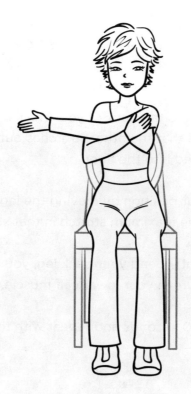

Exercise 16 / **SEATED SHOULDER STRETCH**

This stretches the shoulder and the triceps.

- Bring your right arm across your chest; keep it straight.

- Bring your left arm under it and gently press on your elbow to get a deeper stretch in your right shoulder.

- Don't let that right shoulder pull forward or hunch up.

- Hold for 20 seconds and repeat on the other side.

Exercise 17 / STANDING CALF AND HAMSTRING STRETCH

This stretches the back of the leg.

- Holding on to the back of your chair, bring one foot forward so that the other stretches out in back with the heel pressed into the floor.

- Adjust your position by moving the leg farther back so you feel the maximum stretch in that straight back leg.

- If you slightly bend your back leg, you will feel the stretch more in your lower calf muscle.

- Hold for 20 seconds and repeat with the other leg.

Exercise 18 / **STANDING HAMSTRING STRETCH**

This stretches the back of the thigh.

- Again holding on to the back of your chair, move one foot forward, resting your heel on the floor and flexing that foot up, while keeping that leg straight.

- Bend the other knee and press your buttocks back so that you feel the maximum stretch up the back of the straight leg.

- Hold for 20 seconds and repeat with the other side.

Basic Exercise Prescription*

The recommendations below are for people not competing in high-level sports.

Minimum Activity for Disease Prevention

CARDIOVASCULAR EXERCISE

Accumulate 30 to 60 minutes of physical activity most days.

STRENGTH TRAINING

Include weight-bearing activity most days.

FLEXIBILITY

Maintain your body's range of motion by bending and stretching during daily activities.

Basic Health Level

CARDIOVASCULAR EXERCISE

Engage in a large-muscle repetitive activity or sport for at least 20 minutes, at least 3 times a week.

*Based on recommendations by Dr. Michael Hewitt

STRENGTH TRAINING

Use Key 3 (see pp. 96–98) or an equivalent program, performing 1 or 2 sets, 2 times per week. Increase the number of sets as you get stronger.

FLEXIBILITY

Perform 2 to 4 large-muscle stretches *after* activity. Hold each stretch for 20 seconds.

Enhanced Fitness Level

CARDIOVASCULAR EXERCISE

Engage in an aerobic exercise or sport for 40 to 60 minutes, 4 to 6 times per week.

STRENGTH TRAINING

Use a whole-body machine or free-weight program, performing 2 or 3 sets for each body part, 3 times per week.

Use weights heavy enough to allow you to do 8 to 12 repetitions but no more.

FLEXIBILITY

Perform 6 to 10 whole-body stretches *after* activity. Hold each stretch for 20 seconds.
Key 3: Double-leg press or squat. Chest press. Lat pull-down or single-arm row.

Tips for Healthy Eating

1. Don't skip breakfast! Feed yourself regularly throughout the day. Ideally, you should have one-third of your daily calories in the morning, one-third at midday, and no more than one-third in the evening—so you don't impulsively grab whatever is around.

2. Keep healthy snacks on hand for between meals—things such as fruit or low-fat cottage cheese or string cheese. Red grapes go well with cheese.

3. Don't shop when you're hungry. Eat an apple or another healthy snack prior to going to the grocery store.

4. Make a shopping list and stick to it so as to avoid impulse buying.

5. Keep a food diary for a while, writing down what you eat at each meal. You will be amazed to learn how much more we eat than we realize.

6. Make sure you've consumed a variety of colors before the day is over, especially the superstar foods high in antioxidants and phytonutrients: dark greens and blues/purples and yellows/oranges. (See pages 117–119.)

7. Make sure that at least half of the food on your plate consists of fruits and/or veggies.

8. Eat slowly and chew well.

9. Eat sitting down.

10. Eat mindfully. Focus on what you are eating, and don't read or watch TV while you eat.

11. Avoid empty calories, like those from sodas, candy, alcohol, and cakes.

12. Get in the habit of reading food labels before you buy.

13. Don't diet! Studies have shown that the majority of people who go on diets gained back more weight afterward than they had lost.

14. Instead, try to eat when you are hungry and stop when you are full. If you have food addictions (bingeing, anorexia, bulimia), you may not be able to recognize when you are full—you eat to satisfy other needs. To help you identify those other needs, read *Women, Food and God*, by Geneen Roth.

HOW TO READ THE NUTRITION FACTS PANEL ON FOOD LABELS

1. How many **calories per serving** are shown? Bear in mind that you want to keep your total caloric intake to between 1,500 and 2,200 calories a day. That means your meals will be about 400 to 800 calories each. If you are on the small side, I recommend closer to 1,500 to 2,000 calories, with meals of 400 to 700 calories each, depending on your schedule, your snacks, and your preferences.

2. How much **saturated fat** is shown? It should be minimal, so that you're not eating more than 10 to 20 grams per day. It will be higher in foods that contain fat (even healthy foods will have some), and may be zero in foods like fruits and vegetables.

3. Is **trans fat** listed? If so, perhaps this is a food you should forgo. Aim for zero trans fat in your diet.

4. Subtract the saturated (bad) fat and the trans (truly dangerous) fat from the total fat content on the label, and you have the amount of **polyunsaturated or monounsaturated (good) fat.**

5. How much **fiber** is shown? Remember, you are aiming for at least 25 to 30 grams of fiber daily. Fiber is highest in

plant foods, such as whole grains, legumes, nuts, fruits, and vegetables.

6. How much **sugar** is shown? The list of ingredients might include corn syrup, dextrose, maltose, glucose, or invert sugar, but it's all sugar, and there should be as little as possible per serving—certainly no more than 7 grams per serving. Your daily allotment of sugar should be less than 30 grams.

7. **Sodium** content should be as low as possible to keep your total daily sodium intake below 2,300 milligrams. If you have high blood pressure, limit your sodium to 1,700 milligrams per day.

8. **Always check the list of ingredients.** Ingredients are listed in order of predominance. Do you like what you see?

Nutrition Facts

Serving Size 5 spears (93g)

Amount per serving

Calories 25	Calories from fat 0

	% Daily Value*
Total Fat 0g	0%
Saturated Fat 0g	0%
Cholesterol 0mg	0%
Sodium 0mg	0%
Total Carbohydrate 4g	1%
Dietary Fiber 2g	8%
Sugars 2g	
Protein 2g	

Vitamin A 10%	■	Vitamin C 15%
Calcium 2%	■	Iron 2%

*Percent Daily Values are based on a 2,000 calorie diet. Your daily values may be higher or lower depending on your calorie needs:

		Calories:	2,000	2,500
Total Fat	Less than		65g	50g
Sat Fat	Less than		20g	25g
Cholesterol	Less than		300mg	300mg
Sodium	Less than		2,400mg	2,400mg
Total Carborhydrate			300g	375g
Dietary Fiber			25g	30g

Calories per gram:
Fat 9 ● Carbohydrate 4 ● Protein 4

Nutrition Facts

Serving Size: 1 sandwich (228g)

Amount Per Serving

Calories 632	Calories from Fat 349

	% Daily Value*
Total Fat 38.76 g	60%
Saturated Fat 12.45 g	62%
Trans Fat	
Cholesterol 77.52 mg	26%
Sodium 1238.04 mg	52%
Potassium 332.88 mg	10%
Total Carbohydrate 41.59 g	14%
Dietary Fiber	
Sugars	
Sugar Alcohols	
Protein 29.41 g	
Vitamin A 620.16 IU	12%
Vitamin C 2.96 mg	5%
Calcium 257.64 mg	26%
Iron 3.63 mg	20%

Calcium

Calcium experts recommend three to four servings of high-calcium milk products per day, each containing about 300 milligrams of calcium per serving. About 1 cup of milk, 1 cup of yogurt, or 1½ ounces of hard cheese are the best examples.

In addition, check with your doctor about supplementing with 500 milligrams per day, taken between meals and as calcium citrate.

THE HIGH-DAIRY CALCIUM GUIDE

FOOD	AMOUNT	CALORIES	CALCIUM (IN GRAMS)
Buttermilk	8 oz.	91	264
Nonfat milk	8 oz.	86	301
Alpine Lace reduced-fat cheddar cheese	1.5 oz.	105	300
Brie cheese	1.5 oz.	142	78
Cheddar cheese	1.5 oz.	171	307
2% cottage cheese	1 cup	203	155
Hard Parmesan	1 oz.	111	336
Plain, nonfat yogurt	1 cup	127	451
Low-fat fruit yogurt	1 cup	225	313

OTHER TIPS:

• Check the Nutrition Facts Panel on your food label. A good source of calcium contains at least 30 percent of your daily requirement. Also, check the calories and saturated fat: How many calories or saturated fat grams does it take to get more calcium from the food? For people watching their health or weight, the more nutrient-dense, calorie-poor, and lower in saturated fat, the better.

• If you're lactose intolerant, talk with your doctor: Some people do well on lactose-reduced products, and some are able to tolerate the relatively small amount of lactose in certain yogurts and cheeses.

Guide to Mindful Meditation

Someone once said, "Meditation is like riding a bike: You can't and you can't and then you can."

What you will read here is excerpted (with a few minor additions) from Elizabeth Lesser's wonderful book *Broken Open: How Difficult Times Can Help Us Grow.*[1] Elizabeth is a spiritual leader and cofounder of the Omega Institute, in Rhinebeck, New York, America's largest adult-education center focusing on health, wellness, spirituality, and creativity.

As I said earlier in this book, it took me a long time to develop a meditation practice. But I just kept at it—quite regularly—and eventually found it easier to relax into mindfulness, learning to not identify with the thoughts that came to my overly busy mind. I am still very much a beginner in meditation practice, and there are weeks when I do not make time to meditate; but, as for many people I know, the practice has helped me expand as a person and heal where I was broken. I find it hard to put words to the ways in which this is so. I simply live how it is so.

While the benefits of meditation are usually talked about in abstract terms—the psyche, the soul, the mind—there are definite physical benefits to it as well. Claire Myers Owens, in "Meditation as a Solution to the Problems of Aging," writes, "Scientific experiments conducted in various laboratories, using yogi and advanced Western meditators as subjects, reveal [that] . . . in the deep relaxation of meditation the heart rate decreases and apparently the muscles of the walls of the blood vessels relax. This allows blood to flow more abundantly to all organs including the brain."[2]

Here, then, is Elizabeth Lesser's guide to meditation. When you read "I," this is Elizabeth talking. She begins with an overview of how to do it:

I. **SEAT**: It is best to sit on a firm pillow on the floor or on a firm-seated chair. If you use a chair, sit forward so that your back does not touch the back of the chair.

2. **LEGS**: If you sit on a pillow, cross your legs comfortably in front of you, with your knees resting on the floor if they can. Be sure your circulation is not cut off. If you sit in a chair, put your feet flat on the floor, knees and feet hip-width apart. Invite the groundedness of the earth into your body and mind. Let your whole body experience the strength of your stable connection with the earth. Relax into the firmness of this stability.

3. **TORSO**: Keep your back comfortably straight, your chest open, and your shoulders relaxed. Zen teacher Philip Kapleau writes, "If you are accustomed to letting the chest sink, it does require a conscious effort to keep it up in the beginning. When it becomes natural to walk and sit with the chest open, you begin to realize the many benefits of this ideal posture. The lungs are given additional space in which to expand, thus filling and stretching the air sacs. This in turn permits a greater intake of oxygen and washes the bloodstream, which carries away fatigue accumulated in the body."

A straight back and soft shoulders is a natural position. It does not have to feel forced or painful. In fact, after time, meditation breeds a sense of overall comfort. But often when we start to meditate, assuming a straight back makes us suddenly aware of discomfort in the body. This is why many people who meditate also practice yoga, or another form of physical exercise that strengthens and stretches the body. One of the best ways to maintain a straight back and open chest in meditation is to repeat silently a phrase whenever you feel physical pain. For example, if you feel yourself tensing your shoulders as you hold your back straight during meditation, you can inwardly whisper to yourself, "soften, soften," or "open, open."

4. HANDS: Sometimes, when meditation gets very quiet, our concentration coagulates in the hands. It sounds strange, but you may experience this yourself. It's not uncommon, as your exhalations dissolve outward, to feel as if all that is left of your body is your hands. Therefore, it is good to position your hands in a way that is both grounding and meaningful. You will notice in statues from a variety of religious traditions that the deities or saints hold their hands in intentional ways. These hand positions are called *mudras* in the Tantric Buddhist tradition—physical gestures that help evoke certain states of mind.

One frequently seen position is the forefinger lightly touching the thumb and the other three fingers flexed outward. Another common mudra is one hand resting in the palm of the other, thumbs touching. Many people like to meditate with their hands in the Christian prayer position of palms together, fingers pointing up. Some people meditate with their hands simply resting, palms down or upward, on their knees.

Each mudra evokes a specific quality that you can experience yourself merely by experimenting with them. For example, resting the palms upward on the knees indicates receptivity—openness to whatever comes your way. Hands placed downward on the knees produce a grounded feeling in the body, a sense of balance and strength. My personal favorite hand position is where the thumb and index finger touch and create a circle. There is something about the thumb touching the finger that reminds me to be *on the spot* in my concentration, yet delicately so. I gently extend the other three fingers and rest my hands on my knees. This position keeps me steady and balanced. . . .

It is a good idea to stick with one position for your hands per meditation session, so as not to get distracted by the switching-mudra game. It's very easy to turn anything into yet another way not to do the simple work of meditation. At the end of a meditation session, many traditions suggest raising the hands palm to palm and bowing. This is a way to indicate respect and gratitude for having meditated. It is also a way to experience a sense of humility as we bow to the universal forces of wisdom and compassion.

5. EYES: Some meditation traditions recommend closing the eyes during meditation; others suggest keeping them open and directing the gaze downward, four to six feet in front of you, focusing on a point on the floor. Some suggest keeping a soft, unfocused gaze. I meditate with my eyes closed. You can experiment and see which way affords you the best relaxation and concentration. If you find that closing your eyes makes you sleepy, keep them open. If you find that keeping your eyes open is distracting, close them.

6. MOUTH: We hold a lot of tension in the jaw. Let your jaw drop right now. Open your mouth wide, stick your tongue out, and then close your mouth. Massage your jaw area from your ears to your chin. Now notice the difference. You can do this often during the day as a way to release tension. During meditation, it is not unusual for tension to gather in the jaw. The Vietnamese Zen master Thich Nhat Hanh recommends smiling slightly while you meditate, a great way to keep the jaw soft. I find that having a slight smile helps bring a subtle sense of openness and love into my being. Or you can drop your jaw and open your mouth several times during meditation.

Understand that the pain or tension you may feel in your body as you meditate is both physical and psychological. If you experience pain, constriction, restlessness, or all of the above, do not be alarmed, and do not take the attitude "no pain, no gain." Adjust your position slowly and mindfully as many times as you want during a meditation session. The point of meditation is to be relaxed and awake. Therefore, make sure you are comfortable, and at same time sit in a way that keeps you alert. . . .

As you sit down to meditate, approach the experience lightly so that your body relaxes, just as it would if you were about to slip into a bath or settle down before the television. Then choose your hand mudra, close your eyes, straighten your back, and at the same time soften your shoulders and expand your chest, so that your posture is also one of gentle openness.

Breath, posture, placement of hands, eyes open or shut: All of these techniques form the container for meditation practice. But none of them eradicates the absurd quantity and aggravating intensity of the thoughts that flood the mind when we sit down to meditate. Please expect this. Good thoughts, bad thoughts, pleasurable ones, disturbing ones—they will come and go as we sit in meditation, watching our breath, maintaining our posture. They are the weather of the mind. Our goal in meditation is not to get rid of thoughts. Rather, the goal is to abandon identifying with each thought as it comes and goes; to watch the thoughts as we would watch the weather from an observation tower. . . .

TEN-STEP MEDITATION PRACTICE

1. **PLACE AND TIME:** Find a private and relatively quiet place where you will not be disturbed by people, children, telephones, et cetera. Choose an amount of time you are going to meditate. Set a timer or keep a clock close by. Begin with ten minutes, and work your way up over a few weeks or months to a half hour or forty-five minutes.

2. **SEAT AND POSTURE:** Assume a comfortable posture, sitting cross-legged on a pillow on the floor or on a simple chair. Keep the spine straight, and let your shoulders soften and drop. Do a brief scan of the body, relaxing parts that are tight. Relax your jaw. Choose a hand position and gently hold it.

3. **BEGINNING:** Close your eyes (or keep your open eyes focused gently on a spot on the floor). Take a deep breath in and let it out with a sigh. Do this three times. As you sigh, release anything you are holding on to. Remind yourself that for these few minutes you are doing nothing but meditating. You can afford to drop everything else for the time being. The pressing details of your life will be waiting for you at the end of the session.

4. **BREATH:** Bring your attention to your breathing, becoming aware of the natural flow of breath in and out of the body. Observe your chest and belly as they rise and expand on the in-breath, and fall and recede on the out-breath. Witness each in-breath as it enters your body and fills it with energy. Witness each out-breath as it leaves your body and dissipates into space. Then start again, bringing your attention back each time to the next breath. Let your breath be like a soft broom, gently sweeping its way through your body and mind.

5. **THOUGHTS:** When a thought takes you away from witnessing your breathing, take note of the thought without judging it, then gently bring your attention back to your chest or your belly and the feeling of the breath coming in and out. Remember that meditation is the practice of unconditional friendliness. Observe your thoughts with friendliness and then let the breath sweep them gently away.

6. **FEELINGS:** When feelings arise, do not resist them. Allow them to be. Observe them. Taste them. Experience them but do not identify with or interpret them. Let them run their natural course, then return to observing your breath. If you find yourself stuck in a feeling state, shift a little on your seat and straighten your posture. Get back in the saddle and gently pick up the reins of the breath.

7. **PAIN:** If you feel pain in the body—your knees, for example, or your back—bring your awareness to the pain. Surround the painful area with breath. Witness yourself in

pain, as opposed to responding to or resisting the pain. If the pain is persistent, move gently to release tension, and return to your posture and breath. If your back is particularly painful, you may want to lean against a wall or the back of your chair, or, if your knees hurt, you may want to straighten your legs for a while. Avoid excess movement, but do not allow pain to dominate your experience.

8. RESTLESSNESS AND SLEEPINESS: If you are agitated by thoughts or feeling, or if you feel as if you cannot sit still, or if you are bored to distraction, come back to your breath and your posture again and again. Treat yourself gently—and with love—as if you were training a puppy. Likewise, if a wave of sleepiness overtakes you, see if you can wake yourself by breathing a little more deeply, keeping your eyes open, and sitting up tall. Sleep and meditation are not the same thing. See if you can be as relaxed as you are during sleep, yet at the same time, awake and aware.

9. COUNTING BREATHS: A good way to deal with all of these impediments to concentration is to count your breaths. On the in-breath, count "one," and on the out-breath, count "two." Continue up to ten. Then begin again. If you lose count at any point, start over at "one." As thoughts and feelings, or pain and discomfort, or restlessness and sleepiness arise, allow your counting to gently override their distracting chatter. Roshi Joan Halifax suggests words to "generate a state of presence and self-compassion" that she learned from the Buddhist teacher Thich Nhat Hanh: On the inhalation, say to yourself, "Breathing in, I calm body and mind." On the exhalation: "Breathing out, I let go." Inhalation: "Dwelling in the present moment." Exhalation: "This is the only moment."

10. DISCIPLINE: For one week, practice meditation each day, whether you are in the mood or not. Even if it is for only five minutes, commit to a regular practice. See how you feel. If you notice a difference (or even if you don't), commit to

another week. Then consider joining a meditation group or taking a retreat and receiving more in-depth instruction and support in your practice.

I am grateful to Elizabeth Lesser for permitting me to include her meditation guide in my book. I hope this practice will be as a meaningful for you as it has been for me.

Acknowledgments

I T TAKES A VILLAGE:

First and foremost, I am forever grateful to my editor, Kate Medina, for her patience, talent, and encouragement.

Her assistants, Millicent Bennett and Lindsey Schwoeri, helped me in countless ways.

Copy editor Bonnie Thompson and associate copy chief Dennis Ambrose performed miracles that helped me organize and clarify. Barbara Bachman created the beautiful design. Thanks also to Paolo Pepe for his front- and back-cover designs, and to Ken Wohlrob for bringing me into the world of eBooks.

A special thanks to Lisa Bennett, who helped me illuminate all the ways that seniors help (rather than hinder) society, and what society needs to do to help make seniors' lives easier.

My thanks to Angela Martini, for her wonderful illustrations.

And to my friend and assistant, Steven Bennett, who put in countless hours on permissions and such, with the help of Carol Mitchell and Laura Masseur.

Deep gratitude to Terry Savage for so generously letting me borrow her financial expertise.

Thanks to the late Dr. Robert Butler, whose commitment to gerontology was responsible for deepening and expanding the entire field. It was he, with his seminars at the International Longevity Center (which he founded), who introduced me to many of the scientists whose expertise deepen this book. Dr. Denise Parks is one of them. She is director of the Center for Vital Longevity at the University of Texas at Dallas, whose expertise about the brain was essential to me. Another is Dr. Richard Sprott, executive director of the Ellison Medical Research Foundation, who explained, in terms I could understand, the cutting-edge research on aging.

Dr. Butler brought me to Dr. Diane Meier, who heads the Center to Advance Palliative Care (CAPC) at Mount Sinai Hospital in New York City. She helped me understand what palliative care means in the most moving, soulful terms.

Thanks to Dr. Michael Hewitt, research director for exercise science at Canyon Ranch health resort. He kindly reviewed my workout chapter to make sure everything was accurate, and allowed me to borrow his Key-3 exercises.

And thanks to Dr. Michael Jacobson, executive director of the Center for Science in the Public Interest, who, together with Katherine Talmadge, kept me straight on the topic of nutrition.

Thanks to Dr. Marion Perlmutter, with the department of psychology at the University of Michigan, who helped me understand some of the great deepening that can come with age.

Dr. Michael Perelman is Clinical Associate Professor of Psychiatry, Reproductive Medicine, and Urology at Weill Medical College, Cornell University, and co-director of the Human Sexuality Program at New York Presbyterian Hospital. Dr. Perelman greatly expanded my understanding of sexuality and aging, as did Dr. Michelle Warren, medical director at the Center for Menopause, Hormonal Disorders and Women's Health, Columbia University Medical Center, New York. She helped me understand women's hormone replacement therapy, among other important things.

Dr. Tom Lue, internationally recognized expert in the treatment of male sexual dysfunction at the University of California, San Francisco, explained to me, with great humor, the ins and outs of male sexual dysfunction, in particular the penile implant.

Dr. Louann Brizendine taught me a lot about the female brain and sexuality in aging women. Dr. Brizendine is a neuropsychiatrist at the University of California, San Francisco, founder and director of the Women's Mood and Hormone Clinic, and co-director of the Program in Sexual Medicine at UCSF.

Dr. Barbara Bartlik, sex therapist and psychiatrist, helped me, in her juicy, forthright manner, with ideas for heightening sexuality as we age.

Dr. Laura Carstensen, founding director of the Stanford Center on Longevity, gave generously of her time and expertise in many areas of aging. She took me around the Center and introduced me to many of their researchers, including Dr. Thomas Rando, Stanford Center on Longevity's deputy director and stem-cell biologist. It was Dr. Rando who helped me understand the role of stem-cell research and aging.

Dr. Ken Matheny, regents professor at the Department of Counseling and Psychological Services at Georgia State University, profoundly helped me to understand much about late life and the spirit.

Thanks to Mary Madden, who generously shared her experience with online dating.

Deep thanks to the staff and clients at the center for WISE & Healthy Aging in Santa Monica, California, who gave me so much of their time and shared their moving experiences.

I am eternally grateful to Beverly Kitaen-Morse, who taught me, with her therapy, the value of a life review.

And to all the friends whose stories enrich this book, I am filled with love and gratitude. Thank you for your trust: Erica Jong, Roshi Joan Halifax, Janet Wolfe, Nat and Jewelle Bickford, Mary Catherine Bateson, Dr. Johnnetta Cole, the Honorable Robin Biddle Duke, Yoel and Eva Haller, Reverend Bill and Kathy Stayton, and those others who shared their most personal intimacies and asked that their real names not be used.

Notes

PREFACE: The Arch and the Staircase

1   Mary Catherine Bateson, *Composing a Life* (New York: Plume, 1990), p. 34.
2   Mary Catherine Bateson, *Composing a Further Life* (New York: Knopf, 2010), p. 12.
3   Bernice Neugarten, "Dynamics of Transition of Middle Age to Old Age," *Journal of Geriatric Psychiatry,* vol. 4, no. 1 (Fall 1970), pp. 71–87.
4   Erik H. Erikson and Joan M. Erikson, *The Life Cycle Completed: Extended Version with New Chapters on the Ninth Stage of Development* (New York: W. W. Norton & Company, 1997), p. 114.
5   George Vaillant, *Aging Well* (New York: Little, Brown, 2002), p. 113.

CHAPTER 1: Act III: Becoming Whole

1   Carl Jung, *Modern Man in Search of a Soul.*
2   Rudolf Arnheim, *New Essays on the Psychology of Art* (Berkeley: University of California Press, 1986).
3   Marion Perlmutter, interview with the author, Ann Arbor, Michigan.
4   Peter Applebome, "Loss of Speech Evokes the Voice of a Writer," *The New York Times,* March 7, 2011, p. A14.
5   Stephen Levine, *A Year to Live* (New York: Three Rivers, 1997), p. 38.

CHAPTER 2: A Life Review: Looking Back to See the Road Ahead

1   From a letter to me from Kenneth Matheny, Regents Professor and director of the Department of Counseling and Psychological Services at Georgia State University.

CHAPTER 3: Act I: A Time for Gathering

1   Vaillant, *Aging Well,* p. 96.
2   Judith Newman, "Inside Your Teen's Head," *Parade,* November 28, 2010.
3   Laura Carstensen, *A Long Bright Future: An Action Plan for a Lifetime of Happiness, Health, and Financial Security* (New York: Broadway Books, 2009), p. 245.
4   Terrence Real, *I Don't Want to Talk About It,* p. 146.
5   Vaillant, *Aging Well,* p. 285.

6   Terrence Real, *The New Rules of Marriage: What You Need to Know to Make Love Work* (New York: Ballantine, 2007), p. 95.
7   Vaillant, *Aging Well*, p. 284.
8   Ibid., p. 285.

CHAPTER 4: Act II: A Time of Building and of In-Betweenness

1   Vaillant, *Aging Well*, p. 96.
2   Suzanne Braun Levine, *Inventing the Rest of Our Lives: Women in Second Adulthood* (New York: Plume, 2006), p. 59.
3   Ibid.
4   Joan Halifax, *Being with Dying*.
5   William Bridges, *Transitions: Making Sense of Life's Changes* (Cambridge: Da Capo, 2004), p. 146.
6   Marion Woodman, *Leaving My Father's House*, p. 194.
7   William Bridges, *The Way of Transition* (Cambridge: Perseus, 2001), p. 196.
8   Gail Sheehy, *Sex and the Seasoned Woman* (Random House).

CHAPTER 5: Eleven Ingredients for Successful Aging

1   Vaillant, *Aging Well*, p. 213.
2   Tom Kirkwood, *The End of Age*, p. 63.
3   Vaillant, *Aging Well*, p. 207.
4   Quoted in ibid., p. 206.
5   Ibid., p. 48.

CHAPTER 6: The Workout

1   Walter Bortz, *Dare to Be 100*, p. 47.
2   Ibid.
3   Jane Brody, "Mental Reserves Keep Brain Agile," *The New York Times*, December 11, 2007.
4   Ibid.
5   *Archives of Internal Medicine*, http://archinte.ama-assn.org/.
6   Michael Hewitt, *Growing Older, Staying Strong: Preventing Sarcopenia Through Strength Training* (New York: International Longevity Center, September–October 2003), p. 4.
7   Scott McCredie, *Balance: In Search of the Lost Senses* (New York: Little, Brown, 2007), p. 189.
8   Quoted in McCredie, *Balance*, p. 214.
9   Joan Halifax, interview with the author.
10 John W. Rowe and Robert L. Kahn, *Successful Aging* (New York: Dell, 1998), p. 98.

CHAPTER 7: Now More than Ever, You Are What You Eat

1   *Nutrition Action Healthletter*, July–August 2008.
2   Jane Brody, "Even Benefits Don't Tempt Us to Vegetables," *The New York Times*, October 5, 2010.

3 For more on yogurt with active and live cultures, I recommend the book *Gut Insights,* by Jo Ann Hattner.

CHAPTER 8: You and Your Brain: Use It or Lose It

1 From a talk I attended at the Age Boom Academy, held at the International Longevity Center in New York on September 24, 2007.
2 Cynthia Gorney, *The New York Times Magazine,* April 18, 2010.

CHAPTER 9: Positivity: The Good News Is You're Getting Older!

1 Published online in the *Proceedings of the National Academy of Sciences,* May 2010.
2 Vaillant, *Aging Well,* p. 206.
3 Carstensen, *A Long Bright Future,* p. 16.

CHAPTER 10: Actually Doing a Life Review

1 Real, *The New Rules of Marriage,* p. 71.
2 Levine, *A Year to Live,* p. 88.
3 Zalman Schachter-Shalomi and Ronald S. Miller, *From Age-ing to Sage-ing: A Profound New Vision of Growing Older* (New York: Grand Central, 1997), p. 98.

CHAPTER 11: The Importance of Friendship

1 Ursula Le Guin, *Dancing,* p. 151.
2 Jean Baker Miller, *Toward a New Psychology of Women,* 2nd ed. (Boston: Beacon), p. xxi.
3 Gene Cohen, *The Mature Mind: The Positive Power of the Aging Brain,* p. 28.
4 *The Diane Rehm Show,* NPR, August 26, 2008.
5 Shirley MacLaine, *Sage-ing While Age-ing* (New York: Atria Books, 2007), p. 239.

CHAPTER 12: Love in the Third Act

1 David Schnarch, *Passionate Marriage: Keeping Love and Intimacy Alive in Committed Relationships* (New York: Owl Books, 1997), p. 56.
2 Real, *The New Rules of Marriage,* p. 257.
3 Jane Loevinger, *The Meaning and Measure of Ego Development* (San Francisco: Jossey-Bass, 1976).
4 Betty Friedan, *The Fountain of Age* (New York: Simon & Schuster, 1993), p. 286.
5 David Gutmann, *Reclaimed Powers: Toward a New Psychology of Men and Women in Later Life* (New York: Basic Books, 1987), p. 153.
6 *Time,* October 12, 2007.
7 Tara Parker-Pope, *The New York Times,* June 10, 2008, p. D1.

8   Paraphrased from Real, *The New Rules of Marriage,* p. 76.
9   Real, *The New Rules of Marriage,* p. 254.
10 Ibid., p. 255.
11 *The New York Times Magazine,* April 18, 2010.
12 Suzanne Braun Levine, *Inventing the Rest of Our Lives,* p. 132.
13 Ibid., p. 131.
14 For more information on Women for Women International, go to womenforwomen.org.
15 Vaillant, *Aging Well,* p. 305.

CHAPTER 13: The Changing Landscape of Sex When
    You're Over the Hill

1   Friedan, *Fountain of Age,* pp. 262–63.
2   Ibid., p. 286.
3   Schnarch, *Passionate Marriage,* p. 79.
4   Ibid., p. 76.
5   Ibid., p. 99.
6   Ibid., p. 134.
7   Ibid., p. 85.
8   Marty Klein, *Let Me Count the Ways: Discovering Great Sex Without Intercourse.*
9   Gail Sheehy, *New Passages,* p. 311.
10 Gail Sheehy, *Passages,* pp. 454–55.
11 Louann Brizendine, *The Female Brain* (New York: Morgan Road Books, 2006), p. 177.
12 "Stimulation of the Libido: The Use of Erotica in Sex Therapy," *Psychiatric Annals,* vol. 29, no. 1 (January 1999), p. 60.

CHAPTER 14: The Lowdown on Getting It Up in the Third Act

1   Jane Brody, "A Dip in the Sex Drive, Tied to Menopause," *The New York Times,* March 31, 2009.
2   E. O. Laumann, A. Nicolosi, D. B. Glasser, A. Paik, C. Gingell, E. Moreira, and T. Wang, "Sexual Problems Among Women and Men Aged 40–80 Y: Prevalence and Correlates Identified in the Global Study of Sexual Attitudes and Behaviors," *International Journal of Impotence Research,* vol. 17 (2005), pp. 39–57.
3   Rowe and Kahn, *Successful Aging,* pp. 80–81.
4   Ibid., p. 82.
5   Marianne J. Legato, *Eve's Rib: The New Science of Gender-Specific Medicine and How It Can Save Your Life* (New York: Harmony Books), p. 204.
6   Susan Rako, "Testosterone Deficiency and Supplementation for Women: Matters of Sexuality and Health," *Psychiatric Annals,* vol. 29, no. 1 (January 1999), p. 23.
7   Legato, *Eve's Rib,* p. 213.

CHAPTER 15: Meeting New People When You're Looking for Love

1   Pepper Schwartz, *Prime: Adventures and Advice on Sex, Love, and the Sensual Years* (New York: HarperCollins, 2007), p. 68.
2   Ibid., p. 70.

CHAPTER 16: Generativity: Leaving Footprints

1   Vaillant, *Aging Well,* p. 4.
2   Vaillant, *Aging Well.*
3   Schachter-Shalomi and Miller, *From Age-ing to Sage-ing,* p. 16.
4   Vaillant, *Aging Well,* pp. 48, 113.
5   Schachter-Shalomi and Miller, *From Age-ing to Sage-ing,* p. 57.

CHAPTER 17: Ripening the Time: A Challenge for Women

1   Gutmann, *Reclaimed Powers.*

CHAPTER 18: Don't Put Off Preparing for the Inevitable:
        One of These Days Is Right Now

1   Carstensen, *A Long Bright Future,* p. 230.
2   Bernice Bratter and Helen Dennis, *Project Renewment* (New York: Scribner, 2008), p. 23.
3   Terry Savage, *The New Savage Number: How Much Money Do You Really Need to Retire?* (Hoboken, N.J.: Wiley, 2009).
4   Terry Savage, *The Savage Number* (Hoboken, N.J.: Wiley, 2005), p. 48.
5   Ibid., p. 84.
6   Study cited in Alan Walker, "Care for Elderly People: A Conflict Between Women and the State," in *A Labour of Love: Women, Work and Caring,* edited by Janet Finch and Dulcie Groves (London: Routledge & Kegan Paul, 1983), p. 123.

CHAPTER 19: Let's Hear It for Revolution!

1   Florian Kohlbacher and Cornelius Herstatt, eds., *The Silver Market Phenomenon: Business Opportunities in an Era of Demographic Change* (Heidelberg, Germany: Springer, 2008).
2   Maxine Frith, "The Woofs: A Graying Generation with Golden Spending Power," *Independent,* September 25, 2003.
3   MetLife Mature Market Institute, *Demographic Profile of American Baby Boomers* (Westport, Conn.: MetLife Mature Market Institute, 2005).
4   Adam Cohen, interview by Lisa Bennett, *Esquire,* April 16, 2010.
5   Carstensen, *A Long Bright Future,* p. 29.
6   K. M. Daniel, L. C. Cason, and S. Ferrell, "Emerging Technologies to Enhance the Safety of Older People in Their Homes," *Geriatric Nursing* vol. 30 (2009): pp. 384–89.

7   Philanthropic Trust, "Philanthropy Statistics," http://www.nptrust.org/
    philanthropy/philanthropy_stats.asp (accessed on April 18, 2010).

8   "How Americans of Different Generations Give to Charity," *Chronicle of
    Philanthropy,* http//www.philanthropy.com/article (accessed on April 18,
    2010).

9   Suzanne Braun Levine, *Fifty Is the New Fifty* (New York: Penguin, 2009),
    p. 182.

10 Susan J. Ellis, "The Dollar Value of Volunteer Time," http://www.energize
    .com/art/dollar_value.html (accessed on March 15, 2010); and Founda-
    tion Center, "Frequently Asked Questions," http://foundationcenter.org/
    getstarted/faqs/html/volunteer_value.html (accessed on March 15, 2010).

11 Milt Freudenheim, "More Help Wanted: Older Workers Please Apply,"
    The New York Times, March 23, 2005; http://www.nytimes.com/2005/03/23/
    business/23older.html (accessed on April 19, 2010).

12 National Committee to Preserve Social Security and Medicare, "Senior
    Income Statistics," http://www.ncpssm.org/ss_senior_income/ (accessed
    on March 1, 2010).

13 NCPSSM, "Fast Facts About the Social Security Disability Program,"
    http://ncpssm.org/disability_fast_facts/ (accessed on March 1, 2010).

14 NCPSSM, "Americans Support Protecting Social Security Benefits: Find-
    ings of NCPSSM Survey," http://ncpssm.org (accessed on March 1, 2010).

15 AARP, "Retirement Income" (Chapter 4, Section 9) in *AARP Policy Book
    2009–2010,* http://www.aarp.org/issues/policies/policy_book/ (accessed on
    March 28, 2010).

16 Benson Rosen and Thomas Jerdee, "Investing in the Older Worker," *Per-
    sonnel Administrator,* April 1989.

17 Freudenheim, "More Help Wanted."

18 AARP, "Employment" (Chapter 5, Section 12) in *AARP Policy Book 2009–
    2010,* http://www.aarp.org/issues/policies/policy_book/ (accessed on March
    28, 2010).

19 National Council on Aging, "NCOA Issue Brief: Older Americans Act
    Appropriations," http://www. ncoa.org (accessed on March 5, 2010).

20 Wikipedia, S.V. "AARP/Blue Zones Vitality Project," http://en.wikipedia
    .org/wiki/AARP/Blue_Zones_Vitality_Project (accessed on February 5,
    2010).

21 AARP, "Health: Medicare Beneficiaries Out-of-Pocket Costs" (Chapter 7,
    Section 38) in *AARP Policy Book 2009–2010,* http://www.aarp.org/issues/
    policies/policy_book/ (accessed on March 28, 2010); and My Medicare
    Matters, "What Is Covered by Medicare Parts A, B and D," http://www
    .mymedicarematters.org/AboutMedicare/whatiscovered.asp (accessed on
    March 1, 2010).

22 Center to Advance Palliative Care and National Palliative Care Research
    Center, "America's Care of Serious Illness: A State-by-State Report Card
    on Access to Palliative Care in Our Nation's Hospitals," http://www.capc
    .org/reportcard/findings (accessed on March 1, 2010).

CHAPTER 20: Facing Mortality

1   Joan Halifax, *Tricycle,* Spring 2008, p. 8.
2   Here's another option instead of cremation: I've read that a Swedish company, Promessa, will freeze-dry your body in liquid nitrogen, pulverize it with high-frequency vibrations, and seal the resulting powder in a cornstarch coffin. The company claims that this "ecological burial" will decompose in six to twelve months.
3   Letty Cottin Pogrebin, *Getting Over Getting Older* (New York: Berkley, 1997), p. 78.

CHAPTER 21: The Work In

1   David Bohm, *Wholeness and the Implicate Order* (London: Routledge, 1980), p. 49.

APPENDIX I: Summary of Main Areas of Anti-Aging Research

1   Robert N. Butler, *The Longevity Prescription: How to Maximize the Three-Decade Dividend* (New York: International Longevity Center).

APPENDIX V: Guide to Mindful Meditation

1   Elizabeth Lesser, *Broken Open.*
2   From the archives of the *Women's Collection,* Texas Woman's University, Denton, Texas.

Index

NOTE: Italicized page numbers refer to picture captions.

PHOTO: © FIROOZ ZAHEDI

JANE FONDA is an Oscar- and Emmy-winning actor and a successful film producer. Fonda revolutionized the fitness industry with the release of *Jane Fonda's Workout* in 1982. In addition to her home exercise videos, audio recordings, and five bestselling exercise books, she is the author of the number-one *New York Times* bestseller *My Life So Far*. In 1995, she founded the Georgia Campaign for Adolescent Pregnancy Prevention, which she chairs. In 2002, she opened the Jane Fonda Center for Adolescent Reproductive Health at Emory University's School of Medicine. She lives in Los Angeles.

ABOUT THE TYPE

This book was set in Requiem, a typeface designed by the Hoefler Type Foundry. It is a modern typeface inspired by inscriptional capitals in Ludovico Vicentino degli Arrighi's 1523 writing manual, *Il modo de temperare le penne*. An original lowercase, a set of figures, and an italic in the "chancery" style that Arrighi helped popularize were created to make this adaptation of a classical design into a complete font family.